THE CRITIC'S DAUGHTER

THE CRITIC'S DAUGHTER

A MEMOIR

Priscilla Gilman

W. W. NORTON & COMPANY
Celebrating a Century of Independent Publishing

We are grateful for Shaina Taub's permission to use lyrics from *As You Like It*.

For information about permission to reproduce selections from this book, write to
Permissions, W. W. Norton & Company, Inc., 500 Fifth Avenue, New York, NY 10110

For information about special discounts for bulk purchases, please contact
W. W. Norton Special Sales at specialsales@wwnorton.com or 800-233-4830

Manufacturing by Lakeside Book Company
Book design by Chris Welch
Production manager: Lauren Abbate

ISBN 978-0-393-65132-4

W. W. Norton & Company, Inc., 500 Fifth Avenue, New York, N.Y. 10110
www.wwnorton.com

W. W. Norton & Company Ltd., 15 Carlisle Street, London W1D 3BS

1 2 3 4 5 6 7 8 9 0

IRINA: (*Sobbing.*) Where? Where has it all gone? Where is it? Oh my God, my God! I have forgotten everything, forgotten everything . . . Everything is confused in my head . . . I am forgetting everything, I forget more every day, and life flies past and never returns, never and we will never go to Moscow . . . I see now that we will never go . . .

—Anton Chekhov, *Three Sisters*

That is what the highest criticism really is, the record of one's own soul.

—Oscar Wilde, "The Critic as Artist"

Everything that's gone before, reaching back to the first moments, all the excitements and subsidings, the musings and expostulations, the innocent or calculated assertions, the flurries of encounter and withdrawal, the little enactments and disclosures of self, the tears and joys, the histories and prospects—all this flowers now into aesthetic logic; the end toward which these means have been moving is taking shape.

—Richard Gilman,
Chekhov's Plays: An Opening into Eternity

FORTY CHARACTERS IN SEARCH OF MY FATHER
(IN ORDER OF APPEARANCE)

The King from Rodgers and Hammerstein's *The King and I*
Rabbit Angstrom from John Updike's *Rabbit, Run*
Holden Caulfield from J. D. Salinger's *The Catcher in the Rye*
Max Jamison from Wilfred Sheed's *The Critic*
Richard Gilman in John Updike's *Bech: A Book*
Daddy Warbucks from *Annie*, the musical
Big Bird from *Sesame Street*
The Nome King from L. Frank Baum's *Ozma of Oz*
Uncle Wiggily from the Uncle Wiggily books
Huckle Cat and Lowly Worm from the Richard Scarry books
Mrs. Piggle-Wiggle from Betty MacDonald's
    Mrs. Piggle-Wiggle series
Cookie Monster from *Sesame Street*
Kermit from *Sesame Street*
Grover from *Sesame Street*
Curious George and Paddington
Drosselmeyer from *The Nutcracker*
The critic from Rachel Cusk's *Kudos*
Willy Wonka

The Captain in *The Sound of Music*

The Wizard from *The Wizard of Oz*

Johnny from Betty Smith's *A Tree Grows in Brooklyn*

Charlie Brown's Christmas tree from *A Charlie Brown Christmas*

The Velveteen Rabbit and the child from
    Margery Williams's *The Velveteen Rabbit*

Eddie Kerrigan from Jennifer Egan's *Manhattan Beach*

Ted Kramer from *Kramer vs. Kramer*

Will Ladislaw from George Eliot's *Middlemarch*

Mr. Darcy from Jane Austen's *Pride and Prejudice*

Gene Kelly as Don Lockwood in *Singin' in the Rain* and
    Jerry Mulligan in *An American in Paris*

Tony from *West Side Story*

Kanji Watanabe from Akira Kurosawa's *Ikiru*

Wilbur and Charlotte from E. B. White's *Charlotte's Web*

The Scarecrow from *The Wizard of Oz*

King Lear

Hamlet

Uncle Vanya

I lost my father for the first time when I was ten years old. In the months and years that followed, I lost him over and over, many times and in many different ways. This book is my attempt to find him.

THE CRITIC'S DAUGHTER

'm in a darkened Broadway theater at a revival of *The King and I* on a balmy evening in the summer of 2015. The production is sumptuous and beautifully sung, the show is stirring and delightful, and my spirits soar with the music. But then, the song "Something Wonderful" begins, and I'm undone.

Sung by Lady Thiang, the King's long-suffering Head Wife, to Anna Leonowens, the tutor brought from England to teach the King's children, "Something Wonderful" is an impassioned plea to accept the King as he is and not desert him despite his many faults. With a simultaneous realism about his flaws and a deep belief in his virtues, Lady Thiang is trying to convince Anna—bothered by the King's peevishness, put off by his egotism, and frightened of his volatility—to give him another chance. Her attempt to acknowledge his darkness but recognize his worth, to plead for mercy and forgiveness, ravages me. I am heaving with sobs. Tears wet the front of my silk summer dress and drip onto the program I'm clutching. Willing myself to stifle the sobs, I let out an involuntary moan, and heads swivel. I drop my head into my lap, thinking of my father.

It hits me in that instant that the King has always represented my father to me. Peremptory but playful, immensely powerful but incredibly vulnerable, witty and smart but naïve and quixotic. My father, in many ways the quintessential intellectual and a deeply cerebral man, was nonetheless a man who thought with his heart. He was an idealist. He was a romantic. He was fun and charming and charismatic, sweet and adorable and endearing. Like the King, he was hampered by pettiness and petulance. Like the King, he was both an autocrat and a radical. He wanted to do and be good, but his limitations—his rage, his defensiveness, his insecurities—had hindered and hampered him at every turn. He was a man who stumbled and fell, but he was a man who tried.

"Something Wonderful" is sung again at the end of the show when the King has died. The death of that king, the strong man brought low, the powerful monarch reduced to a frail and mortal body, had always devastated me. Just like my father, he was a man on the brink of a breakthrough but was felled before he could achieve it. All of Lady Thiang's devotion couldn't save him. All of Anna's influence couldn't save him. It was too late.

I saw myself in Lady Thiang, ardently pleading with Anna to see the King holistically, as more than just his temper and his weaker moments. All my life I'd sung a version of "Something Wonderful" about my father to my mother. But unlike Lady Thiang with Anna, I had never managed to convince my mother to give my king a chance, acknowledge his virtues, see beyond his flaws. She hadn't relented. She still shuddered when she spoke of him. She still dismissed my missing him as "obsessive." I needed my mother to acknowledge my father's virtues. I needed her to see him in the round.

But I also saw myself as Anna. Frustrated and saddened and exhausted by a demanding and mercurial man, be he my father or romantic partners over the years. What had been the price of telling difficult and depressed men they were wonderful over and over again because they needed my love? Of protecting them when they were wrong? What was the cost of such protection? And how could I be both Anna—critical, ethical, self-protective—and Lady Thiang—loyal, empathetic, loving?

On that night of overwhelming sadness in the theater, I realized that I had never been allowed—and in some ways had never allowed myself—to truly grieve my father or reckon with his legacy to me. And now I knew I must.

I am haunted by my father. He has made me the thinker, writer, parent, human that I am, brought me to my knees, led me into dangerous romantic entanglements, buoyed me during times of crisis, informed my reading and writing and parenting in ways I am only now realizing. I am both drawn to and wary of places, people, works of art that will touch that sore spot in me, unleash that tide of sadness.

In college, I studied the literature of trauma. We read of how those who suffer trauma experience a bewildering discontinuity, an absolute break between before and after and spend their lives attempting to mediate that gap. We explored how the traumatized both yearn to be free of their pain, heal their wound, and resist forgetting, healing, getting over it.

The grief has stopped me in my tracks time and time again. Years after my father's death, a street corner in New York City, a clip from *Singin' in the Rain*, a song from *West Side Story*, a tender note from a former student of his, could send me into unstoppable crying. I hated his smoking when he was alive, but after he died, cigar and cigarette smells made my knees buckle. I have struggled against the flood of tears that threatened to engulf me as I prepared to teach a class on *The Assistant* (a book he loved by a dear friend of his) or read a Paddington book to my younger son. My sister, too, was subject to these irrational eruptions of grief. A few years ago, she saw my father's friend André Gregory (he of *My Dinner with André* and *Vanya on 42nd Street*) at a public reception, and as she walked up to say hello, she found herself bursting into tears. Was it simply seeing one of our father's close friends? Was it seeing one of the last of a dying breed of eccentric artists and intellectuals? Was it his kind, welcoming smile, the way he reminded her of our father?

Fifteen years after my father died, at age eighty-three, in a suburb of Kyoto, Japan, he is disappearing faster and faster. His friends, colleagues, adversaries, compatriots are almost all gone. His New York City is disappearing. Middle-class Flatbush, Brooklyn, where he grew up; the bohemian, literary, electric West Village where he lived as a young man; industrial and still-unchic SoHo where he moved in with my mother and brought me home from the hospital in May of 1970; the liberal, affordable, and diverse Upper West Side of rambling rent-controlled prewar apartments inhabited by therapists and academics and artists, where my parents raised me and my sister; the then slightly sketchy neighborhood near Columbia University where he ended up after my parents divorced. I walk the city's streets in search of him and am turned away and turned off by glistening, imperious apartment towers, by one Duane Reade or bank or expensive clothing store after another moving in to replace small businesses, mom-and-pop stores, bookstores. How horrified my father would be by the loss of New York City's edge, affordability, neighborhood stores, diversity, and artistic fecundity.

As one by one my father's colleagues, friends, enemies, and now even his students die, as many of his books go out of print, as his life recedes into the distance, I wonder not *how* he will be remembered, but increasingly, *if* he will be remembered. Or will he simply vanish? I feel an urgency that drives me onward in search of traces, spirits, glimmerings.

This book is an attempt at exorcism at the same time that it is a plea to be haunted. I don't want my father's light, the light that emanated from him, the light he had access to, to die away and fade into the light of common day. I don't want my father's voice, sensibility, values "in darkness lost, the darkness of the grave."

And yet, I must look at him critically too. I must acknowledge that he wasn't always wise, that he stumbled and fell, that his weaknesses made him difficult to handle and sometimes difficult to love. How he would hate a sentimental or sanitized portrait of the complicated and unclassifiable man he was.

As his daughter, I have the privilege—or the burden—of making the final assessment of my father's life. And my loyalty is at stake.

> "Loyalty in a critic," Bernard Shaw wrote, "is corruption" . . .
> From the true critic the theater generally gets what can only be interpreted as gross infidelity, the reason being, as Shaw and every other major observer of drama makes abundantly clear, and as our own sense of what is civilized should tell us, that the critic cannot give his loyalty to men and institutions since he owes it to something a great deal more permanent. He owes it, of course, to truth and to dramatic art.
>
> —Richard Gilman,
> "The Necessity for Destructive Criticism," 1961

In this early essay, one his first major pieces, my father laid out both an intellectual defense of his profession and a manifesto reflecting his larger approach to life. He insisted that the highest form of love demands rigorous honesty. He never whitewashed, never tiptoed around, never equivocated or resorted to euphemism when giving his opinion or rendering his judgments. Can I attain that level of truth-telling and rigor in my own reflection on my father? Can I see him clearly but with compassion? How can I be at once truthful and loyal, both to him and to my mother, who bitterly divorced him and remained hardened against him until his death? Can I make an act of bracing honesty also an act of love? Am I betraying him if I reveal his flaws, his weaknesses, his "sins" (to use his own Catholic language)? Alternatively, am I betraying his critical standards if I put too romantic a sheen on him? For despite his elevation of truth as the highest critical value, despite his emotional openness, he hid things, kept secrets, told lies.

My father's sense of human beings as flawed, frail, imperfect creatures, his resistance to black-and-white judgments, is exemplified in his claim that "Chekhov's devils have at least the rudiments of wings and his angels the beginnings of horns." How can I hold on to the best of what he taught me, do him justice, depict him in all his messy, complex, contradictory being, with neither wings nor horns?

> When biography enters the realm of interiority, syntax always has to use the conditional, and thought can only be speculative; in conjectures like these we're asked to stretch sympathy and shrink credence, to trust our intuition, sometimes against likelihood.
>
> —Richard Gilman, *Chekhov's Plays: An Opening into Eternity*

As I attempt to portray my father, to understand him, as I enter the realm of his interiority, I will resist labels and categories, pronouncements and declarations. I will use the conditional. I will stretch my sympathy and trust my intuition. And as he wrote about interpretations of Ibsen, "mysteries will remain, as they should." I don't want to solve the mystery, or lay bare the reality, or provide a definitive account of my father. Even as I strive to capture him, I will remind myself of the virtues and value of his remaining elusive, unable to be resolved or solved.

ACT 1

APPARELLED IN CELESTIAL LIGHT

There was a time when meadow, grove, and stream,

The earth, and every common sight,

To me did seem

Apparelled in celestial light,

The glory and the freshness of a dream.

—William Wordsworth, "Ode: Intimations of Immortality"

And so I start, picking out memories, sifting and sorting, trying to reconstruct past time and vanished states of mind and to construct, on the slippery site of language and with its recalcitrant tools, at least the shape of what happened, its difference from what didn't.

—Richard Gilman, *Faith, Sex, Mystery: A Memoir*

My first memory of all is also my first memory of my father. I'm three years old, it's a hot summer night in Spain, and a loud, dramatic thunderstorm has awakened me. I must have cried out in terror, because the memory begins with my father, behind me, at my bedroom window, the two of us gazing out into the stormy night. Framed by the window, the scene before us is like a little theater, the garden behind our rental house strangely unfamiliar, the dark blue night sky intermittently scored with silvery streaks of lightning. With one arm wrapped around me, the other gesturing skyward, my father narrates what we're seeing and hearing. "Look at the tree!" he exclaims as the wind whips its branches. "And . . . *thunder!*" he cries in a thrillingly dramatic voice. He shows me how the lightning lights up corners of the garden, makes different kinds of seeing possible, uncovers things we haven't noticed before. He never explicitly soothes me or calms me, he doesn't say reassuring things, he doesn't comfort me. But in his presence, with his voice in my ear and his arm around my waist, my fear melts away.

My father didn't give me a hug and a kiss and send me back to sleep, he brought me to the window. In the face of the unexpected, the frightening, the disorienting, he was a madcap sportscaster, a wise sage, an ebullient enthusiast. As one arm embraced me, the other helped me face a world beyond him, a world of challenge and intensity and wonder.

I don't think of myself as a critic or teacher either, but simply—and at the obvious risk of disingenuousness—as someone who teaches, writes drama criticism (and other things) and feels that the American compulsion to take your identity from your profession, with its corollary of only one trade to a practitioner, may be a convenience to society but is burdensome and constricting to yourself.

—Richard Gilman, from a 1970 *New York Times* article about his directing a play at Yale Repertory Theatre

Despite my father's aversion to being categorized as a critic or teacher—he'd been the theater critic at *Commonweal* and *Newsweek* and taught at Yale Drama School from 1967 to 1997—he indisputably *was* a certain kind of New Yorker in the 1970s. Liberal, passionate, intellectual, clad in denim shirts or turtleneck sweaters, bell-bottom jeans or corduroys, sneakers or Wallabees, a pack of cigarettes bulging out of one pocket or another, with black clunky glasses and wild curly hair, my father cut a dashing yet unpretentious figure. He was as at ease discussing the travails of the New York Giants as he was debating the merits of the latest Eric Rohmer film.

He loved classic New York deli food—pastrami, pickles, corned beef sandwiches—Chinese takeout, pizza. He shopped at Zabar's, Barney Greengrass, H & H Bagels, and the local mom-and-pop stores in our Upper West Side neighborhood. He had next to no vanity about his appearance—bought cheap sneakers and jeans at an outlet store on Broadway, had his hair cut by our neighborhood barber, and exercised only when my mother cajoled him into playing doubles tennis with friends. He loved New York City's independent and used bookstores, its libraries, zoos, and museums; Central Park, where he pushed me and my fourteen-months-younger sister, Claire, on precarious metal swings, bought us soft pretzels, and chased us up and down the rocks; Riverside Park, where he watched us zoom down slides and run through sprinklers. His idea of a great evening would include a poker game with cigar-smoking buddies, a spirited discussion of a novel or play, and reading aloud to his daughters.

Thirteen years younger than my father, my mother, Lynn Nesbit, with her almond-shaped dark eyes, stick-straight jet-black hair, and slender, small-boned frame, had a piquant, gamine beauty. When I was born, she wore her hair long and parted in the middle, but around the time we began preschool, she cut it very short, which gave her a more professional air and a harder, less feminine edge. She wore elegant A-line shift dresses and fashionably clunky bead jewelry at work, cotton sundresses, bell-bottom jeans with clingy T-shirts or poncho sweaters, and skimpy bikinis on weekends. Unlike my father, who smoked and ate red meat for breakfast, lunch, and dinner, my mother watched what she ate, did Pilates at a studio several times per week, played tennis for hours, used a stationary bicycle set up in her and my father's bedroom while watching the news in the evenings, and jogged around the Central Park Reservoir to maintain her figure.

The same discipline and intensity she brought to her diet and exercise regimens, she demonstrated in her career. She'd come to

New York from a tiny town in Illinois as a wide-eyed girl of twenty-two, gotten a job as an editorial apprentice at *Ladies' Home Journal*, then a seventy-five-dollar-a-week job as the assistant to literary agent Sterling Lord. She worked as Lord's receptionist, typist, and file clerk, weighing his packages and stamping his letters. But by the time I was born, when she was thirty-one, she'd risen to become a high-ranking agent at International Creative Management, representing icons of the New Journalism from Tom Wolfe to Hunter S. Thompson, cult literary figures including Donald Barthelme (her first great love), who once referred to her as "the mother of postmodernism," Robert Caro and Toni Morrison, whose first novel, *The Bluest Eye*, came out the year I was born, and Michael Crichton, who signed with her to do *The Andromeda Strain* and became a close friend and client for his entire career. Strong and capable, my mother always performed at a high level, whether it was in heated negotiations for her clients or in the kitchen before a dinner party for illustrious guests.

We lived amidst stacks of *The Nation*, the *New Republic*, *Partisan Review*, the *New York Review of Books*, the *Village Voice*, and *The New Yorker*, walls and walls of bookcases, back copies of the *New York Times Book Review* and *Times* Weekend and Arts & Leisure sections, and pile upon pile of books, manuscripts, student papers. The soundtrack of my childhood: the theme songs from *Mister Rogers' Neighborhood*, *The Electric Company*, and *Sesame Street*, Pete Seeger's voice, the tinkle of the Mister Softee truck outside our window, and the aggressive, even frenetic, yet also somehow comforting and optimistic sound of my father's typewriter.

Our apartment at 333 Central Park West on West 93rd Street had "good bones"—high ceilings, herringbone wood floors, and fabulous Central Park views through its large bedroom and living room windows—but the paint on its prewar moldings was chipping, its exterior hallways were dark and dingy, and its two tiny, windowless bathrooms had tubs whose glaze came off in bits every time we took a bath. The neighborhood around our building was gritty—the streets were littered, drug dealing took place on stoops, muggings were frequent, and we never took the subway (always the bus). Today the apartment would be called a Classic Seven and sell for many millions of dollars; then, my parents paid under two hundred dollars a month to rent it. Our best friends in the building included *New Yorker* writer Jane Kramer and her anthropologist husband, Vincent Crapanzano; legendary editor Richard Seaver, who'd translated or published everyone from Samuel Beckett to Henry Miller, *Story of O* to *The Autobiography of Malcolm X*, and his French wife, Jeannette, who'd had a career as an opera singer and now wrote cookbooks; writer and *Nation* and *Newsweek* editor Dick Pollak and his PBS producer wife, Merle. All of these couples had children my age who became my playmates.

My parents entertained frequently, so our apartment was full of writers and critics, actors and artists, who came for cocktails, dinner, a party, a strategy session with my mother or my father. Their voices—discussing, arguing, exulting, scolding, pleading, expatiating—wove in and out of my dreams.

In a 1974 *New York Post* piece called "At Home with Lynn Nesbit and Richard Gilman" (complete with a sidebar offering my mother's recipe for Chile Relleno Puff), my mother says that they entertained often as a way of simultaneously sustaining their friendships and being present for their children. My mother loved to cook from Julia Child and somehow managed to produce impressive dishes like *Veau Prince Orloff* and *Daube de Boeuf* despite her stressful work schedule. At our modest weekend house in Weston, Connecticut, my father usually grilled, animatedly discussing a provocative *New York Times* article or new play while deftly flipping burgers or marinating steak. I loved my father's Yale students (everyone from Mark Linn-Baker to Skip Gates) who came to parties at our Weston house. The rangy, intense, mostly male graduate students jockeyed for position nearest the grill while my father made their hot dogs, sat on the floor to play jacks with me and Claire, or accompanied us down to the swimming hole, where they'd give us shoulder rides and flip us into the water.

Our favorite Connecticut friends were *New York Times* book critic Anatole Broyard, with his cap of tight graying curls, tanned, lithe body, wry humor, and zest for both assessment and fun, and his lovely Nordic-looking wife, Sandy. My father and Anatole went way back—they'd both served in the Pacific Theater during World War II and had met a few years later in the Village. They'd shared girlfriends, books, social idealism, and a dedication to forging their identities free of the shackles of convention, history, and expectation. I felt they knew things about each other that no one else did.

In one of her books, my mother's client and close friend Jill Schary Robinson recalled a Weston lunch with the Broyards in which Martha Stewart and my mother "battled their way through a conversation about real estate prices in Weston and Fairfield, like high school champions going for the trophy," and Anatole suggested that my father turn it into a play. "Dick," Jill wrote, "encouraged everyone except himself." According to Jill, my father would "find the flaw and gently point it out," but "Lynn's sharp insights made . . . [her] flinch." And as Martha and my mother duked it out for conversational supremacy, so did Anatole and my father: "Anatole enjoyed taking stances in opposition to Dick, mostly to tease him and to enjoy the wordplay. Like star students, they jousted, positioning ideas for battle." As Anatole and my father sparkled in conversational skirmishes, I listened and imbibed their fervent commitment to ideas.

Participants in my parents' gatherings flitted in and out of my and my sister's bedrooms. We got bedtime stories from gentle, courtly, enigmatic Uncle Bern (Malamud), whimsical and witty Aunt Ann (Beattie), earthy and affectionate Aunt Toni (Morrison).

Publicly austere intellectuals morphed into very different creatures when they crossed the threshold of our bedroom doors. Elizabeth Hardwick and Susan Sontag, both of whom my father admired enormously, generously appraised our drawings and singing and poems with none of the severity that marked their worldly personae. Novelist Jerzy Kosinski, a great pal of my father's during the seventies, reacted to meeting our stuffed animals with exclamations of delight, although I always saw pools of sorrow in his arresting dark eyes. Frizzy-haired, disheveled jazz critic, civil libertarian, and *Village Voice* columnist Nat Hentoff was always up for a game of hide-and-seek with us; zany *Sesame Street* writer and composer Christopher Cerf would come bearing a stack of albums signed by the cast and humming his newest ditty. Impossibly tall and movie-star handsome Michael Crichton squeezed his six-foot-eight-inch frame into our tiny chairs with an awkward charm and even did some coloring when we handed him crayons. Tiny but formidable Lore Segal, whose first novel my father had reviewed favorably in the *New Republic*, brought us her new translation of *The Juniper Tree and Other Tales from Grimm*, illustrated by Maurice Sendak, and dedicated her 1977 children's book *Tell Me a Trudy* "to Priscilla and Claire." To us, these luminaries were just people: complicated, endearing, real.

At my parents' low-key cocktail parties, Claire and I would be enlisted to pass around bowls of nuts or trays of my mother's spicy deviled eggs; after early dinner parties, we'd bring out the amaretti cookies and get good-night hugs from the assembled guests. Sometimes I'd be trotted out in my pastel polyester nightgowns (made in my father's uncle Wally's Brooklyn nightgown factory) to show his buddies that I could enact all the NFL referees' signals or recite a poem for his literary friends (these groups often overlapped, and *A Fan's Notes* author Fred Exley was an especially raucous member).

I saw the humanity, the frailty of these powerful intellectuals, these imposing authors, these towering cultural figures. I saw them hurt, frightened, rejected, confused, angry, lost. I saw them as exuberant and childlike. I saw them lauded; I saw them leveled. I saw them drunk, dejected, despairing. I saw the vulnerability behind the powerful pens, the insecurity, the weaknesses. I saw acclaimed authors devastated by savage reviews, groveling for praise, beset with self-doubt. I saw them felled by illness and infirmity. I saw them buck each other up and tear each other down, commiserate and criticize, laugh and lament, bask in glory and shrivel up in disappointment. I saw them flirt with women who were not their wives, and I saw the wives' drawn, despairing, or contemptuous faces. And most of all I saw my father as an enormously powerful figure, a fount of wisdom, a locus of authority.

> CRITIC. Always "eminent." Supposed to know everything, to
> have read everything, to have seen everything.
>
> —Flaubert's *Dictionary of Received Ideas*

> Authors are partial to their wit, 'tis true,
> But are not critics to their judgment too?
>
> —Alexander Pope, "An Essay on Criticism"

Surrounded by creative writers, did my father not feel inadequate? No, because he was the judge and they the judged, he the one they all turned to for advice, wisdom, validation. My father's approval meant everything to those who wanted to please him. He gave confidence to those who lacked it, courage to those who were fearful, reticent, or retiring. But he also destroyed confidence, inspired fear, and issued stinging put-downs in print. You wanted to be on his good side.

Harold Brodkey, one of my father's closest friends during the 1970s and the dedicatee of *The Making of Modern Drama*, was the kind of writer they call a critics' darling. *First Love and Other Sorrows*, his first story collection, had been rapturously received, and the stories he subsequently published in *The New Yorker* were discussed reverentially by the literary types who came to my parents' cookouts in Weston and dinners in New York. The New York publishing world, in fact, held Harold in the highest esteem, and was waiting, somewhat less breathlessly over time, for him to turn in the long, autobiographical novel for which he'd had a series of book contracts negotiated by his agent, my mother. I knew that it was taking an inordinate amount of time for him to complete the book, but that my mother and his editor, Gordon Lish, believed it would be well worth the wait. Gordon, an acerbic enthusiast, described it as the next Great American Novel and Harold as the American Proust. The American Proust and the Eminent Drama Critic often commiserated over their mutual struggle with getting words on the page as the Prominent Literary Agent clucked over their mutual inertia.

Harold, dark, intense, forbidding, was a frequent visitor to our apartment, and Claire and I were somewhat afraid of him. Sometimes when he'd come over, we'd barricade ourselves inside Claire's closet and hide from him. He asked penetrating questions and often gave us what Paddington would call "a hard stare" as we pranced about in our play. Once when my mother made a spinach soufflé that failed in dramatic fashion, Harold's eviscerating comments had made her tear up. My father, however, brought out the droll side of Harold and knew how to put him in his place. After initially wincing at the first bite, Daddy had shoveled the offending spinach soufflé into his mouth and cracked a joke about Harold's "impossibly high critical standards." Harold, chastened, took a few penitent bites.

One afternoon in our living room at 333 Central Park West, I was playing in a corner while my father and Harold conversed. Harold said, in a teasing yet deadly serious tone, "Dick, am I not the greatest writer since Proust?"

My father stared at him incredulously.

"No, let me rephrase that," Harold added. "Am I not the greatest writer of the twentieth century *including* Proust?"

My father, smilingly, drew out his response so as to savor his role as judge and sage and critic. "Harold, the short and the long answer to your question? *No*."

Harold laughed ruefully, noticed me, and asked me who my favorite writer of the twentieth century was. I told him Norton Juster (author of *The Phantom Tollbooth*).

My father told that story over and over again, ostensibly as a critique of Harold's narcissism, but also as a testament to his own power. He, Richard Gilman, was the Proust expert, the one who determined greatness, the ultimate authority.

> To grapple with [Gilman's] perspective is to grapple with one's own flaccid preconceptions; to be roused from torpor for a cultural wrestling match and to find oneself a gastropod pitted against a Viking. What's more, the Viking wears hobnailed boots.
>
> —John Leonard, review of Richard Gilman,
> *The Confusion of Realms*, 1969

I knew that my father was powerful, that what my father was doing was important. Not in the way that bankers or lawyers, businessmen or politicians were "powerful" or "important." My father almost never wore suits and ties, carried a casual shoulder bag rather than a briefcase, didn't go to an office or have a secretary like my friends' fathers and as my mother did, didn't wear expensive shoes or drive an expensive car. But he was doing work of the highest importance, the most important kind of importance. That I was certain of. I knew it from the hushed or earnest tones in which he discussed books, films, politics, issues of social justice. I knew it from the way everyone around the table would quiet when he spoke, pay special attention to his opinions, gaze at him worshipfully. Writers, some famous, some not, hung on his every word, begged him to read their work, asked him for his opinions and his judgments. I knew it from the way otherwise intimidating or imperious men would pander or clam up, hover or retreat in his presence, the way his students clustered around him, working hard for his approval.

I knew of my father's power from the way the words "Yale" or "*Newsweek*," where he'd been the theater critic before coming to Yale, would inspire instant respect in everyone from a friend's parents to a teacher, to a flight attendant.

I knew of my father's power from the challenging subjects, commanding titles, and magisterial covers of his books. *The Confusion of Realms* (1969) and *Common and Uncommon Masks* (1971) both had dramatic silver covers with the titles in large, aggressive block letters. *The Making of Modern Drama* (1974) also had an all-caps title and was emblazoned with a quite frightening photo of a screaming woman (I later learned it was from a production of *Mother Courage*). My father worked on innovative, difficult, avant-garde art; the names of his favorite authors and plays—Strindberg, Brecht, Pirandello, Handke, *Waiting for Godot*, *Ivanov*, *Woyzeck*—were hard to pronounce and came out sounding guttural, intimidating, highbrow. But because my mother was a powerful agent, I knew that being published by Random House meant my father was not just a fringe intellectual; he was right there at the center of culture.

I knew of his power from the mystique and drama that surrounded his writing: his need for privacy and solitude, the intensity of his typing, the elation when he had finished a piece or submitted a book. Moreover, my mother seemed to fully believe that what he was doing had vital significance. She chided us if we interrupted him, put on her most serious face when urging him to get to work, spoke of his work to others in awed tones. There were articles about him in the newspaper; a reporter observed our afternoon and evening routines and gave me the last line in her *New York Post* piece about my parents: " 'I want three peanut butter sandwiches,' said Priscilla." Teachers and friends' parents told me they'd seen my father on PBS or *The Dick Cavett Show*, read his pieces in the *New York Times* or the *New Republic*.

And I knew that my father was an especially fastidious critic, difficult to please, demanding, rigorous. Friends would joke about how tough he was. He'd complain to my mother about being unable to give blurbs for friends' books—"It's just not good enough, Lynn!"— or about their dissatisfaction with the carefully hedged, insufficiently admiring blurbs he did manage to produce. I knew he'd been uncomfortable as a *Newsweek* critic because he had to review so much "middle-brow" stuff.

It's said that critics criticize because they are thwarted artists or creators. But my father was not a frustrated artist or a failed creator. He had no interest in playwriting. Instead, he passionately believed in the worth, the indispensability, the nobility, even, of the critical endeavor. In the cultural milieu of his professional life, criticism *mattered*.

> By a process we naturally cannot trace, Büchner modulated from a scientific outlook that was highly imaginative and open to an artistic procedure that obtained its data and worked out its methods through a pragmatic freedom from preconceptions, a liberation from the expectations and mechanical traditions of literature. As is always the case, such freedom meant that literature might therefore be renewed, made possible again through an act of life-giving heresy.
>
> —Richard Gilman, from *The Making of Modern Drama*

Like the playwrights, authors, and characters he loved, my father sought a freshness of perception, a freedom from conventional thinking, a penetrating directness that defied expectations and challenged the status quo. Defining the renewal of literature in modern drama as "life-giving heresy," he was both a spiritual seeker and an irreverent heretic. He especially loved this line—talk about life-giving heresy!—from Büchner: "The word *must* is one of the curses with which Mankind is baptized." My father hated musts, shoulds, imperatives, rigid definitions. In his 1979 book *Decadence: The Strange Life of an Epithet*, he inveighed against the "insidious power which all moral and spiritual terminology inevitably exerts over us." He despised academic cant and jargon. He served as an expert witness in the Lenny Bruce obscenity trial and can be heard on a recording resolutely defending (in the face of furious badgering by the prosecution's attorney) the necessity of "obscurity" and openness of interpretation for what he called "imaginative workers."

My father was a champion of freedom. Freedom to imagine and create oneself unshackled by convention, history, origins; freedom to be, express, signify in a multiplicity of ways; freedom to resist being pinned down, labeled, mastered, interpreted definitively. His review of John Updike's most iconic novel contains a passage that strikes me as a veiled description of his own values and nature, his apotheosis of freedom as a paramount virtue:

> On one level, *Rabbit, Run* is a grotesque allegory of American life, with its myth of happiness and success, its dangerous innocence and crippling antagonism between value and fact. But much more significantly, it is a minor epic of the spirit thirsting for room to discover and be itself, ducking, dodging, staying out of reach of everything that will pin it down and impale it on fixed, immutable laws that are not of its own making and do not consider its integrity.
>
> —Richard Gilman, "A Distinguished Image of Precarious Life," *Commonweal*, October 28, 1960

The "minor epic of the spirit" he describes could be applied equally to my father's own circuitous, idiosyncratic path. Born in Brooklyn to conservative Jewish immigrant parents, he was the only person in his family with leftist leanings and a passion for the arts, who studied literature and philosophy, and experimented with drugs. His first wife, Esther, was a fellow nonconformist, a feisty visual artist, avant-garde set designer, and modern dancer whom he met in the Village and married at City Hall. In the 1950s, they traveled frequently to Mexico and Europe in search of literary idols and political heroes; horrified by McCarthyism, they moved briefly to Italy before returning to New York. My father once wrote of what he was searching for in those years: "style, antipsychology, antidomesticity, a noncommercial spirit, Europe." Esther told an interviewer: "I didn't care much about the accumulation of money, possessions, or following old traditions"; my father didn't either. He would often refer to himself as "an intellectual hobo" in his twenties, and in the *New York Post* profile, he told the reporter: "I didn't know what I wanted to be. I was a Bohemian bum for a while. I went to Europe, lived in the Village, wrote some poetry." What he didn't tell that reporter—and never told his parents—is that in his late twenties he also underwent a rhapsodic conversion to Catholicism. In the late 1950s, he began writing for left-leaning Catholic magazines like *Jubilee* and *Commonweal* on everything from the pope to plays. But he would soon fall away from the church and channel his hunger for the divine, the beautiful, and the sublime into an obsession with art, drama, literature.

What's being tested is our own originality against the pull of received wisdom.

—Richard Gilman, *Chekhov's Plays: An Opening into Eternity*

My father was all about finding and forging "our own originality against the pull of received wisdom." He celebrated originality in artists, in students, in friends. The epigraph to his first book, *The Confusion of Realms*—"We must get behind the masks of common vision"—from one of his favorites, Jerzy Grotowski, exemplifies his aesthetic. He valued modern dramatists because they were "revolutionaries [and] innovators," lauded them for their "creation of radically new styles and patterns of consciousness," their heroic "effort to renew drama, to combat its tendency to inertia and self-repetition." He championed idiosyncratic, difficult, daring authors: Susan Sontag, William Gass, Donald Barthelme, Renata Adler, John Barth; my mother represented all of them but Susan. My father liked art that had a strong critical bent, assumed a counterposition, a stance of opposition, questioning convention and cliché. He liked people who were nonconformists, but not in any kind of stagy or calculated way; authenticity was crucial to him. He was a champion of difference, oddness, individuality.

But it wasn't enough to be different or odd in his book. You also had to be good. He had no patience for people who called themselves poets or painters but lacked real talent or were more hung up on the persona of an artist and the coolness of a pose, a role, an identity than on actually making good work. And as a critic, Richard Gilman was all about puncturing pretension, dispelling hype, and delivering the cold hard truth. In an early piece, "What Keeps Us Going," he declared that "telling the truth about the theatre's shame and boredom and death is very nearly the central activity and radical justification for a journalist-critic of drama in our time." He was famous for his ruthless, implacable judgments: no pity, no sympathy, no partiality at all. He simply couldn't politely demur, bow out, stay silent. He felt an obligation to tell the truth as he saw it, and he wasn't afraid to be peremptory. The word "nonsense" pops up frequently in his writing, as do "absurd," "preposterous," and "foolish." Of Dustin Hoffman's much-debated performance in *The Merchant of Venice* in a 1987 *New York Times* Arts & Leisure piece, he wrote: "To say that Mr. Hoffman lacked a tragic quality or a sense of Shylock's evil is nonsense." No beating around the bush, no equivocation. It was nonsense, pure and simple.

That's not to say that my father didn't sometimes find gleeful delight in taking down what he felt was unworthy, pompous, or foolish. He would often repeat some of his most stinging zingers, savoring, relishing, luxuriating in the wit and grace and archness of each clever turn of phrase. Two of his—and our—favorites: "Directing Jason Robards must be like pushing heavy furniture around the stage"; and "Like an enormous fake elephant, an inflated contrivance to elicit oohs and ahs from the children, Eugene O'Neill's *Strange Interlude* has come into view again on Broadway, after having been in storage for nearly thirty-five years. And the children have responded beautifully, walking around the astonishing object with awed faces." Everyone would laugh at his cutting wit and beg him for more. A story he especially liked to tell was how one day while sitting at his desk in his *Newsweek* office, he got a phone call from an actress's aunt who indignantly informed him that his review was "just plain cruel" because her niece had "never had an acting lesson in her life!" "Well, thank you very much for calling," my father told the woman in a chipper voice. "That explains everything!"

Richard Gilman could be extraordinarily harsh in print. In review after review, he indicted the "incompetence, vulgarity, pretension, mendacity, and cowardice . . . on exhibit" year after year on Broadway. Reading his work now, I'm struck over and over again by how he holds nothing back as he absolutely *demolishes* lauded playwrights, actors, and directors, thereby perfectly fulfilling Shaw's dictum—"Loyalty in a critic is corruption."

And the energy that animated his lash, the galvanic force that motivated and spilled out in his criticism, was at its essence a righteous indignation on behalf of truth and art. "To be any sort of useful critic means one has to resist bullying from whatever direction it comes," my father once wrote, and he resisted it fiercely. His criticism, at its best, was fine discernment, a championing of the unusual or the unnoticed, characterized by a bracing honesty, a fiery eloquence. It could sometimes be hostile and aggressive, and that anger could be liberating, electrifying.

Criticism for my father was a diagnosis of false seeing, a diagnosis of false *being*. He loathed plays that pandered to an audience's comfortable view of itself or loaded every rift with highfalutin ore; he despised people who put on airs, were pretentious, dishonest, hypocritical. He was a critic of what he referred to disparagingly as "bourgeois" culture (and Broadway's prominent role in it), of celebrity for its own sake (part of his resistance to star vehicles, vanity projects, and puff pieces), of material acquisitiveness and ostentation. As an adolescent, I fell head over heels in love with Holden Caulfield in large part because his hatred of phonies, his anger, intelligence, distaste for (failure at?) conventional life, his great reserves of sweetness and longing reminded me of my father.

And like Holden, my father could apply his strictures too severely. Anyone who went to law school or business school was craven, mercenary, or both. My father bemoaned his student Henry Winkler's "selling out" by taking the role of the Fonz on *Happy Days*. "Henry was a great actor, he could do Shakespeare!" my father would lament. Until the night he was at a New York City restaurant and Henry Winkler came up to him, adoringly, calling him "Professor Gilman" in a reverent tone, telling him how much his tutelage had meant to him. From that point on, he was *fine* with anything Henry did.

In his *New York Times* review of my father's first book, John Leonard described the experience of reading him as being "roused from torpor for a cultural wrestling match and to find oneself a gastropod pitted against a Viking." "The athletic metaphor is employed advisedly," he wrote, "for Mr. Gilman practices a kind of confrontation criticism." My father was brave, so much braver than I have ever been, in thrusting himself into the arena of debate, taking unpopular stances, unmasking hypocrites and charlatans, taking down sacred cows. He was always up for the challenge, game for a fight, unrelenting in his commitment to advocating for the worthy and exposing pretenders. He wielded his verbal weapons with a gleeful savagery and thrust himself into the fray. The protagonist of Wilfred Sheed's 1970 novel *The Critic*, who declares "that good theater is more important than individual feelings" and writes with a "corrosive style" and "biting merciless wit," was thought to be based on my father.

Ironically, my father was often himself the target of harsh criticism. *The Confusion of Realms* received infamously scathing reviews from Philip Rahv in the *New York Review of Books* and from Gore Vidal in a piece called "Literary Gangsters" (my mother would later take Gore on as a client). John Updike, who once declared that "critics are like pigs at the pastry cart," wrote in a *New Yorker* piece: "If a harsh Providence were to obliterate, say, Alfred Kazin, Richard Gilman, Stanley Kauffmann, and Irving Howe, tomorrow new critics would arise with the same worthy intelligence, the same complacently agonized humanism, the same inability to read a book except as a disappointing version of one they might have written, the same deadly 'auntiness.'" In the bibliography at the end of Updike's 1970 novel *Bech: A Book*, an article by Richard Gilman is pretentiously entitled "Bech, Gass, and Nabokov: The Territory Beyond Proust," and in *S*, the nasty lawyer representing the protagonist's estranged husband is named Gilman.

But my father laughed about Updike's digs and barbs; indeed, he often found amusement in negative responses to his work. One story that he relished about himself was the time he appeared on television, some show on PBS, and the next day, while out shopping, he noticed that a woman wearing a raincoat and a dowdy cloche hat was following him. Finally, she caught up to him and asked: "Are you Richard Gilman? I saw you on TV last night!" When he answered "Yes," preparing to receive the expected compliments, she simply said: "Well, you stunk!" and walked away.

My father saw himself as an anti-romantic critic, stern and unsparing, unbewitched and unbenighted. He celebrated his beloved playwrights for their tough-minded realism, praising Büchner's freedom from "prejudice and distorting idealism" and "brilliant cold refusals of fantasy and myth-making," Ibsen's "anti-romanticism," and most of all Chekhov and his "grave anti-romanticism," his understanding that "beneath our ideas and values, our ambitions and dreams, lies fact, the rock-hard actuality of what we are and must do."

But even as he made a name for himself by being discerning, hard to please, hypercritical, my father was also and always an enthusiast, a passionate believer. Of Ibsen, he once wrote: "I must confess to feeling . . . like a lover whose beloved draws mostly unappreciative stares. I can't imagine why everybody doesn't see what I do, and I conclude that they are simply not looking at the same person." He saw his as a sacred task, an act of radical honesty, unshakable integrity, and impassioned advocacy. He wanted to protect the plays and playwrights he loved from benighted interpretations, reductive assessments, and wrongheaded or insufficiently realized enactments. In "What Keeps Us Going," he described the profession of drama critic "as a service to one's public . . . and even more sustaining, in all modesty, as a service to dramatic art." When he won the George Jean Nathan Award in Dramatic Criticism for 1970–71, the committee's citation praised *Common and Uncommon Masks* for its "intellectual scope, practical knowledge, and genuine concern for the state of the theatre in our times." That genuine concern could sometimes shade into indignation, outrage, and condemnation of those who didn't come up to his standards, but its genuineness was never in question. In his criticism as in his parenting, idealism and love were the foundation and the wellspring.

An unparalleled joy was the birth of my daughters, to whom this book is dedicated: Priscilla on May 1, 1970, and Claire on July 14, 1971 . . . [T]heir childhoods were a renewal and replenishment for me.

—Richard Gilman, *Faith, Sex, Mystery*

n her eulogy for my father, Claire wrote of the surpassing value of childhood to him:

Fatherhood was not simply a wonderful part of Daddy's existence. Nor was it a compartmentalized role that he occupied parallel to and apart from his intellectual and creative pursuits. Rather, fatherhood spoke to the core of who he was as a person. It resonated with his basic faith in creativity. His love for the life of the mind. His deep imagination. And his quest for spiritual enlightenment and beauty. My father *believed* in childhood. And he infected my sister and me with this belief, leading us to develop the rich, imaginative life that we had as children, and that continues to sustain us . . . Throughout his life, my father sought something higher, something beyond the dross of the everyday—that elusive opening into eternity to which his book on Chekhov refers and which impelled his conversion to Catholicism as a young man. I believe that the world of childhood provided him with a secular equivalent to what religion ultimately could not deliver. I think, more specifically, that my brother, sister, and I provided him with that as well. We were more than just his children. We represented all that was good in the world.

In the very years when he was at his professional peak as a cultural warrior, our father was dedicated to giving me and Claire a childhood free of worldly strife. My father was the priest of the cathedral space that was our childhood even as he submitted to its power as a devout congregant, a wonder-struck parishioner.

He had a number of roles of gentle yet formidable authority in our vast imaginative universe. As the Great Finder, he conducted searches for lost library books, hairbrushes, and toys with all the flair and sangfroid of his detective heroes Hercule Poirot, Sherlock Holmes, and Perry Mason, calming our flustered nerves with his poise and invariably locating the missing item, which he'd present with an electrifyingly dramatic: "The Great Finder . . . strikes again!" As the Reverend Gilman, he officiated at the weddings of our stuffed penguins, horses, and Pooh Bears to our Madame Alexander dolls, offering the newlyweds his hearty congratulations and a marriage certificate on Yale Drama School stationery. As esteemed Director Gilman, he'd pop in for a look at and listen to auditioning bears and seals when Claire and I would line up our menagerie of stuffed animals and hold open-call auditions for a production of *The Sound of Music* or *Annie*. (Years later, he told me that long before we summoned him into the room for the final group of auditioners, he would eavesdrop on the whole process, silently rolling with laughter as we made poor Snoopy sing dreadfully off key and then dismissed him with a "Don't call us, we'll call you" or made a snobby ballerina doll throw a hissy fit when she didn't get a callback for Anita in *West Side Story*). During weekends and summers at our house in Connecticut, he'd warmly open his writing studio (a ramshackle barn-like structure next to a vegetable garden, its knotty pine walls hung with our crayon drawings, cards we'd made for him, notes we'd written to him) to our visiting Paddingtons, who'd come by for a hot cocoa or piece of chocolate and a chat with kindly Mr. Gilman about books they were reading, troubles they were having, or ideas they wanted feedback on. At our New York City apartment, his office—a tiny maid's room filled with filing cabinets, papers, and clouds of thick cigarette and cigar smoke—was a welcome destination for a slew of stuffed animals who'd stop by to say hi, offer encouragement, or report on the day's news to Professor Gilman, known to them as a noted authority on drama but in need of support when what my mother called "writer's block" struck (I'd always imagine a big wooden block slamming down on my father's head or on his typewriter keys).

And then there was Maestro Ricardo Gilman.

The summer I was seven, my parents rented a house in Siena, Italy, with their good friends anthropologist Lionel Tiger and his English professor wife, Virginia. Claire and I were best buddies with their son, Sebastian. Sebastian, intellectual yet roguish, was the same-age brother we didn't have. Claire and Sebastian and I splashed and swam in the pool and roamed around the property in all sorts of invented games. We read side by side, tucked into Lionel's famous grilled cheese sandwiches for lunch, played pranks—at Sebastian's instigation—on our Italian babysitter.

And late each afternoon, we went to circus practice with Maestro Ricardo Gilman. After his writing day was over, our father would summon Claire, Sebastian, and me to his office on the top floor of our airy house. As we climbed the narrow spiral staircase that led to his lair, I'd feel my heart leap up.

Maestro Ricardo Gilman would welcome us with a flourish, a gallant wave of the wrist, a deliciously pregnant phrase, and then we'd get to work. He'd solicit ideas from us about acts (based on our yearly trips to the Ringling Bros. and Barnum & Bailey Circus at Madison Square Garden), put us through our paces, marvel at our abilities. He coached us through both mastering tough tricks and imitating the performance of tough tricks. I was a tightrope walker, mimicking a slow, tentative walk complete with balance checks and a triumphant arrival on the other side. Claire was both a bareback rider on my father's equine back and the human cannonball, launched from my father's arms onto an overstuffed chair during practice and ultimately into the swimming pool. Sebastian juggled and deftly executed physical comedy as a waggish clown. He and my father coaxed the two dogs who came with our rented house to fetch, dance, and jump over obstacles. During rehearsals, my father was a bewitching combination of experimental European theater director (complete with the puffing on cigarettes and barking of commands) and hammy American ringmaster.

The act we all loved most, that we felt was most ingenious, most amazing, most guaranteed to wow the three remaining parents—our audience—was the clown car. Gesticulating and grinning, Claire, Sebastian, and I ran in circles in and out of our small Italian car. On the last go-round, my father, who had lain unseen on the floor (with us scurrying over and sometimes stepping on him), rose in dramatic fashion from the floor and emerged, with a triumphant smile, from the impossibly tiny space.

With his enthusiasm, his exuberance, his ability to notice and take pleasure in the tiniest aspects of experience, my father could make anything, any activity, exhilarating, uncanny, invested with an electric charge. Simple games where he'd throw us on our parents' bed or chase us became rip-roaring romps named "Flip Flop" and "Catch 'Em." At our rented summer houses in Spain and Italy, my father spent hours in the pool with us, pushing us in a floaty choo-choo train, carrying us on his shoulders, then flipping us off into the water. He got me to swim in the deep end by making my labored progress seem like an athletic feat—as I determinedly kicked and scissored and stroked toward him, he'd excitedly narrate my progress in his best Jim McKay or Howard Cosell imitation, then take me into his arms in a laughing hug when I got to the "finish line." And always there were word games—opposites, synonyms, sentence completions, metaphor-making—all ways in which he was honing our language skills and fostering our appreciation for words, but they felt like pure play. I lived with a sense of delighted anticipation; there was always more to read, more to see, more to invent and create and realize.

"Sidda, Swanee!" he'd call with a happy lilt in his voice whenever he laid eyes on us. I was Sidda because as a two-year-old, I'd called myself what sounded like "P'Sidda" instead of Priscilla. Claire was Swanee because her middle name was Swan (my grandmother's maiden name). And for us, he was always Daddy, never, ever Dad.

Our country weekends were shaped by the rituals my father created. When we got off the train from Grand Central Station to Westport every Friday evening and caught sight of him on the platform, he'd open his arms as wide as he could and we'd run at top speed toward him, laughing and squealing as he picked us up, one under each arm, and kissed the tops of our heads over and over again. Once in the car, my parents would begin their catch-up conversation about the week in literature and publishing, politics and art. When we got to the house, Daddy would build a roaring fire in the large stone fireplace, cook London broil for dinner, and read to us before bed. On Saturday mornings, while my mother rested or caught up on manuscript reading and my father wrote, Claire and I played with our dollhouse and our stuffed animals. Careful not to disturb my mother, Daddy would make us sandwiches for lunch, and then take us to the Weston and Westport libraries, delicious sojourns sandwiched around a stop at Friendly's for ice cream. When we'd get home, we'd watch the *Wide World of Sports* on ABC, absorbing ourselves in the thrill of victory and the agony of defeat. Saturday nights, the three of us would usually have dinner at a small pizza place on the main street in Westport, then walk a half block over for an ice cream cone at Baskin-Robbins. My mother was a peripheral figure on these weekends. She had no interest in sports, or ice cream/pizza outings, or reading aloud to us. She needed time to rest and to work, and the three of us made sure to give it to her.

My father unequivocally supported my mother in having a major career and happily took on child care duties, working from home much of the time. He brought us up to admire female trailblazers like Amelia Earhart, Golda Meir, Marie Curie, Althea Gibson, and Billie Jean King. He adored Brearley, the rigorous, empowering, feminist all-girls school my sister and I attended. Women others considered plain, even unattractive, he found beautiful because of an intelligent gleam in their eyes, a warm smile, a noble mind. For him, beauty was tied to something interior, incorporeal; he found it in character and intellect and vibrant appreciation of life. When I was a seven-year-old tomboy who hated wearing dresses and having my hair combed, he told me that I might not be as pretty as some of the white pinafore-clad, blond-ringleted little girls in my Sunday school class, but I was something more important: I was "smart." "Your brain is more valuable than any pretty face," he said, running his hand affectionately over my head.

And despite my father's daunting intellectual prowess, he never intimidated us. And he never talked down to us either. In conversation with him, any idea I had was acceptable and worthy of being taken seriously. I loved to write, and he was always the first, and often the only, person I shared my writing with. He didn't go into rhapsodies of praise, he didn't tell me I was brilliant or gifted or amazing. He read my first novel, an homage to (rip-off of) *The Phantom Tollbooth*, earnestly, seriously, and offered constructive feedback. Recently, I found a photo of us from Christmas morning, 1978. He's sitting in a chair in my grandparents' living room, and I have one hand lovingly resting on his head and the other on his arm. He's reading my second "novel," which I'd scribbled in a composition book every day for three months in Brearley Language Arts class. Heavily influenced by L. Frank Baum's *Oz* books, it recounted the epic story of King Ketchup and his love for a beautiful damsel named Julianna. In the photo, my father looks engaged, and I look happy and calm, waiting for what I know will be his considered reaction. My father's admiration was hard won, and this is why I trusted his judgment so. I knew he would never tell me something was good if it wasn't, I knew he would always help me make my work better.

Other than reading and writing, writing plays and putting on shows for my parents and other relatives was what I loved most to do. Claire would only perform in these shows on the condition that she play the glamorously dressed heroine or princess or prima ballerina. She wore my mother's old prom dresses, my grandmother's lacy and silky negligees or diaphanous nightgowns, and flowers or a tiara on her head. I took the decidedly less flashy role as her paramour, usually attired in bell-bottom jeans or cords and my grandfather's bowler hat and tie; my grandmother had all the other roles (witch, fairy godmother, angel, dog). My father, the venerable and exacting critic, ate these shows up.

Claire and I loved books about child performers, from family friend Jill Krementz's *A Very Young* series (Dancer, Gymnast, Skater, Actress) to Noel Streatfeild's *Shoes* books. And from a young age, I got solos in music class, at camp, and in school performances. But I was always aware that while my father reveled in my talent, he did not want me to take that talent anywhere professionally. He and my mother agreed that I should not be given any voice lessons or cultivated as a child performer. Daddy hated what he called "those bratty kid singers," and when a family friend who'd heard me sing suggested that my parents get me an agent and have me audition for Broadway shows, he was horrified.

The musical *Annie* opened on Broadway in 1977. Posters were plastered everywhere; classmates raved. My parents finally gave in and took us to see it in the spring of 1979; the show was already on its third Annie, a lovely, unaffected fourteen-year-old named Sarah Jessica Parker. That seven-year-old Claire and eight-year-old me were absolutely enchanted is not surprising, but how surprising was it that my champion-of-the-avant-garde father succumbed entirely?!

As a kid, he'd read the *Little Orphan Annie* comics, of course, and the show is set in 1933, in the New York City of my father's childhood, so the nostalgia factor was strong for him. Plus there was a dog, an adorably disheveled and endearingly unprofessional one. One of our most prized Christmas gifts in 1979 was *Sandy: The Autobiography of a Star: A Homeless Mutt Steals the Spotlight in Broadway's Smash Hit "Annie."* My father hated the words "smash" and "hit" and everything that they entailed, implied, and made possible. He hated machines of stardom and what he once referred to as "refulgent names which stand in the place of talent." He couldn't keep a mainstream theater critic position because he refused to boost Broadway with "raves" and blasted what he called the "the soul-killing popularity hunt of Broadway" in much of his writing. But he loved homeless mutts, and he loved Sandy.

He also loved plucky, optimistic, resilient little Annie who brought sunshine to gruff, depressed Daddy Warbucks and stood on a desk in the Oval Office to cheer the entire political establishment out of the Depression. He squeezed my hand during Daddy Warbucks's poignant ballad "Something Was Missing," and whispered, "You and Clairey are my Annies," as Daddy Warbucks and Annie sang their exultant duet "I Don't Need Anything But You."

After we all three fell in love with *Annie*, Daddy bought me and Claire the cast album and we played it over and over on our little red record player. We held auditions for our own production of the show with our dolls and stuffed animals, belted out "It's the Hard-Knock Life" and "You're Never Fully Dressed Without a Smile" while dancing around our room with mops and brooms, and each of us adopted one of Annie's ballads as our own anthem. In a strange role reversal, moody little Claire's chosen ballad was "Tomorrow" and optimistic, smiling little me chose "Maybe." I wasn't an orphan, I didn't have to scrub floors or worry about having enough to eat. But there was something about the plaintive "Maybe," with its imagining of a beautiful mother and father united in domestic happiness, that resonated with me. I sang it wistfully, with an ache in my heart, and sometimes tears would inexplicably spring to my eyes as I sang. What was I wishing for? I had my parents—both of them—an intact family, a comfortable life. But there was something I still yearned for, or something I feared I'd lose?

His strange, difficult task was to compel the world to yield up unheard-of and demoralizing truths. The imagination's triumph would lie in wresting such truths from the obduracy of mere events and the closed system of historical time. He would shape counter-truths to those of history and in this way establish a new morale and a new kind of hard-looking, unruly, unlofty "beauty."

—Richard Gilman on Büchner, from *The Making of Modern Drama*

Despite his passion for the strange and the difficult in art, my father never tried to smuggle the arcane or the adult into our childhoods. Or rather, he saw and honored the marvelous, uncanny, profound aspects of childhood itself. He had as much affection and respect for William Steig's Amos and Boris or Beatrix Potter's Hunca Munca and Jeremy Fisher as he did for Beckett's Vladimir and Estragon or Chekhov's Olga, Masha, and Irina. For him, *Sesame Street* was as valuable a source of wisdom and pleasure as *A Doll's House* or *Hedda Gabler*. And he treated the characters as would a child who doesn't realize that they are characters. One day he spied the actor who played *Sesame Street*'s warmhearted grocery store owner, Mr. Hooper, across the aisle at a store in our neighborhood and revealed his familiarity with the show by referring to the man not merely by his character's name but by Big Bird's jumbled version. "Hi Mr. Dooper, I mean Mr. Looper, I mean Mr. Pooper!" he called out amiably. When he reported the encounter to us afterwards, it was with the glee of an accomplice in a special understanding.

Every day my father was in New York (he spent Wednesdays and Thursdays in New Haven), he'd watch *Sesame Street*, *The Electric Company*, and *Zoom* with us and read to us for hours on end, animating each character with a distinctive voice. He'd channel L. Frank Baum's evil Nome King, Ruggedo, when coaxing Claire and me to brush our teeth; impersonate the dapper and ingenious Uncle Wiggily when confronted with a challenge or predicament; and invoke Richard Scarry's Huckle Cat and Lowly Worm at opportune moments. He'd emulate Mrs. Piggle-Wiggle when discipline was needed: our messiness was met with "I think you girls need the Won't-Pick-Up-Toys

Cure!"; our resistance to taking a bath with "Time for the Radish Cure!" He'd speak in the voice of Cookie Monster when he was hungry, or preface an announcement with "Hi Ho! Kermit the Frog here, for *Sesame Street News*, reporting to you today from . . ."

The rule was that my father was never to be disturbed when he was hard at work in his study, but to this rule there was one exception: we could always knock on his study door with a worry. I trusted his judgment above all others'. I knew he wouldn't dismiss me out of hand, or belittle me, that he'd give whatever I told him serious consideration. A strange bump on my ankle, a math test, a tricky situation with a friend—my father was the one I went to. He solved problems, he found things, he dispelled worries. And he did so not by being practical or conventionally "reliable," but by assuaging the worry with warmth and boundless good humor. He'd address my worries in the voice of his favorite Muppet and alter ego, the intrepid yet vulnerable Super Grover—"Do not worry, little girl, I will solve de problem!" In and of themselves, his crinkly-eyed smile, his expressive and dynamic voice, which rose and fell and swooped and soared, crackled and hummed and sang, made me feel better. He was the one who removed ticks, took our splinters out, bandaged our cuts. As my mother fretted or anxiously oversprayed us with Bactine, he stayed steady and calm. On airplanes, my mother closed her eyes tight and gripped the armrests as we'd take off or land, but my father pointed out the sights below and encouraged us to imagine jumping on the clouds.

But my father was no sunny, blind optimist, and when something was really wrong, he knew—instantly. One wintry morning in 1973 or early 1974, I was at the top of a slide in Riverside Park, waiting my turn to go down. A little boy in my class came racing up the stairs behind me, he jostled and pushed me, and somehow I went over the side of the slide and landed on the asphalt below. I broke my fall with my hand and felt a surge of pain. I didn't scream or call out; I have always had a high tolerance for pain. Only the boy had seen me fall and he raced off, probably afraid he'd be blamed. I got up slowly and went to find a teacher. When I told her what had happened, she smiled, a bit condescendingly, and said: "But you seem fine." I could tell she thought I'd made it up. When our nanny, Carrie, picked me up from school an hour or so later, the teacher didn't report anything to her. I told Carrie that I'd fallen off the slide and that my wrist hurt. Given that the teacher hadn't seemed at all alarmed, Carrie probably assumed I'd fallen off the bottom of the slide. She put ice on my wrist and set me up in my parents' bed to watch *Mister Rogers* and *Zoom*. When my mother came home from work, she kissed me absentmindedly and told me it would be better in the morning. My father arrived from New Haven late that evening, just as I was getting ready for bed. The instant he laid eyes on me, he asked in a stricken tone: "Sidda, what's wrong?!" I described what had happened, and he immediately bundled me up, took me downstairs where the doorman helped him hail a taxi, and we were off to the ER. X-rays showed that I had badly shattered my wrist and would need to be in a cast for months. My father knew me. My father believed me.

My father protected me also by brooking no nonsense or disrespect from others as far as I was concerned. He was usually the only father who served as a chaperone on school field trips, and he enjoyed the outings almost as much as we did. On a nursery school outing to the Bronx Zoo, my father scooped up a young rapscallion (one of my father's favorite words) who'd been bothering me, dangled him near the tall fence around the lion area, and said with a mischievous grin: "I think it's feeding time, and if you don't stop pestering my daughter, it's into the lion's den for you!" Sam looked at once aghast, petrified, and impressed. Who was this bold and funny father anyway? Needless to say, Sam never bothered me again, and in fact became a close pal (my father also loved the word "pal") who followed my father around like a puppy dog when he was over for playdates.

In his stories about his own childhood in Flatbush, Brooklyn, my father cast himself as an irrepressible, plucky kid who listened avidly to radio serials—"Who knows what evil lurks in the hearts of men? The Shadow knows!" he'd dramatically intone—played stickball and stoop ball, touch football and roller hockey in the streets with his pals, delivered papers, and gobbled up the Rover Boys, Hardy Boys, and Ted Scott aviation series. We were enthralled by our father's stories about eating at automats, watching newsreels and cartoons at the cinema, working as the sports editor on his college newspaper, and serving in the Marines during World War II. Stationed on a remote island in the Pacific, he formed deep friendships with his comrades, read all of *Remembrance of Things Past* while sitting in a shell hole, and survived a close call with a shark (his fellow marine, sitting in a boat, shot the shark dead just a few feet away from my swimming father), a Japanese kamikaze bomber who missed his boat by inches, and a monkey raining coconuts down on the marines' heads (two were knocked out with concussions, but my father dodged all the nuts).

These survival stories were part of a series of near misses that made up the legend of my father's "nine lives." They included driving away from Three Mile Island the morning it blew, canceling a flight on the doomed Korean airliner days before it went down, and a childhood fall facefirst onto a broken milk bottle that left a permanent scar on his nose. His classmates dubbed him "Scarface," after Al Capone, which made him both ashamed and proud. My father saw himself as a survivor.

He emphasized his intrepidity and his independence in all the stories he told. He hated being called "Little Dicky" by his doting mother, sought refuge from family tensions in a reading cave he constructed between the back of the sofa and the wall, and dreamed of a larger life. In his memoir, he described Joan of Arc and Amelia Earhart as "the Beatrice[s] of my youth." It was their bucking of convention and bravery in forging new, untried paths, their life-giving heresy, that most appealed to him.

Such courage and daring took on a comic cast in "The Time I Tried To" stories he told of his own childhood, each one more hilarious than the last. There were "The Time I Tried To" cut my own hair (it kept getting shorter and shorter the more he tried to even it out), make my own breakfast or dinner (toast burned while water boiled over, shell fell into the eggs as bacon grease spattered the kitchen), do my own laundry (he dyed his clothes a horrible color and flooded the basement with soap suds), clean the house (he slipped on a wet floor while mopping and broke semi-precious objects while dusting). These were tales of both audacity and incompetence, about a boy with a Curious George- or Paddington-like penchant for mischief, propensity for getting into trouble, and ultimate resilience. In them, he poked fun at himself even as he presented himself to us as a bit of a rebel, a risk-taker, a boy who did things alone and wanted to make his own decisions.

It occurs to me now that his parents never appeared in his stories except as shocked and horrified adults reacting to his escapades. My Gilman grandparents were already in their eighties when Claire and I were born. My grandfather's parents had come from Russia or Lithuania; my grandfather, Jacob, had been born and raised in Brooklyn. Jacob had been an attorney, voted conservatively (I knew we were never to bring up politics in conversation with him), and still kept an office in the front of their house, complete with rolltop desk, a framed law degree, and impressive-looking accouterments. My grandmother, Marion, was an immigrant from Belarus; she was short and plump, with a round laughing face surrounded by a halo of tight white curls. She wore loud print dresses, knee-length hose, and sensible shoes; on our outings to the theater or restaurants, she proudly broke out her heels, fur coat, and shiny leather purse. She greeted us with whoops of joy and covered our heads with kisses. My grandfather by contrast was taciturn much of the time, although being around me and Claire warmed him up considerably.

We'd visit them once every few months, usually for Sunday lunch or dinner. We'd drive from the Upper West Side to their two-family house in Flatbush; my father's older sister, Edith, and her husband, Sid, lived upstairs. On our arrival, my grandfather would give me and Claire quick, violent hugs. He'd make a show out of offering us a plastic banana or plum from a bowl on the dining room sideboard, we'd pretend to be fooled, only to have him smilingly snatch it out of our hands just as we were about to take a bite. There was also a ritual involving a toy red bird in a metal cage—it chirped and sang quite realistically, and we'd ooh and aah over it until he showed us the key underneath the cage with which he'd wound it up.

My grandmother would serve her homemade liver pâté on crackers, and Claire and I were allowed to drink ginger ale (we were never allowed soda or sugared drinks of any kind at home unless we had a stomach flu) out of fancy goblets. Then we'd repair to the dining room for a lunch or supper of deli food: rolls of turkey, salami, and bologna, potato salad, coleslaw. We'd sit around the dark wood table spread with a white lacy cloth and Claire and I savored the food we wouldn't get at home (my mother never permitted luncheon meat or any food that was heavily mayonnaised).

After the meal was over, while the grown-ups had coffee and my father and grandfather enjoyed cigars, Claire and I would race down the stairs to the basement, where we'd dress up in my grandmother's old clothes, gaudy costume jewelry, and hats that were kept in boxes and bags and on racks. We'd do "fashion shows" for the adults, taking on sharp-talking, funny personae from previous decades as we strutted around. Sometimes when we'd emerge from the basement outfitted to the nines, giggling and beaming, a tension between my father and his father seemed to dissipate.

I sensed my father's alienation from his parents in the stilted conversations between my father and my grandfather, in the way my grandmother would profusely thank my mother for arranging the get-togethers, in the palpable relief on my father's face as we got into the car after another "successful" visit to Brooklyn. I can remember once hearing my father—they'd thought we were asleep in the backseat—comment to my mother on how strange it was to see our grandfather hug me and Claire since he had no memory of ever being hugged or kissed by his own father. I felt a pang of sympathy for my father, and gratitude that he did things differently, lavishing us with physical affection and encouraging an easy, cozy intimacy.

I could tell that he felt different from his family members. His sister, four years older, had married a dentist and been a home-maker. My mother would say things like "Aunt Edith could have had a career; she's very smart, you know." My father himself never commented on his difference from his family, never complained about his childhood to us or uttered a negative word about his parents. But one night after an especially tense visit with my grandparents, in which my grandfather had brusquely changed the subject when my mother mentioned the National Book Critics Circle award nomination for *Decadence*, my mother told me that my grandfather didn't understand my father, hadn't supported his artistic leanings, hadn't ever believed that one could make a career out of being a critic.

Religion was another barrier. My Gilman grandparents as well as Aunt Edith and Uncle Sid were Jewish; somehow I knew that my father had been a Catholic before he met my mother, and now believed in no traditional religion as far as I could tell. He never accompanied us to church on Christmas Eve (we always spent Christmas in Dundee, Illinois, where my mother had grown up), but he deeply respected my maternal grandparents' strong Protestant faith.

My mother's parents, Merle and Peg Nesbit, were Illinois natives and Protestant midwesterners through and through. Merle lost his father at a young age, couldn't afford college, and worked as a traveling salesman, eventually rising to become president of his own company selling dried milk as animal feed. He was a tall, strong man, an upright gentleman who wore cardigans and ties and had a Mister Rogers-like decency. Peg, warm and effusive, was a dutiful housewife who taught Sunday school and thought Nixon had been wronged.

The two families should have had trouble merging. But surprisingly and joyfully, my two sets of grandparents got along well—the grandfathers bonding over a mutual love of fishing and fiscal conservatism, Marion and Peg giggling over their granddaughters' antics or admiring each other's desserts (Peg's custard and hot fudge sauce, Marion's blueberry blintzes with sour cream and an array of butter cookies).

My four grandparents were also united in their love of Nicky, my half brother. Nicky was my father's son from his first marriage, and twelve years older than me. My mother had met Nicky and my father for the first time at exactly the same moment as they came striding across the lawn of their mutual friend Gordon Rogoff's rented summer house to greet her on her arrival from New York City. That first image of my father—*as* a father—may have been crucial for her. She had been enchanted by the six-year-old little boy, pale, dark-haired, and vulnerable, from the start. And Nicky, whose mother was depressed and somewhat unstable, was hungry for siblings, grandparents, family.

My father was fond of repeating what I'd supposedly said when I was about five: Nicky "doesn't feel like half a brother to me." And it was true. When he visited us in Connecticut or came for holidays, Claire and I trailed after him like faithful little sprites attendant on their magnificent master, their Oberon. He was tall and well built, with lush dark hair and a strong Roman (Jewish) nose. He was irreverent and funny, with loads of energy for playing with two adoring little girls as well as managing difficult people and situations. In Weston, he tirelessly pushed us on the rickety wooden swing hung from two trees at the bottom of the hill, gave us piggyback rides, threw balls with us on the lawn. Nicky was prized by both sets of grandparents for his puckish sense of humor, his warmth, and his fondness for the same old movies and music they—and my father—loved. He'd spearhead viewing parties for Fred Astaire and Ginger Rogers, Shirley Temple, Judy Garland and Mickey Rooney, and Marx Brothers movies, put on Glenn Miller or Bing Crosby records and twirl my grandmother around, and play endless rounds of Crazy Eights or poker with Merle and my father. He also had a talent for calming both grandmothers down—one Thanksgiving at our apartment, Grammy Gilman got lost in the onrush until Nicky saw her waving her arms frantically above her head and crying "No one's paying any attention to me!" Nicky paid attention to her. Peg was scatterbrained and apt to misplace her glasses, her purse, her dinner. Nicky had patience for her, and he always found whatever she had lost.

Nicky came out as gay soon after he went off to college at Hampshire. No big deal at all in the New York artistic and literary world of my childhood. My mother said she'd always known, and Claire and I adored Nicky's boyfriend, a pale, bookish sculptor named Glen Seator. Neither set of conservative grandparents was ever told that Nicky was gay.

But despite their essential conservatism, my mother's parents utterly embraced my father, whose down-to-earth warmth and ease made him fit in seamlessly. He and Merle bonded over sports and poker; he was much more patient with Peg than my mother was, and he and Peg could easily bring the other to tears of laughter as my mother tapped her nails restlessly on the kitchen table. My father happily gobbled up the calorie-laden treats Peg served while my mother nibbled on cookies, then whipped out the fiber crisps she'd brought in a Baggie. Oddly enough, it was my mother, increasingly glamorous, high-profile, and impatient with everyone's love of hanging out and "visiting" (as my grandmother called conversation), who stuck out as different.

Our two standing outings with my Gilman grandparents were Sunday lunch at Windows on the World or lunch in the Theater District followed by a Broadway matinee. My tiny white-haired fur-coated grandmother would always proudly tell the coat check girl, the maître d', and the waiter: "My son used to be the drama critic at *Newsweek*, and now he teaches at *Yale*!" My grandfather, who had next to no interest in anything artistic or academic, would look in the other direction and bite down hard on his bread.

Despite his reputation as a champion of the avant-garde and an enemy of schmaltz, my father had the ability to fully surrender to the pleasures of uncomplicated fun, daring feats, charming entertainment. He loved introducing his girls to the magic of live performance. As a family of four or sometimes three (my mother would bow out due to her heavy workload), we attended Gilbert and Sullivan operettas and Little Orchestra Society concerts, and every year we'd go to the Paper Bag Players and Moomenschanz, the circus, and the New York City Ballet's *The Nutcracker*.

> Do we really have to say once again that the theatre is only alive today when it is being brash, irreverent (or imaginatively reverent), disturbing, antic, dangerous, and even cruel? When it introduces cracks in the glacier of our public images and private fantasies? When it manages to leave off being a rear-view mirror? When it fills the air with rain, hailstones and flying objects instead of with fog and weak sunshine?
>
> —Richard Gilman, "What Keeps Us Going," 1961,
> in *Common and Uncommon Masks*

From the first time we saw it as tiny girls, Claire and I were enchanted by Balanchine's *The Nutcracker*. We yearned to be one of the children who cavorted and capered, chasséed and chased each across the stage (we always knew a few in the cast), but our parents forbade us to audition for the School of American Ballet, from which the cast was drawn, because they saw it as pre-professional education. Nonetheless, we studied ballet at a less prestigious institution because it was "good for our posture," and whenever we put on shows for our parents, we performed numbers from *The Nutcracker*.

I longed to be a part of this shimmering tapestry of wonders, and I wanted to play Marie, the little girl heroine, in part because I saw myself in her. She was the well-behaved child whose younger sibling makes mischief and causes scenes. She was dreamy and loving, warm and friendly, maternally protective of her Nutcracker. But Marie's father, a prosperous, elegantly attired man who hosted a grand holiday party in his sumptuous home, didn't remind me one whit of my own.

It was Marie's godfather, the elusive and enigmatic Drosselmeyer, who reminded me of him. His arrival at the party injects a note of mystery and magic into a conventional gathering. The children swarm him just as my friends and his students always crowded around my father. Performing magic tricks, leading them through games with charismatic confidence, Drosselmeyer blurs the line between reality and fantasy. He stokes young imaginations by breathing an air of "life-giving heresy" into a polite and proper party.

A gifted showman, Drosselmeyer is ostentatiously performative, a figure of high drama. But not with Marie. The two of them have many private moments of sincere, fond connection. When jealous Fritz breaks the Nutcracker in a fit of pique, Drosselmeyer immediately soothes Marie, and with a comforting smile and a histrionic flourish, he repairs it. Like my father, Drosselmeyer is both the magic maker and the problem solver.

He seems to completely understand Marie, to see that she needs something beyond the decorous, staid, conventional world. And later that night, he provides it. While Marie sleeps on the living room sofa, Drosselmeyer returns to complete his repair. Once, when one of the dolls in our dollhouse lost her head, my father found a top doll hospital in the UK and sent our doll there to have her head put back on. He enlisted the author Alastair Reid in this plan and had Alastair write us a series of long newsy letters in the doll's voice ostensibly sent from the doll hospital. For me, Drosselmeyer's coming back to fix the toy, tucking the good-as-new Nutcracker into Marie's arms as she sleeps, then tenderly kissing her head, epitomizes how my father worked tirelessly to sustain the sanctity of our imaginative world and loved us all the more for believing in it.

As a gift during one of his frequent visits to our Weston home, one of my father's favorite Yale Drama School students, Rocco Landesman, gave me and Claire an intricately painted wooden nutcracker that stood at least a foot high. Nutty the Nutcracker was married to Ellen, a cloth doll Harold Brodkey had given me, and installed as the gatekeeper between the homes of Mrs. Gilman and Mrs. Filton, the names Claire and I gave ourselves in our roles as mothers to almost a hundred and fifty stuffed animals and dolls—and we were single mothers, no less! Nutty occasionally cracked walnuts, but rarely left his post in the middle of our shared country bedroom. His smart martial uniform made him a spiffy doorman who could turn to either side adroitly. To knock on each other's "door," we used his lever. He was a bulwark of protection and a beacon of magic.

To our squeals of delight when we'd unwrapped Nutty, Rocco had laughingly proclaimed: "You are both my Maries!" then added with a smile: "But Dick's the real Uncle Drosselmeyer!" In a *New York Times* article about my father's memorial service, Rocco, who'd gone on to become a major Broadway producer and the owner of Jujamcyn Theaters, was quoted as saying: "For those of us taught by him, he was our intellectual conscience. He was a very funny guy, but there was a fundamental seriousness about Dick that kept us on our toes." *The Nutcracker*'s Drosselmeyer, too, combines humor and ethical force in his being and keeps all the characters on their toes. He is the Brechtian disrupter, the one who dismisses bourgeois proprieties and explodes generic clichés, the director and actor and playwright who would have fit right in alongside those my father most admired. His is the theater my father revered: "brash, irreverent (or imaginatively reverent), disturbing, antic, dangerous, and even cruel."

Claire and I were little girls who fervently believed in magic. We loved books with magical themes: the Mary Poppins series, *Half Magic* and its sequels by Edward Eager, Roald Dahl's *James and the Giant Peach* and *Charlie and the Chocolate Factory*. After reading of Betsy, Tacy, and Tib's flying practice in one of our favorite children's book series, we embarked on such training ourselves, flapping our arms wildly while jumping off the stone porch behind our country home, certain we had levitated just a little bit. And our father confirmed our belief: "You hovered!" he'd cry as he strode toward us across the lawn. We were certain our dolls and stuffed animals talked and walked around while we slept, and when we were awake we gave life to them by speaking in their voices and treating them as members of the family. My father was delightfully complicit in this fantasy. He'd engage in long conversations with our Paddingtons, offer them sips of juice or bites of bacon at the breakfast table, tell the customs agent that we were a family of six and have the Paddingtons checked through, invite them to accompany him and his girls to the movies and restaurants. He'd reinforce the reality of the imaginary friends Claire and I created for them: redheaded brothers Harry and Tommy Teelock and Michelle Googyagyoogyagyoogyagyoogy. While out at the beach, my father would excitedly cry,

"There goes Tommy Teelock!" as he gestured across the sand at no one in particular; while making us lunch, he'd ask earnestly how Michelle had done on a school test. He helped maintain the illusion. He never broke the third wall.

Children and animals alike adored my father. My memories are of children clustering around him, dogs flocking to his side, babies reaching out their arms to be picked up by him. In photos from my childhood birthday parties, my father is invariably surrounded by a gaggle of girls hanging on his every word.

So powerful was my father's charismatic spell that a dog who never went within ten feet of a pool followed my father all the way to the edge, and when Daddy jumped in, the dog, begrudgingly but determinedly, jumped in too. This dog was Georgie, a black-and-white mutt who'd come with the house in Italy we were renting and formed an instant, deep bond with my dog-loving father. Each morning, Georgie slowly climbed the steep, winding stairs to my father's top-floor study so he could lie next to him while he wrote, and then followed him down at day's end. Only my mother's barring the door to their bedroom could have kept Georgie from sleeping by my father's side. The day we packed up to depart for the US, Georgie, sensing imminent heartbreak, refused to eat, whimpered every time my father walked a few feet away from him, and tried to get into the rental car as we loaded it with our bags. As we drove away, down a dusty Italian road, I looked out the back window to see Georgie galloping toward our car at top speed, desperately trying to catch up with us. A month or so after we returned to New York, my mother received a letter from the friend who'd rented us the house. She read this bit aloud to us:

> Georgie has been in a deep depression since Dick departed. Tell the children that he has eaten away the telephone cable— he has given a definitely antique look to the outside dining

table, has gnawed away the legs—he has chewed up three
cushions and torn up two bedcovers and, worst of all, he has
eaten the duck!!!

Claire and Daddy and I laughed uproariously. "Good for Georgie
for eating the duck!" my father cried. That duck, a pest par excellence,
had been taunting Georgie all summer, nipping at his heels as he
walked around the perimeter of the pond and breaking into our house
to poop on the stone floors, only to be punted out by my father. Georgie's revenge on his—and our—inveterate adversary delighted us. His
sadness was another matter. My mother thought the litany of Georgie's grieving actions absurd. But Georgie's despair at losing my father,
which would have seemed insane to some, made total sense to me.

When we were very little girls, Claire and Daddy and I invented a
term we used only with each other: streaks of love. I don't remember
who came up with the phrase, but for all three of us it meant a sudden, piercing jolt or bolt or sudden rush of overwhelming love that
stabbed us at our core. I imagined the streaks looking like those
silvery flashes of lightning that had lit up our garden in Spain the
night my father and I had stood together at the window. And the idea
of a streak of a love encapsulates the way our father loved and how
he taught us to love: unabashedly, ardently, with the whole of our
beings. When you love like that, you can get your heart broken.

Once a year or so, during the winter months, my parents would
take a week or ten-day trip alone together, usually to the Caribbean—
St. John's, St. Barts, Bermuda—places Claire and I never went, locations that were hazy in our minds. They needed "warm weather
and relaxation," my mother would tell us as she made orderly piles
of bikinis and sundresses to put in her suitcase. Claire lived in
dread of their leaving, her anxiety ratcheting up as the hour of their

departure drew closer. To help assuage her worry and give us both comfort, before they left they'd each give us an article of their clothing to sleep with until they returned. A filmy or quilted nightgown of my mother's—they smelled of the cocoa butter she slathered on her body and the Georgette Klinger creams she used on her face— and a T-shirt of my father's, redolent of cigarette smoke, Speed Stick deodorant, and his sweet homey smell. Claire would sleep with one clutched in each hand. I'd lay my mother's nightgown next to my pillow so I could smell it when needed, but I'd take my father's shirt and hug it to my chest.

When my parents went away, Grandmother Peg would come to stay with us. She would sweep in in a kind of Auntie Mame fashion with an abundance of floral quilted suitcases and heaps of ideas for fun with us. Every day, we had candy hunts, excursions for hot cocoa or pastries, and endless endless imaginative play with her. She distracted Claire from her worry and sadness with humor and indulgent bolstering—we'd get to have food our parents didn't allow, stay up later than they permitted, listen to our grandmother read from our favorite books for hours on end.

Sometimes when I lay in bed breathing in my father's smell, I'd wonder how the vacation was going for my parents. For some reason, it was hard for me to imagine the two of them together nonstop, without anyone else, for that long. Would they be more like normal husband and wife when removed from the stresses of ordinary life? What would they do or talk about alone together? They didn't call or write so it was total silence, a silence I filled with imaginings and wonderings.

As the day of my parents' return approached, we'd plan an elaborate celebration for their arrival. We'd make "Welcome Home Mommy and Daddy!" signs and affix them to the apartment's front door; our grandmother would buy special treats and we'd hang streamers and balloons.

And then: at last! At last! My parents would come through the door and we'd run to them in a wild rush, flinging ourselves upon them. Claire would always burst into tears and clutch at my mother's coat, hand, bag, anything to assure her that this was real, that Mommy was back. Our grandmother would restore a sense of light-hearted celebration, beckoning them to the living room, where show songs from *Annie*, *Oklahoma!*, and *West Side Story*, dances from *The Nutcracker* and *Swan Lake*—awaited them. And then we'd all repair to the dining room for a feast.

There's a family photo of the four of us—Claire, my mother, me, and my father from left to right—at the dining room table after my parents have just returned from a Caribbean vacation in 1977 or 1978. Claire is in a quilted red-and-blue vest tied at the neck over her white ballet leotard, and her little face is woebegone. She's sitting on my mother's lap and both of my mother's hands are pressed protectively into Claire's chest, her head leaning in to almost touch Claire's. Claire's glum face belies the festive aura of the photo—a yellow balloon springs from a silver candleholder, a chocolate cream pie my grandmother had made is positioned in front of my chocolate-loving father, a fuchsia lei is draped around my mother's neck, paper party plates and napkins sit in front of us. My father, deeply tanned, wearing a plaid flannel shirt and craggily handsome in a Marlboro Man kind of way, holds onto Claire's arm, which she's outstretched past my mother and me toward him; her hand clings to my father's arm. I have an orange lei wrapped around my head twice as a "crown," and yellow streamers attached to an elastic band around my waist as a flowy skirt over my white ballet leotard and tights. I am the only one standing. I am stretching my arms wide so that I can reach them around both my parents' shoulders. My arms are the bridge between my parents; my bright smile the antidote to Claire's melancholy. Three of my parents' four hands are on Claire. No one's hands are on me.

Even as he cultivated the pristine and protected sanctity of our childhood, even as he was the one I'd go to for reassurance when I had a worry, I never felt entirely secure about my father. He seemed physically vulnerable: prone to colds and coughs, hobbled by bad feet, a compulsive smoker, given to cigar-smoking and scotch-drinking to take the edge off a mood. Despite his essential good nature, my father could also be testy, irritable, defensive. The success of a "mediocre" or "fraudulent" author or play irked him no end. Like the critic in Rachel Cusk's *Kudos*, "what he couldn't tolerate above all else . . . was the triumph of the second-rate, the dishonest, the ignorant." My father would perceive slights—not being a regular contributor to the *New York Review of Books*, not winning awards he was nominated for—that would make him depressed. More frighteningly, he could explode in fits of volcanic anger, often about what to me seemed like silly, inconsequential things: my mother forgetting to buy orange juice, a car horn blaring on Central Park West.

He was especially frustrated by and short-tempered with Claire. As an infant, Claire cried all the time. She was a fussy, peevish, colicky baby. Nicky laughingly called her "the cranky old man." The photo album of her first year is filled with shots of various people looking down in consternation at a swaddled infant. Carrie would joke that she could hear Claire's crying from outside the front door of the building. Carrie had taken care of hundreds of babies, but never one that cried more than Claire. "A difficult baby," "a handful," "a fussbudget," "a hollerer," family friends would cluck to my parents. The doormen would smile sympathetically when Claire was pushed out in her pram. As a toddler, however, she suddenly became angelic, with tight blond curls, pale, smooth skin, light green eyes, and little rounded, dimpled legs and arms. But appearances were deceiving. She was Shirley Temple without the sunny personality. She didn't sleep through the night until she was three or four. My parents would shut their bedroom door and turn the television up as loud as they could so they wouldn't hear her wails. I'd be woken up both by her cries and by the blaring television. When she didn't get her way or was upset about something, she would have tantrums so violent she would shake all over, tremble, quiver with rage, and heave without tears. Claire spilled her milk, knocked things over, broke things, ate with her fingers, drew on the walls. In the supermarket, if Carrie or my grandparents told her they wouldn't buy sugary cereal, she'd go back and get it herself. After repeated warnings not to climb the bookshelf in her bedroom, she did it again and it fell down on top of her. Luckily, it was made of light plastic with open shelving and she wasn't badly hurt. I admired her for her pluck and determination even as I lived in fear of the consequences her actions would bring.

Claire spoke up, cried, complained, voiced her needs, didn't suppress her feelings. Her resistance terrified me because of the anger I knew it would provoke. If she didn't agree with my parents' decisions, she talked back. "I don't like zucchini and I won't eat it." "Well, you're damn well going to eat it," my father would retort. I didn't want to eat it either, but I forced it down and fought the rising nausea, or sometimes hid it in my napkin and then flushed it down the toilet when my parents weren't looking.

"I don't want to wear that, do that, see that," Claire would protest.

During car rides, she would loudly announce she was tired, bored, hungry, thirsty. "How much longer?" "When will we be there?" "I need food NOW." "I can't wait until later." "I need to pee now. You'll have to stop the car." How many times did I force myself to go hungry, hold it in, hunched over in pain, in order to avoid stirring things up with a request to find a rest stop? Claire made scenes. I envied her lack of self-consciousness, her insistence on advocating for herself, her ability to be herself without apology. Yet I dreaded her setting my father off.

But although Claire spoke up and out, she was much more emotionally fragile than I, more dependent on my parents. Along with crying when my parents left for or returned from trips, Claire clung to my mother on the first day of school, didn't find it as easy as I did to navigate social interactions. And I loved her with a fierce, helpless tenderness. She was my little Clairey, whose vulnerability and innocence it was my duty and my honor to protect. Other than my father, there was no one I loved more.

A famous story from our childhood goes that my father was waiting for five-year-old Claire to get her shoes tied so we could go out to the park. As she ostentatiously took her time, intricately looping the shoelace to make the prettiest bow, my father grew impatient. "Hurry, Claire!" he cried repeatedly. Stalking around the living room, sighing and expostulating, he finally yelled: "You'd better hurry up and get this over with, Claire, or let me do it for you." Carrie overheard little Claire defiantly muttering to herself: "Maybe if you'd quit hollering for a minute, I could get them tied!" When Carrie told my dad, he laughed, and we all admired Claire's unshakable faith in herself. She could get them tied, and she did get them tied. That story put a charming, funny spin on a darker dynamic— my father's frustration with Claire's strong will, her defiance, and the growing tension between them, which often exploded into full-fledged rage on both their parts. Sometimes after she'd talked back to him and he'd raise his voice at her, she'd run to her room and slam the door, refusing to open it even to me. When she'd emerge, it would be only to slip notes signed "Hate, Claire" under the door of his study. I'd wheedle them both into forgiving the other so I could have them back again.

My father favored me over Claire, my mother told me, because I never fussed or fretted, never made trouble. I was careful not to make trouble. When his moods went black, my father needed to be strenuously pulled back into good humor, composure, life. I sensed his needs with an almost preternatural sensitivity, and I rushed to meet them. I felt a responsibility to calm him down or cheer him up. And that was in part because I never felt that my mother really understood, appreciated, or loved him the way I did.

> And his eyes—his eyes were most marvelously bright. They seemed to be sparkling and twinkling at you all the time. The whole face, in fact, was alight with fun and laughter.
>
> And oh, how clever he looked! How quick and sharp and full of life!
>
> —Roald Dahl, *Charlie and the Chocolate Factory*

Willy Wonka, especially as incarnated by Gene Wilder in the 1971 film, has always uncannily evoked my father for me. Of course, my father was far from a wealthy entrepreneur, and he wasn't a loner or a natty dresser. But those marvelously bright eyes, sparkling and twinkling, the face alight with fun and laughter, the quickness and sharpness and countenance bursting with life—oh how they reso-nated for me with my father!

All the complexities and contradictions of Willy Wonka, they were my father's as well. At once the magician who presides over his realm with serene control and the vulnerable man prone to outbursts of anger, paranoid about spies and thieves. Dynamic and charismatic, yet strangely sad and lonely. Great reserves of energy and exuberance, but also a world-weary resignation. Easily irritated, easily moved. Capable of dismissing people as bad eggs and calling people's comments absurd, and also of effusively expressing affection and love. Effervescent and haunted, nimble and gay yet melancholic. So much fun and somewhat frightening. The rages that came out of nowhere, the integrity that underlay that anger.

Like Wonka, my father was put off by pushy, shallow parents and would brook no naughtiness or nastiness, brattiness or egocentrism from children. Claire would have a tantrum—and lose my father's love momentarily as a result—but she wouldn't whine or wheedle. My father wouldn't allow us to watch any TV other than PBS kid shows, *Wild Kingdom*, and *The Hardy Boys* and *Nancy Drew*, or listen to any "banal pop music"—a phrase he always uttered in a voice dripping with contempt. He wouldn't buy us conventional or expensive toys. His one concession was a Baby Alive doll I begged for the Christmas I was seven, and when it peed on his pants leg, he laughingly said: "This is why we don't buy you girls silly toys like this!" He entirely shared Wonka's disdain for and disgust at Violet's rudeness and self-importance, Mike's glazed eyes and zoned-out fixation on screens, Veruca's petulance and greed, Augustus Gloop's messy and mindless gluttony.

When Charlie brings back the Everlasting Gobstopper and Wonka murmurs, "So shines a good deed in a weary world," I invariably sigh in recognition. I was the one who made the saving gesture, I was the redemptive innocent who gave my father a sense of hope and possibility. And for him the purity of untainted childhood was always the antidote to pessimism or despair. My father and I knew of no life that could compare with pure imagination. Living there, we were free.

It was an ostensibly happy ending—what happens to the boy who gets everything he wants? He lives happily ever after!—but I always struggle to contain a sob when Wonka tells Charlie that he's leaving the factory to him:

> I can't go on forever, and I don't really want to try. So who can I trust to run the factory when I leave and take care of the Oompa Loompas for me? Not a grown-up. A grown-up would want to do everything his own way, not mine. So that's why I decided a long time ago that I had to find a child. A very honest, loving child, to whom I could tell all my most precious candy-making secrets.

As a little girl, I wondered, Was Mr. Wonka sick? Did he know he was going to die soon? I felt like the Charlie to my father's Willy Wonka. I was that honest, loving child he had found. I knew he had chosen me, singled me out, entrusted his ethic, his aesthetic, his candy-making secrets to me. I felt both the honor and the weight of that obligation. And I feared, always, that he would float away in a glass elevator, leaving me bereft.

I lived shadowed by an uncertainty about my parents' marriage and a sense of some fundamental instability lurking just beneath the surface. "Lynn and Dick" were held up as a model couple by many of their friends, and were profiled as such in several newspaper pieces, celebrated especially for the ways my father made my mother's business success possible. They complemented each other well: my father the extravagant romantic, my mother the cool realist. As my father would give disquisitions on a new play, or whoop excitedly with his buddies as they watched a sports game, my mother would break in to summon everyone firmly to the dinner table. If my father luxuriated in meandering after-dinner conversations that continued even after coffee and dessert, it was my mother who reminded everyone how late it was and briskly ushered guests out the door.

One day, when I was about seven, a client of my mother's called in tears over a bad review. My mother was empathetic and comforting, reassuring the client that one review did not a success or failure make. When she hung up the phone, my father said: "Lynn, why did you lie to her? That review was spot-on, and it will hurt her career." My mother sighed in exasperation. "I was doing my job, Dick," she replied.

But at other times and in other ways, it was my mother who was the flinty realist, the one described as tough in numerous newspaper and magazine articles. A 1973 *Newsweek* piece called her "smart, pretty, and tough" and praised her for reading "her writers with a sharp critical sense." A 1980 *Daily News* article about her as one of "the New Superwomen" juggling high-powered careers with marriage and children, deemed "unsettling" what they called her "compulsive efficiency" (my father defended her in print). My mother grimly urged her authors to take day jobs and worked hard to "manage their expectations"; by contrast, my father consolingly threw his arms around his former students when they suffered professional disappointment, bucked up insecure author friends, rhapsodized about a play, an actor, a production.

My father gave my mother both intellectual credibility and the ability to be a powerfully ambitious career woman. With him, she could discuss Proust, explore Kierkegaard, and get up to speed on experimental European fiction. And marrying my father—a much older, divorced, cerebral, liberal, Jewish man—was a strikingly effective way for my mother to signal her difference from her conservative, Republican, straitlaced, Middle American parents.

As different as their backgrounds were, my parents shared a commitment to Art, a passion for and faith in Literature. Agent and Critic would seem to be opposed roles in the literary firmament, but both of my parents were advocates and both believed in the redemptive and transcendent value of great art. My father greatly admired my mother's work ethic and her literary taste. Although my mother did represent big commercial writers like Crichton and Anne Rice, she, like my father, fought on behalf of art against the relentless tide of commerce. In the *Newsweek* piece, my mother declared: "Agents have a real responsibility in this increasingly commercial world of publishing, and we have to take it seriously. We have to stand up for literature."

If my father spent his twenties as a self-described "Bohemian bum" and his thirties as a struggling freelance journalist and a lonely divorced man who smoked too much, in his forties and especially in his relationship with my mother, he got his act together. She made sure of it. She believed wholeheartedly in his "genius" and urged him to apply for prestigious posts, write important books, and position himself as a major player on the cultural scene. She pushed him to exercise, sprinkled wheat germ on his cereal, made nice with his parents. My mother never played with us or watched PBS with us; she never took us to movies or museums; she never read to us. She used to joke that her job was to "make the trains run on time," and boy did those trains run on time. With my father, she cracked the proverbial whip—hard—and he didn't emerge from his office until the page limit or word count she'd set for him had been achieved. She nurtured, bullied, dragged his books into being. His first book, *The Confusion of Realms*, is dedicated to "my wife, Lynn, without whose loving impatience this book might not have come about."

In my eyes, impatience often won out in the way my mother related to my father. She was impatient with the painstaking research he did before writing—"Just start writing, Dick!" she'd say—his predilection for luncheon meat and other unhealthy fare, his love of digressive conversations. He thrived on her briskness, her matter-of-fact, let's-get-on-with-it attitude. But at what cost? They enabled each other to be parents and to succeed professionally, but what was the special realm between them, the sacred space of connection and love? I could discern very little steady affection or tenderness, let alone passionate intensity.

What passionate intensity there was came in the form of arguments. They never insulted each other in a cruel or belittling way, never put each other down or mocked each other, but they did yell and curse at each other. Nicky would joke about their yelling—"Here they go again!" he'd impishly grin as the volume began to rise—but to me, it was often terrifying. I'd feel torn between staying in the room so as to prevent them from going too far and running to my bedroom to put on an upbeat record so I could block out the sounds of their argument. Or I would grab Claire's hand and run off with her to play with our dollhouse.

The Christmas I was six and Claire five, we got our very own dollhouse. A bare-bones wooden structure, the house was made by a parent at our school and sold at the annual fair. Our grandparents gave us a family of dolls: a mother, father, pretty blond teen daughter, to whom we affixed the to-us-mature-and-alluring name Melissa, and a twin boy and girl, whom we dubbed Patrick and Patty. To these we added two small plastic babies we'd received in our stockings; they were simply known as "the Babies," and each of us voiced one as they got into all sorts of mischief and scrapes. Later, twin girl dolls were added to the family as adopted sisters Molly and Mary. Seven children, all effortlessly managed and tended to and adored by their ebullient Mother and their emotionally sturdy Father.

Mother, we decided, had been a concert pianist in her twenties, and while she still played the miniature piano (which wound up to play Beethoven), she'd put aside her professional ambitions to devote herself to her large, happy family. She home-schooled the children in literature and music, flitted about the house dispensing wisdom, breaking up quarrels, and bestowing kisses, treated guests (a mouse or Weeble Wobble or Fisher-Price Little People family) to concerts and parties.

In an ironic twist given who we were aligned with in our own family, I voiced Mother and Claire voiced Father. I gave Mother a cascading laugh, a voice charged with feeling, a talent for singing and for soothing ruffled feathers. I made her in many ways everything my mother was not: warm, artsy, nurturing, a homebody. This Mother never got silent or tense or pursed her lips in disdain, and she never cursed at her lazy husband. Claire gave sandy-haired Father a steady, calm demeanor and a comfortingly reliable presence. This Father never grew irritable or yelled, never struggled with writer's block or feelings of inadequacy, never smoked or drank. But this Father, like ours, was funny, devoted to his children, a down-to-earth intellectual. He was, in fact, a Critic. He reviewed books and plays for a prominent newspaper. He had a mini typewriter and would bang away on it until his review was complete. He'd get phone calls from his editor. He'd lament the mediocrity of the cultural productions he'd been enjoined to report on. And then he'd give the children piggyback rides, grill hamburgers and hot dogs, joke with and delight in his family.

These parents, this Mother and Father, were madly, wildly, crazily in love with each other. They'd kiss at the breakfast table. Lie in bed with their arms wrapped around each other. Stand together and watch their brood cavort on the front lawn (shag carpet) while Mother leaned her head on Father's shoulder. They argued sometimes, but in the way Claire and I did—quickly, directly, with the uncomplicated and easy restoration of warmth and love.

And often when our parents started arguing, we'd get up and run to our dollhouse, where we'd work to sustain the gossamer web of its fictions, exult in the abundance of its familial security and love.

A major source of the tension between my parents was my father's love of—what my mother would call his "mania" for—sports. My father loved all kinds of sports, but he reserved his greatest love for football and his New York Giants. When I was a small child, he'd watch football alone, hunched in front of the television, lost in a world that signified only to him. My mother had absolutely no interest in sports and was quite contemptuous of what she deemed my father's "frivolous" and "trivial" obsession. She couldn't understand his desire to spend six hours straight in front of a television set watching grown men crash into each other. Claire, a girly girl, would rather draw, play with paper dolls, or shop with my mother. I felt my father's loneliness in his fandom and wanted to give him some companionship. So one Sunday afternoon, when I was about six, I decided to try this football thing out. I cuddled up next to him on the sofa, asking tentative questions at first, not wanting to disturb his enjoyment or distract him from what was clearly a matter he took very seriously indeed. But he was disarmed by my innocent interest, and soon saw that I was a willing pupil and a quick study. Once I understood the basics, I was hooked, obsessed, an avid reader of the *New York Post* sports pages along with my father. "The son your father never had," my mother would wryly call me, in pointed reference to Nicky, who painted and played jazz piano and had no interest in sports of any kind.

But my father didn't just love football. He liked to bet on games, on teams he had no allegiance to, and almost never the Giants since they were abysmal for most of the 1970s. Every Friday, when the point spread was released, my father and I would play what we called "the Betting Game." He'd tell me who was playing whom and which team was the home team, and I'd guess the point spread. He was proud of my ability to guess correctly or near correctly most of the time, and I loved both the challenge of figuring out the right number and the smiles I brought to his face as we played our game. But betting was no game once a game he'd bet on was actually underway. On the occasions when he'd bet, he'd typically watch with his close friend and fellow bettor, publishing executive Victor Temkin, and the two of them would yell, flail around, curse, and drink and smoke heavily if their team wasn't beating the spread. I'd stay with them as long as I could, but when the smoke got too thick and the yelling too savage, I'd flee to the kitchen, where I'd find a worried Susie Temkin and my mother conferring about how to calm them down. My parents would often have screaming fights about "your bookie," who I imagined as a human-sized book with a cute smiley face and boxing gloves he pulled out when my dad didn't pay up on time.

Sometimes after especially bitter arguments, Claire and I would ask my parents if they were going to get divorced; they would peremptorily dismiss our concerns. No one in either of their families had ever been divorced, and both sets of grandparents were in long, stable, conventional marriages. Very few of our friends had divorced parents, but divorce was in the air in the late seventies, and after Lionel and Virginia Tiger announced their divorce just a few months after one of our summers with them in Italy, my worrying intensified. Rather than being alarmed or saddened by the news of the Tigers' split, my mother seemed quietly thoughtful, ruminative. I wondered where her mind was going. But every time we asked, they'd always reassure us that they would never divorce. They were explicit and definitive. I believed them, yet I still worried about and puzzled over their marriage, which seemed both fraught and flat.

For it was the silences and spaces between my parents that were more unsettling to me. I never saw them express physical affection toward each other. No hugs, kisses, or hand-holding for them. And that seemed especially odd given that they were both warmly demonstrative with Claire and me. Yes, he'd sometimes call her "Lynna" in a fond way, praise her cooking, beam with pride when she closed an especially tricky deal or signed an especially notable writer. And yes, she'd speak glowingly of his parenting to their mutual friends, listen with rapt attention when he delivered a verdict on a new play or book. But they never seemed like a symbiotic unit.

I felt an imbalance of feeling between my mother and father. He wanted to impress her, win her adulation. And if he seemed a little too importunate, a little too solicitous of her good opinion, she seemed a little too distant, a little too chilly. She never seemed to miss him when he was in New Haven, or need him, really, at all, except to take care of us. I never saw him tend to her emotional needs, perhaps because she never asked him to. Although my father was an immensely funny man who loved playful banter, I never saw my parents joke around with each other, tease each other, laughingly needle each other or engage with a sense of lightness and whimsy. I wondered why my father, who had a great ability to make people laugh, almost never made my mother laugh. I wondered why my mother, who could be so snuggly and relaxed with me and Claire, was never like that with my father. And I worried about my mother, who often seemed overworked, exhausted, tense and terse. When I was six, she came down with viral pneumonia that left her bedridden for six weeks and gaunt for months afterwards.

Carrie was a beacon of stability for us all, a steady, soothing, comforting presence. She set a predictable schedule for meals, baths, and outings to the park. She was the only one who could handle Claire when she had a tantrum, and my parents happily deferred to her expertise. She was maternal with all of us. She'd urge my mother to rest more, gently nudge my father out of a bad mood, and provide us all with delectable meals, calming energy, and rock-solid devotion to our family. When Carrie arrived in the morning, we all

breathed easier, and when she left at night, we all felt a little less protected. But even Carrie's ministrations and my parents' assurances
that they would never split up couldn't entirely assuage that nag-
ging anxiety that our family culture, our way of life, was precarious,
dependent particularly on my mother's goodwill. I knew that my
father depended on that secure, well-ordered, comfortable life, on
my mother's strictures and structure, exhortations and regulations,
to stay healthy, productive, happy. The smoothness and stability of
our domestic life seemed fragile, because its foundation—my parents' marriage—was marred by cracks, flaws, fissures.

ACT 2

THE WOUNDED GIANT

It is not now as it hath been of yore;—
Turn wheresoe'er I may,
By night or day,
The things which I have seen I now can see no more.

> —William Wordsworth, "Ode: Intimations of Immortality"

The crickets felt it was their duty to warn everybody that
summertime cannot last for ever. Even on the most beautiful
days in the whole year—the days when summer is changing
into autumn—the crickets spread the rumour of sadness and
change.

> —E. B. White, *Charlotte's Web*

Being a fan means practicing a form of sympathetic magic,
by which you suffer with . . . and generally share in the
vicissitudes . . . of modern-day champions and heroes.

> —Richard Gilman, "The Wounded Giant Regains His Dignity,"
> *New York Times*, January 25, 1987

One October night in the fall of 1980, when I was ten years old, my parents shut themselves in the kitchen and spoke in alternately hushed and heated tones. I knew disaster was imminent. In my room with its cheerful wallpaper—a pattern of goldenrod I'd picked out when we'd moved into the apartment two years earlier—I sat on my yellow bedspread and wrote in my little Holly Hobbie journal: "Please don't let this happen. Please don't let them get divorced. I'll do anything if they'll just stay together." My breath came quickly in short, loud gasps, and my hands were shaking so hard I could hardly hold the pen. I would alternately strain to hear what my parents were saying to each other and attempt to block the sound of their voices from my mind. I felt the blood rushing to my cheeks and my face begin to burn. My writing trailed off into a jumble of squiggles. I stood up, but instead of going to Claire, I picked up our collie puppy, Rosie (we'd recently bought her from a breeder near our house in Weston, over my mother's strenuous objections), and squeezed her so hard she began to whimper. I knew that if my eyes met Claire's, the reality of what was happening would have to be acknowledged.

An hour or so after my parents had begun their conversation, the kitchen's folding doors creaked ominously as my mother pushed them back and called us. "Girls? Girls?" I jumped off my bed and ran out into the hall, only to see my mother beckoning me from the kitchen doorway and my father heading in the opposite direction, toward his office, his shoulders heaving. Claire and I dutifully trotted down the hall, and our mother ushered us into the part of the kitchen we called "the breakfast nook." We sat down at the round table, my mother between us. She looked calm, composed, resolute. "So, girls, your father and I have made the decision to separate." Claire immediately began to cry. "But you said you never would! You promised us!" "It's not a divorce, Claire. He'll still live here until after Christmas. And you'll see him often, even after he's moved out. It's just a trial separation." This did not appease Claire. "What do you mean Daddy's going on trial? What did he do??" My mother laughed. "No, no, sweetheart, trial meaning we're going to try out what it feels like to live separately. He's still going to see you and Sid a lot." Claire continued to press my mother. "But where will Daddy live? How will we see him?" "We don't know yet, Clairey, but we have lots of time to figure it out. Remember it's not a divorce, it's not even a separation. It's just a *trial* separation." I had been silent this entire time, digging my nails into my tights so hard I could feel them breaking through the weave of the fabric. Because I knew this separation was not an attempt, an experiment, a trial anything. I knew, from the look of quiet elation on my mother's face, that her decision had been made, that their split was a done deal.

Even though I was terrified to face the reality of my father's desolation, I knew I had to go to him. As my mother took a somewhat mollified Claire back to her bedroom to help her get ready for bed, I walked with trepidation into my father's study. When we'd moved from 333 into this new, larger, grander apartment at 44 West 77th Street, my father was given the best room in the house. Designed as an artist's studio, it had double-height ceilings and enormous windows that looked out onto the Museum of Natural History. It had seemed to signify just how important my father's work was that he had floor-to-ceiling, wall-to-wall bookshelves (and a custom-built wooden ladder on a track that zoomed down the wall so he could access even the highest books), a custom-made desk that looked fit for a president, and a historically significant view. But now he seemed dwarfed by the majestic surroundings, a lone figure who'd lost control of his domain and was soon to be evicted. "Sidda!" he cried when he noticed me in the doorway. "Daddy!" I ran toward the massive white desk behind which he was sitting, tears streaming down his face. I had never seen him cry before, and it frightened me. As I approached him, he leaned forward, pulled me up onto his lap, and said in a choked voice: "I don't want this, this is your mother's decision." As he pressed my head to his chest with his hand, I felt as if I was stifling. "I don't want to lose our family," he moaned. "Oh, I don't know how I can bear it!" I just hugged him tighter and said nothing, wetting his shirt with my own tears even as I desperately tried to snuff them up so I wouldn't upset him more. I needed to be strong for him. I needed to reassure him that everything would be OK. That I would never desert him as my mother had. That I would always love him more than anything in the world.

My confidence in my parents' word was shattered. Their decision to separate, after so many years of telling us they never would, felt like an immense betrayal of trust. But I had no time or opportunity to express, or even to really acknowledge, my dismay, and my sense of having been misled and falsely appeased. I didn't want my mother to feel guilty, so I made sure not to cry in front of her, not to complain to her, not to give her anything but support for a decision I could tell she'd needed to make for her own peace of mind. Meanwhile, my father was so clearly ravaged that I instantly sprang into action to bolster him and cheer him up. I spent more time than ever with him, wrote him comforting notes, snuggled with him and Claire in his swivel armchair while we watched movies (and tried to pretend I didn't notice his sobbing during *The Sound of Music*'s gazebo scene where Maria and the Captain declare their love for each other). My father had never shared Claire's and my love for the film, reminding us that his friend, Yale Drama School colleague, and illustrious film critic Stanley Kauffmann had dubbed it "The Sound of Mucus," but now its sentimental romance reduced him to helpless tears.

Both of our parents sternly admonished us not to mention their impending separation to anyone, not even Carrie. Claire didn't want to talk about it with me. I didn't want to bring it up with my parents. And I guessed that my father didn't want anyone to know because he was hoping to prevent it from happening. For the next few months, my father was more demonstrative and attentive toward my mother than he'd ever been before, complimenting her to anyone who would listen, trying to hug her often, praising her to me and Claire in an ostentatious way designed for her ears. He stopped betting, cut down on his smoking, ate more vegetables. My mother was indifferent at best, icily rebuffing him at worst. I saw and heard him woo, grovel, beseech, but she was implacable.

That Christmas in Illinois, none of our relatives knew about the looming split, and everyone greeted my father with their customary enthusiasm and affection. I could see my father hoping that love would rub off on my mother: maybe she'd finally understand what the rest of us saw in him, appreciate him, realize she was making a mistake. But my mother seemed impervious to the hugging and backslapping going on around her; her tight smile and clipped voice made it all too clear that she was just trying to get through these days, the last she'd ever have to spend pretending to be in a happy marriage to my father. All the joyous holiday rituals were tainted that year by my keen awareness of my father's barely suppressed anguish and my sense that this was the last time he'd ever experience them. My father, who had never attended church with us before, insisted on joining us for the Christmas Eve service; as he quietly wept, I tried to shield him from my grandparents' notice. On Christmas morning, I exclaimed over my gifts—the new taffeta dress, the books, the Madame Alexander doll—to distract him from his assiduous efforts to ingratiate himself with my mother, efforts I knew were doomed and which made me embarrassed for him. He'd asked Jill Robinson to help pick out an antique brooch for my mother (the first and only time I ever remember him giving her something really special as a gift), and he hovered over her as she opened it, the desperate eagerness on his face painful to witness. She thanked him politely for the gift but recoiled from his touch, turned her lips from his. She was beyond baubles and brooches, praise and pleading. She was out, it was done, our family was over.

My first divorce had been mutually agreed upon, while the second, twenty years later, had been imposed against my will, its terms bitterly fought over. After the first, I was ready for a new life; while in the aftermath of the second, I was lost, not nearly so hopeful, and, naturally, being considerably older, much less resilient.

—Richard Gilman, "The Sorrow and the Need," in the anthology
Men on Divorce: The Other Side of the Story, 1997

One night in early January of 1981, my mother was away in California on business, and my father was especially irritable, grousing about this, grumbling about that. When Claire spilled her apple juice all over the Monopoly game board after having been told repeatedly not to put the glass so close to the board, my father lost it, slamming his hands down on the kitchen table and storming out of the room. Claire burst into tears and I jumped up, not knowing which of them to go to first. Should I comfort Claire or go calm down my father? I ran to get some paper towels and carefully wiped the board and the table, reassuring Claire all the while. "I'll go talk to Daddy, Clairey," I told her. "Don't worry. He won't be mad for long.

Go to your room and I'll be there soon, OK?" She snuffed up her tears and headed to her room.

I found my father in his office, sitting in his desk chair, his head in his hands. I ran up to him and put my hand tentatively on his shoulder. He raised his head and the expression in his eyes was so contrite and sad that I felt my own heart pierced. "Sidda, I'm sorry I got so angry," he said. Tears dangled at the corners of his eyes and I found myself willing them not to fall. "But you know I had warned her not to put her glass there!" "Yes, Daddy, I know, you did warn her, and she shouldn't have done it. I know she won't do it again. She's very sorry, Daddy." "I didn't want to get so angry," he said, his voice cracking. "You know, I love you girls more than anything in the world, don't you?" He looked at me imploringly. "Yes, Daddy, of course! We love you too, sooooooo much!" I patted his arm soothingly and leaned my cheek against his. But he was not to be comforted. He pulled away and stared into space, anguish scoring his face. "Sometimes I think I'd kill myself if it weren't for you girls!" I felt a cold desperation pervade my body, and tears came to my eyes.

I never forgot his words. They became a kind of mantra, a rule to live by. "If it weren't for you girls." My father's survival was my responsibility. And I would do any and everything in my power, use every ounce of my energy and ingenuity and love, to make sure he survived.

In mid-January, my father moved out. Where he would now live, Claire and I weren't told, other than that he'd be staying with various friends until he could find an apartment where he could have us visit. The country house in Connecticut, a sacred spot that exemplified the freedom and wild, untrammeled bliss associated with our childhood, would be rented out to strangers and eventually sold. My mother refused to allow us to keep Rosie, and since my father had no apartment of his own to keep her in, we would have to find her a new home. Fortunately, the breeder agreed to take her back. The afternoon we dropped seven-month-old Rosie off at the breeder, I looked back through the car window and saw her standing, frozen, at the mouth of the driveway we had just left. The breeder was trying to coax her away from the road, but she refused to budge. I bit the inside of my cheeks to keep from crying; I could taste blood in my mouth. My father grimly hit the accelerator and said nothing during the twenty-minute ride back to our house in Weston, where we were staying that weekend without my mother, one of the last weekends we'd be there before the house was rented. When we got back, my father, his face ashen and set in a grimace, told us he needed to pack up the things in his studio and headed down the hill; Claire settled onto the couch with a book. I ran upstairs and squeezed myself into the linen closet. Curled up on a wide, deep shelf, lying amidst the towels and bedding, burying my face in the fabric, I sobbed and sobbed.

That's the only time I ever remember really crying, in an uninhibited way, about my parents' split. I certainly didn't ever cry in anyone else's presence. I never said: "I'm sad," "This is hard," "I miss Daddy," never. Not to my mother, not to Claire, not to Carrie. Claire didn't want to talk about it, and I didn't want the grown-ups to have to worry about me. I was appealed to for comfort, consolation, reassurance, by both my parents, but never comforted or hugged consolingly myself. Carrie and Addie, a School of American Ballet student and freshman at Fordham University who'd moved in that fall—living for free in our maid's room in exchange for babysitting—were comforting presences, but we never openly discussed what had happened. I worried that both of them, devout Christians, might judge my mother for breaking a marriage, and I didn't want to put them—or her—in an uncomfortable position.

No one at my school ever mentioned the split to me. Neither did my grandparents. There was something hush-hush and shame-ful about it. I felt embarrassed and protective of my parents. I felt ashamed of my family's brokenness, my father's vulnerability, my mother's aggressive power.

In the following weeks, I lost my father to a custody schedule that severely reduced his presence in my life to one weekday lunch or dinner, to depression over his inability to provide a comfortable home for us, a near-suicidal despair. I was also losing my percep-tion, my grasp of, my *belief* in my father. Physically, emotionally, and ideationally, he began to seem or was revealed to be a differ-ent person than I'd thought. He was no longer the lighthearted and resourceful parent who'd been the one to soothe my worries; now he was the locus *of* my worries.

When Claire and I met Daddy for meals at the Cherry Restau-rant on Columbus, the Excelsior Coffee Shop on West 81st Street, Tony's Italian Kitchen on West 79th Street, or the Chinese restau-rant across the street from Tony's, he'd be waiting outside, pacing back and forth, looking tired and sad and old in a way he never had before. He'd redden when he caught sight of us and I'd see that he was about to cry, so I'd rush into his arms armed with a silly story or a piece of good news (100 on my math quiz! a good part in the class play!), anything to keep him from breaking down. During the meal, he'd seem harried and distracted, alternately gruff and teary. He rarely joked with us, often snapped at us, and yelled at waitresses about overcooked food. He forced me and Claire to split a dish, usually spaghetti and meatballs. When the meal arrived, he'd carefully cut the third meatball in half and divide the spa-ghetti onto two salad plates. Claire would often protest—"This isn't enough food"—or after finishing what was on her plate: "I'm still hungry." I'd kick her under the table and push the bread basket toward her. Then I'd get things back on track with an anecdote to distract the two of them. At the end of the meal, I'd slip a loving note into my father's bag for him to read later. Each one was a version of this: "Do not worry, Daddy, I will see you soon! Try to keep yourself busy and remember I am thinking of you all the time and love you so so much!"

We'd have fun sometimes. There was a little boy with adorable chubby cheeks at the Chinese restaurant across the street from Tony's whose antics always relaxed my father. We'd run into sweet dogs who'd make a beeline for my father. McDonald's on the corner of 71st and Broadway (still there forty years later!) was a special treat with minimal anxiety for me since it was cheap and quick and there were no waitresses to worry about. But it was also in McDonald's that my father would furtively pour packets of salt and pepper, sugar and ketchup, into his shoulder bag. He was a child of the Depression and had always been frugal and cost conscious, but this was new and alarming. I pretended I didn't see.

He began to cancel plans with us at the last minute, show up an hour late with little explanation, rush us through our meals so quickly that Claire once came home and vomited up the hamburger she'd been forced to wolf down to meet his timetable. Gentle, nonjudgmental Carrie was so mad she wanted to "shoot him in the foot!" As the minutes ticked by and Daddy didn't show up, or as he urged Claire to eat faster, I'd feel mounting anxiety and worry— about him, about Claire, and about my mother's sure-to-be-biting reactions to information she'd take as confirmation that he was lazy, irresponsible, a ne'er-do-well she was happy to be rid of. But I wasn't really angry, then or now. Daddy had no home, no moorings, he had been stripped of his power. I knew he was hanging on by a very thin thread, and that simply getting through a meal with us without breaking down was a victory for him.

In the fall of 2017, I unearthed a bin of old things from my mother's basement. In it was a diary I'd kept in middle school. Here is a page from that diary:

Things Not to Do When I'm w Daddy:
1) Don't Cry
2) Don't Complain
3) Don't Be Difficult
4) Don't Tell Him Anything But Good News
5) Don't Mention Mommy
6) Don't Expect Him to Be the Daddy of Old

A few months after he'd moved out, my father came back to stay in the apartment with Claire and me while my mother was again in California on business. One afternoon I stumbled across a woeful and sexually explicit letter to his first wife, Esther. He'd left it lying out on the white desk that had once been his and was now where Claire and I drew, colored, and did homework. I read a few sentences, enough to see that he was pouring out his sorrow over losing my mother and asking Esther to humiliate him, to subject him to her whims and her control. He even asked her to urinate on him. But almost more disturbing was that he was asking these things of Esther, whom he had divorced twenty years earlier and with whom he had no real relationship as far as I knew. What did these bizarre requests suggest about the nature of his self-loathing? I was confused and frightened. I knew I needed to ensure that my father never found out that I'd seen this, so I hurriedly returned the letter to its spot, plastered a smile on my face, and rejoined him and Claire in the living room, throwing myself into our game of Clue with such giddy abandon that I was sure my father would never suspect I'd caught him in this act of self-abasement.

When, on my mother's return, I told her about the letter (after making her swear she would never mention it to my father or anyone else), she was horrified but, to my surprise, not at all surprised. She confessed that she'd been protecting us from this kind of thing for years.

"He used to stash these awful photos and magazines under the cushions of the sofa in our Weston living room!" she said. "Pornographic magazines with dominating women, whips and chains, that sort of thing."

"Really?" I asked, internally aghast but maintaining a calm demeanor so my mother would keep talking.

"Yes, I'd find them while I was straightening up and rush to hide them before you girls discovered them.

"I mean, you were always playing there," she added, "and it would have been so easy for you—or Grammy and Grampy, or Carrie—to uncover them.

"I never did those things he asked Esther to do in that letter," she added.

I nodded silently. She was furious that my father had accidentally exposed me to what she considered his "perversions." I didn't want to stoke her fury by agreeing. And besides, I didn't really agree. There was something in that letter that had rent my heart. He seemed so desperately sad, so fragile.

One night a week or two after the discovery of my father's letter to Esther, I was hanging out with my mom in her bedroom, enjoying the one-on-one time with her (Claire had gone to sleep). I could see that she wanted to tell me something she felt Claire shouldn't hear. "So

Sid," my mother began, slowly, "you know that letter to Esther you found . . . Well, I want you to know something about your father. He had affairs during our marriage." I flinched as if I'd been struck, but willed myself to stay still. "I couldn't give him what he wanted and he went elsewhere," she said. I was able to muster a few words. "What do you mean, 'what he wanted'?" "The things he asked Esther to do!" she said, then added, more slowly, "Affection, love." I didn't ask her why she couldn't give him love. I didn't want to know. "I think he had affairs in part because he needed more than I could give him." Some of the affairs, she told me, had been with his graduate students; his three days a week in New Haven had provided him with ample opportunity to have a secret, double life. "I know it sounds strange," my mother said, "but the affairs were in a way a relief for me. These women took him off my hands! They gave him what I couldn't."

I felt light-headed, dizzy, nauseous. But I listened calmly and nodded appropriately. I didn't want to freak out in front of my mother, and I didn't know quite what to do with the information she was giving me. I understood why she wouldn't want to humiliate my father; I didn't understand why she could never give him love. I remember thinking even as she ripped back the Wizard's curtain, exposing the shivering fraud behind it, that I couldn't say anything terrible about my father to her because she'd jump all over it. And I didn't like the way she rolled her eyes and shuddered when she spoke about him. Even as a little girl, I didn't judge my father for what he called in *Faith, Sex, Mystery* his "erotic nature and proclivities"—they just seemed a little silly and sad to me. But I did judge him, harshly, for his infidelity. My image of my father as an innocent, childlike being, honest and honorable, a family man above all else, was now shattered.

Scenes went tumbling through my mind: talking to him on the phone in his hotel room on Wednesday and Thursday nights, running into his arms on the Westport train platform on Friday afternoons. Had there been someone else in that room with him? Had his halcyon weekends with me and Claire been a kind of cleansing of adultery's taint?

While I'd seen other married men behave badly and overheard my parents discuss some of their friends' compulsive womanizing, my father hadn't seemed to be like those men. My father's best friends Anatole Broyard and Stanley Kauffmann were both infamous for attempting to seduce attractive women, and had made crass comments about women in my presence that my father chided them for. Harold Brodkey, who dubbed himself a latter-day Byron, was sexually flirtatious with both women and men; he boasted of his conquests, and his sexual desires oozed out of him. As soon as I was a teenager, he'd leer at and ogle me. My father didn't ogle or leer, at real women or at women on TV or in films, ever. He wasn't lecherous. I'd never seen him hit on a woman in the way that so many of my parents' married friends did right in front of their spouses and children. But now, images of my father with women would come to me at strange moments, distracting me in the middle of a science lab or a kickball game, knocking the breath out of me while I was singing in music class.

My father, for all his celebration of freedom and originality, now seemed like a self-indulgent stereotype. He'd taken advantage of the freedom his time at Yale gave him to live a double life. He was anything but original—he was nothing but a pathetic cliché: a predatory professor! And for all his vaunted feminism, he was unfaithful with many women many years younger than he! While at lunch with my father a few days later, I looked at his hands and imagined them touching students, then at his lips, imagining them kissing students, and I felt overcome by nausea. Many years before universities had any strictures against faculty-graduate student relationships and at a time when most of his colleagues were doing the same thing, I instinctively knew it was Wrong.

A few nights later, my mother came to my bedroom to tell me

something else; again Claire was asleep before I was. "Your father was impotent a lot of the time," she began. "You know what that means, right, sweetheart?" I knew what "impotent" meant, but I didn't want to know this about my father. "It's part of why he was unfaithful. It didn't work with us. He needed things I didn't want to give him," she added. "He's not like Anatole or Stanley! Anatole would seduce anything that moved! And Stanley's a rake. He mows through these women, and Laura's the long-suffering wife who looks the other way. Your father isn't a womanizer like they are. He's just so insecure. And he had those strange desires!"

That night, I fell asleep with visions of my father's ineffectual fumbling, his fruitless efforts to be the man he thought he should be. I woke repeatedly from dreams in which my father was powerless or inadequate. Trying to scale a wall and falling back down. Attempting to lift a boulder and collapsing in a heap. Racing toward my mother with his arms open and stumbling before he reached her.

Each time my mother had disclosed more damning things about my father, she'd warned me not to share any of it with Claire; although just fourteen months younger, Claire was considered by both my parents to be fragile, incapable of handling "adult" information. I was a dutiful and obedient little girl; I never told anyone what I'd learned that day until I was much older.

But while Claire was to be protected, my mother was determined to deceive me no longer. She was an anti-romantic, a no-nonsense, direct truth-teller. She must have seethed as she watched her innocent children playing with, revering, adoring a childlike man she knew to be far from innocent. Part of the strain of being married to my father, she'd made clear, was covering for him, hiding his darker side. She was tired of deception. Tired of secrets. And I think she thought she was giving me Truth. She saw it as a gift, a healing blast of arctic air that in its bracing purity would do away with illusion, or a scalding light that purified as it burned away masks and façades. No more gauzy fairyland for my father and me. No more seeing only part of a person. Enough with unquestioning love. It was time for criticism. It was time to grow up.

But what she was actually giving me was *her* truth. Partial truths. Truths I probably shouldn't have been given at my age and in the way she delivered them. She both turned me against my father and turned me toward him. I knew she was right about some of it. I wanted to prove her wrong about the rest.

And even as I shuddered at his darkness and deception and empathized—keenly—with my mother considering what she'd had to cope with, I stayed loyal to and protective of my shaky, struggling, and very sad father. I sensed that Claire and I needed to remain my father's pure and uncomplicated place of love and tenderness. He had made it clear that he relied for his very survival on our steadfast affection and innocent faith in him. He had said he would kill himself were it not for us. So I never let him know I noticed anything unsavory about his behavior or had learned anything that might defile him.

My mother spun the split as her attempt to save Claire from his rejecting anger and both of us from his strange sexuality. As she would natter on about how much his rage must have scared us girls, I'd nod in silent agreement. But I didn't point out that that was a tiny fraction of who my father was for me, that his occasional anger was a small price to pay for his overwhelmingly loving presence.

I could sense that I was not to question her decision in any way. That it had been agonizing for her, and that she was immensely relieved to be on the other side of it. She was waking up and coming back to life emotionally. My mother made it clear that we weren't supposed to think of the split as a bad thing. And so I protected her too. I didn't cry, complain, or express any sadness to her. I didn't want her to feel guilty or worry about me.

What nurturing energy my mother had went to her clients, who gobbled up her attention, advice, and reassurance and begged for more, and to Claire, whom she saw as vulnerable and needy. I was the good girl. The easy one. The mini adult. "I worried so much about taking him from you when you were younger, Sid," she'd confide. "I wanted to wait till you were old enough to handle it. But you're so strong and mature now. I'm so proud of you." I liked being her confidante. I liked the praise she gave me for my behavior. My mother tenderly loved Claire, her little chick or cub in need of protection from the darker things of the world. But I was the one she needed to validate her decision. I was the one she counted on.

And now that she was sharing things with me, I felt closer to her than I ever had before. My mother had been a bit of an aloof and sphinxlike mystery to me when I was a young child. If she wasn't on the phone with a client, she was dashing out to an event, stirring a pot on the stove, or reading a manuscript. Now she was a human being, with problems and worries and lots of love to give. And as my childhood receded, her utter disinterest in dolls and stuffed animals, imaginative play and PBS kids' shows, wasn't disappointing as it had been when I'd longed for her to show some interest, any interest, in what was important to me and Claire. Now she was taking us out to neighborhood restaurants like Anita's Chili Parlor, Indian Oven, and the Museum Café, or to Elio's with her clients and dear friends John Gregory Dunne and Joan Didion, whose symbiotic marriage I always held up as a beacon. On other nights, she'd have Carrie buy green gazpacho and salmon mousse at the Silver Palate or spinach quiche and homemade tortellini at the Green Noodle for a girls'-night-in dinner with me and Claire. She'd take us clothes shopping at the chic stores cropping up on Columbus. For the first time ever, she was reading aloud to us: adult books like *David Copperfield* and *Jane Eyre*. She was making us Ovaltine and cinnamon toast or banana milkshakes in the mornings after racing back from a 6 a.m. exercise class and before donning her power suits and applying her makeup. I don't think I'd ever gone to a movie with my mother before my parents split (other than *Star Wars* as a family), but now she was taking us to special movie premieres—*Grease 2*, *Dragonslayer*, *Superman II*, *Poltergeist*, the restored *Thief of Baghdad*, *Tron*.

In general, my mother smiled so much more, was sparklier, lighter. And she took over my father's role as chief worry-allayer. "Don't get nervous in the service or twitchy in the itchy!" she'd playfully advise. After Toni Morrison encouraged anxious little Claire to imagine putting her worries in a balloon and watch them float away, my mother repeated Toni's line often, as much for herself as for us. I could see anxiety and strain lift from her shoulders and a peace I'd never seen before suffuse her face.

Good things were happening for my father too. That spring, he secured a job as the drama critic for *The Nation*, which would give him a little more income and the chance to take me and Claire to the theater as his companion! And in June of 1981, my father was inaugurated as the president of PEN America, an organization that celebrates artistic expression and works to protect freedom of speech for writers. This was an extremely prestigious post, and it would give my father an opportunity to work on behalf of both literature and human rights. When my mother told me that he would be succeeding his close friend Bernard Malamud as PEN's president, a wave of relief and happiness flooded my body. We, his girls, were to be his escorts to the event. There's a photo of us taken by Carrie before our father picked us up. We're both in pretty, girlish dresses, mine white eyelet, Claire's pink and blue with puffy sleeves, a full skirt, and a velvet belt. Our long hair is pulled back by headbands. We're holding hands, smiling shyly. I look tall and tan and lanky, my long skinny arms sticking out of the too-short sleeves of my dress and the hem rising almost above my knees, and I tower over Claire. I have very few memories of that night; what we ate, what my father said in his acceptance speech, how the night ended—I can't remember any of it. I do remember that for once he was right on time to pick us up. I remember seeing Uncle Bern, I remember my father's glowing pride in his two daughters, one on each arm, I remember thinking this was major, this was bolstering, this would help.

That June, we were also introduced to my mother's new boyfriend. Bill was a tall, strapping, ruggedly handsome and effortlessly cool documentary filmmaker with mirrored sunglasses and lustrous black hair. The first time we met him, he'd accompanied me and Claire roller-skating in Central Park, then cooked us an elaborate dinner. He had a vast repertoire of impressive or exotic dishes: on future visits, he made biscuits from scratch, complicated stews, delicately seasoned fish. Unlike our father, he could cook, really cook—not just ham sandwiches and scrambled eggs but entire menus for dinner parties—he had a tool kit he actually knew how to use, he knew how to sail, and he looked right in tennis shorts. Virile, athletic, Bill was sporty and preppy, big and well built and tanned. He looked at ease in polo shirts and khaki shorts and sunglasses as our father never had. He had a promising project about an all-female pop group in development with Dick Clark—a very early example of reality television, it would air on NBC and draw a lot of media attention.

In all these ways, he was everything our father was not. But in other ways, he was all too reminiscent of him. He smoked like a chimney (he made my father's smoking seem moderate) and drank a little too much with (and before) dinner. Despite his physical strength and athleticism, he seemed so much weaker than my mother. I could tell that he relied on her for his sense of self, to keep him motivated, to prop him up when he had career setbacks or felt blocked creatively. He and Claire quickly began sparring in much the same way she and my father had.

The strange summer after my parents' separation, Claire and I, in New York for the first summer of our lives (we'd spent past ones in Europe or at the house in Connecticut), turned to new pursuits to fill the time and, I suppose, ease our aching hearts. In Weston, we'd taken swimming lessons and gone to Soaring Eagle and Singing Oaks day camps, where we made woven baskets and gimp bracelets and performed in shows (I played Richie Cunningham and sang "Day by Day" in *"Happy Days" Puts On "Godspell"*). By contrast, in the summer of 1981, my mother scheduled us for nothing except tennis lessons on the courts in Riverside Park with our friend Katie Anthony (who fortunately had long-divorced parents and with whom we could be open without shame or embarrassment). We were essentially home all day most days and nights with nothing on the agenda.

Claire and I begged my mother for a pet, but she loathed animals of all kinds and only agreed to a fish. Carrie took us to Woolworth's on 79th and Broadway, where we bought a goldfish for fifty cents and carried him home in a clear plastic bag. We tried to make the fish exciting, but it was difficult. For the first few days, we debated names, talked and sang to the fish, meticulously timed his feedings, and carefully sprinkled the correct amount of fish food flakes into the bowl. However, after the novelty had worn off and it became clear that the fish had no personality to speak of and no use for the intricate structures or singing and talking we lavished on him, we lost interest in being the mother of a goldfish.

But there were new domestic pursuits we became passionate about, and making desserts topped the list. We boiled up Jell-O pudding on the stove and poured it into stoneware cups, checking with delight as it grew a skin and firmed up so we could eat it. After tying aprons around our necks, we'd bake chocolate chip cookies and butterscotch brownies from the recipes on the Toll House chips packages. Sometimes we used our mother's old-fashioned cookbooks: *Betty Crocker's Cookbook*, laughable in the hands of our most un-Betty Crocker like mother, was a gold mine for us. We also got a kick out of devising our own recipes for cake—we'd haphazardly pour cups of flour, sugar, milk, and baking powder into mixing bowls and bake up the batter—producing lopsided, strangely salty concoctions. Creamy Deluxe frosting made even the most bland or implausible cake delicious. We loved serving what we made to my mother's dinner guests; Harold Brodkey was an especially big fan of our butterscotch brownies.

My mother was becoming more lax when it came to food. When Claire and I were little, snacks were prunes, dates, cottage cheese on fiber crisps; "dessert" a sliced banana floating in a bowl of milk, a plate of almonds, a handful of Acerolas, a Dannon frozen yogurt bar, or a Tiger's Milk cookie. Now, there was a kind of liberation post separation. My mother still didn't allow soda, white bread, or candy, but she allowed us to bake sugary treats to our heart's content and go out on Columbus for a Häagen-Dazs or Sedutto's ice cream cone or gourmet jelly beans (and later David's or Mrs. Fields cookies) every night.

And without my father around to monitor or judge our television watching, we all felt free to indulge. A few months earlier, Addie had introduced us to her favorites: *Magnum, P.I.* (she had a huge crush on Tom Selleck), *The Greatest American Hero*, and *Nero Wolfe* on Friday nights, *The Love Boat* and *Fantasy Island* on Saturday nights. I remembered when my father had gotten angry at a babysitter in

Weston because she'd turned on "a stupid, idiotic TV show" (*Fantasy Island*) one night. Now we were the *Fantasy Island* fans. Carrie had only watched TV on days my father was at Yale and we were at school or camp, but now she happily shared her favorite programs—game shows, soap operas—with us. Claire and I began guessing the costs of cat food and dishwashers on *The Price Is Right* alongside Carrie. After getting turned on to *As the World Turns* and *Guiding Light* by Carrie, Claire became a soap opera nut—swept up in the romantic plots and melodrama—and began devouring Harlequin romances. I never got hooked on either show, but I wholeheartedly shared her obsession with *The Brady Bunch*, which we began watching three times a day on TBS. We hankered for the stability and boisterous happiness of a large family with madly-in-love parents and a home in the suburbs, complete with den, family room, and garage.

That summer, I reread my favorite books about big happy families: the *All-of-a-Kind Family* books, the Melendy series by Elizabeth Enright, *Little Women* and its sequels, Maud Hart Lovelace's Betsy-Tacy series. But now I was reading the high school volumes in the Betsy-Tacy series, and Betsy was no longer innocently climbing the big hill but rather "beautifying" herself—winding her hair on Magic Wavers, buffing her nails, using freckle cream. I gave up Beverly Cleary's Ramona and Henry Huggins and *The Mouse and the Motorcycle*, and read instead Cleary's books about and for teens: *Fifteen*, *The Luckiest Girl*, *Jean and Johnny*, and *Sister of the Bride*. These featured girls for whom going steady with a popular, attractive boy was the height of achievement, who spent hours picking out outfits, who painted their nails and curled their hair.

Perhaps partly inspired by Lovelace's and Cleary's beauty-obsessed heroines, and with a delicious feeling of maturity, Claire and I plunged into the world of "beauty products": Jean Naté After Bath Splash, Jergens body lotion, Noxema and Sea Breeze astringent and Clearasil for pimples we didn't yet have, Flex and Finesse shampoo and conditioner (to replace the Johnson's Baby Shampoo we'd used without embarrassment until that point), Ban deodorant, Bonne Bell Lip Smackers. We knew about these things thanks to the commercials we were now seeing and the magazines we were now reading—our great-aunt had given me a subscription to *Seventeen* for my eleventh birthday, and Katie got us into *YM*, *Tiger Beat*, and *Teen*. Claire and I would make expeditions to one of the Love drugstores that dotted the city and pick out what we (thought we) needed, then arrange the bottles and tubes artfully on our bureaus. Needless to say, we never spoke of these beauty products in conversation with our father.

I began to read *Rolling Stone*, *Variety*, and the *Hollywood Reporter*, which my mother brought home in stacks from the office, and the world of music, movies, and pop culture thrillingly opened up to me. I joined the Columbia House record club, a subscription service that sent records to me in the mail on a regular basis. I learned through Addie about the Top 40 countdown with Casey Kasem on Sundays and began listening religiously and trying to guess which song would snag the top spot each week. The songs I especially liked, I'd go to Tower Records (ten blocks south of our apartment) and buy as 45s, then play them over and over on my new record player, a cool-looking adult stereo that had been in the Weston house and was given to me when my parents split. I was discovering classic rock too, listening to WPLJ and WNEW on my little clock radio every morning as I got ready for school.

As I sought refuge in rock music, pop culture, baking, and beauty products, I became a different person. I imagine that embracing these things with such fervor was in a way a rejection of my father's critical values, or if not a rejection, then a swerving away in a different direction, a swerve that made the pain of his loss less acute, or that papered over pain with breezy, lighthearted, adolescent fun.

On my sister's tenth birthday, July 14, 1981, we gathered as a family of four for the first time since my father had moved out. I hadn't seen my father on my own birthday a few months earlier, but he'd called from New Haven, and I'd tried to ignore the break in his voice. He'd always been the leader of my birthday parties, and Addie had gamely tried to fill his shoes. There was the same praline ice cream cake from Grossinger's bakery, the same gang of friends, the same goody bags from Paper House. No one mentioned my father.

That summer, my father was subletting an apartment over by the UN. Although we never spent the night there, we'd visited it briefly after an outing to the UN with him. As a baby, I'd received a book about the UN, *Penguins, of All People*, inscribed to me by the author, Don Freeman (he of *Corduroy* fame), and I'd always longed to see it in person. But the experience felt more like a "buck up Daddy" day than an exciting adventure. The UN was interesting, yes, but it was more about *telling* my father how interesting it was. He wanted to be clapped on the back and thanked for the special treat he'd given us. To me, it was more surreal and disorienting to see his tiny, impersonal sublet in a tall tower on the far East Side. Daddy's forced cheerfulness and hunger for approval and praise gave me an uneasy feeling in the pit of my stomach. It was a brilliantly sunny June day, the resplendently bright UN flags waving proudly in the balmy air, but I felt cold inside.

We'd always spent Claire's birthday either in Weston—with an outdoor party complete with Slip 'N Slide and Grampy Merle's angel food cake festooned with strawberries—or in Europe. The plan this year was dinner at a restaurant followed by the Broadway musical *Barnum* with Jim Dale and Glenn Close. Carrie brought me and Claire from the Upper West Side to the Theater District to meet our parents at the restaurant. My memory is of oak-paneled walls, dim lights, and a bustling sense of conviviality and urgency. My mother ordered a Shirley Temple for Claire and a ginger ale for me; we spread butter thickly on the delicious rolls, and still my father hadn't arrived. I began worrying, smiling nonchalantly but checking the time on my Mickey Mouse watch under the table. Just as my mother started to fret, my father rushed in, dressed in his best but with sweat dripping from his brow. As he caught sight of my mother—perfectly polished and pretty in a sleeveless shift dress and heels, with a mildly irritated look on her face—I could see he was thrown off his game. He seemed both attracted and abashed, he stuttered, he went to take a seat, and I watched in horror as he missed the chair and fell on the floor. Heads swiveled, a waiter rushed over to help him up, Claire cried "Oh no!" Brushing off the concern, my father insisted: "I'm fine, I'm fine." But he clearly wasn't fine. "Happy Birthday, Swanee," he said as he eased himself off the floor and into the chair.

Somehow that embarrassing image of my father lying on the ground summed up who he had been since my mother had decided to end the marriage. He was trying his hardest, he was looking his best, but it was never good enough and his attempts to impress only backfired and made him even more of a hapless, helpless fool. Now the president of PEN, the august drama critic, was sprawled on the floor in a Theater District restaurant, humiliated in front of his contemptuous ex-wife and his paralyzed children.

What I remember of the rest of the meal is strained silence punctuated by my calculatedly chipper comments about how good the food was, how pretty Claire looked, how excited I was about an upcoming visit from my grandparents. When the waiters brought cake with a candle and my father sang "Happy Birthday" off-key with tears glistening in his eyes, I couldn't help but notice my mother's scorn for what I knew she would consider his sloppy sentimentality.

Later, in the theater, typically his domain of utmost power, my father was reduced to a quivering, weeping mess. He had no notepad, no pen to scribble with, no responsibility to assess or judge. He was at the mercy of the spectacle. During one of the love songs, I heard sniffles and looked out of the corner of my eye to see tears coursing down my father's cheeks. I took my cardigan sweater off, arranged it into the highest pile I could, and sat on it, leaned forward, pulled myself up to my full height, and tried to be the best buffer I could between my crying father and my mother's view. Every time I heard a sniff or a strangled sob, I rustled my program loudly to block the sound from my mother's ears. And I pretended to my father that I hadn't noticed. I didn't reach out to comfort him. I knew he was trying to hold himself together, and that he wouldn't want me to see or know.

This was our first and last outing as a nuclear family post separation. In fact, I only saw my parents in the same room three times again: at my high school graduation, at my wedding rehearsal, and at my wedding. They came to my plays and performances on different nights, and only my father attended my college graduation.

The only time we saw our father for more than a quick lunch or dinner that summer was a weekend in the Hamptons at his former student David Epstein's house. Years later, in his eulogy for my father, David would describe that weekend in a way that startled me:

Over the years as I grew to love Dick, I experienced his vulnerability, and his otherworldliness, which could be almost childlike, and often painful to witness. It made me want to protect him. There were phone calls, long calls at night when his emotions were frayed, and he needed comforting, which I fumbled around trying somehow to provide, never feeling as if I had done enough.

It could also be humorous. He came to visit us one weekend with Priscilla and Claire, they were maybe ten or twelve—sparkling, remarkable girls. But having Dick as a house guest was like hosting an extremely large third child, not nearly as competent as the other two. He left drinks in precarious places, ashes overflowed ashtrays, and live cigars were spotted in odd locations—Kate and I worried he'd fall asleep and burn the house down. It's not a small house, but it seemed to shrink around Dick, because every time he turned, something hit the floor, a bottle, a dish. We left sponges in strategic spots.

His girls seemed tuned in to his obliviousness; like guide dogs, they managed to keep him in the world outside his head, alerting him to the moment—"Daddy, that glass!" "Daddy, your plate!" At the end of the visit, when they all got into the rental car, Dick was of course behind the wheel, but I had the oddest sense that the girls were doing the driving.

Although I have very vivid memories of that weekend, from the huge waves we'd ridden to the games we'd played with David's young daughters, I have no memory of being especially vigilant or of my father being especially clumsy or inattentive to matters of safety. So habitual and natural was that kind of behavior for me vis-à-vis my father, I suppose, that I'd forgotten it or never grasped that it was unusual, worth noting or commenting on. And then there was that "never feeling as if I had done enough"—oh, how familiar that was when it came to my father!

I was so grateful to the friends who stayed faithful to my father after the split and those who made it possible for us to have fun experiences with him. Fellow divorced fathers Lionel Tiger and Dick Pollak, who'd bring Sebastian and Amanda along for outings to the Museum of Natural History, where we'd stroll through the magical Hall of Gems or stand, awestruck, under the giant blue whale, or the Met, where we'd pretend to be Claudia and Jamie of *From the Mixed-Up Files of Mrs. Basil E. Frankweiler* and take dibs on which furniture we'd want to have in our own homes as we ambled through the American Wing. We'd have dinners at Dick's and Lionel's apartments, where Amanda and Sebastian stayed every other week, for the full week. Each parent had a viable apartment for the child to visit—they worked it out so that they could do a real fifty-fifty custody split. I envied Amanda and Sebastian their far greater access to their fathers, the cool rooms they had in both apartments, and the relative peace between their parents. At the same time, though, I was grateful that I didn't have to be around my father more in his fragile state—it took so much out of me—even as I felt overwhelmed by guilt thinking that way. Often after outings with him, I'd have to lie down and count quietly in order to calm my racing heart.

But when we made visits to the sprawling Riverdale home of *New York Times* book critic Christopher Lehmann-Haupt and poet-journalist Natalie Robins, I could relax and let the Lehmann-Haupts do the work. Christopher was one of the small group of my father's friends who could break down the New York Giants' draft picks as deftly as he could assess a contemporary novel, and he accorded me the same respect my father did when it came to discussing both football and books. Natalie lovingly called my father "Nelson" after he told her how he'd looked up to Nelson Eddy as a teenager, and she had a knack for bringing out my father's sweetness. Carrie had come to us via the Lehmann-Haupts, who'd used her as a baby nurse for their daughter, Rachel, six months before I was born. Rachel was funny and sharp. She had an enormous playroom filled with toys and closets filled with the coolest clothes. She taught me and Claire about Valley Girl lingo—"Gag me with a spoon!"—and gave us fashion shows, prancing around in her sexy outfits and chattering about boys as Claire and I watched, agog. The Lehmann-Haupts had cats, a grill in the backyard, affection and esteem for my father. Being with them was a balm.

If these friends served as buffers, so did movies and theatrical productions. On Saturday afternoons, our father took us to movies (often at his friend Dan Talbot's Lincoln Plaza Cinemas), ones he'd always loved and wanted to share with us as well as new ones he'd heard good things about from Stanley Kauffmann. Stanley, the film critic for the *New Republic*, was our cinematic guru, although he occasionally misfired. During *On Golden Pond*, my father covered our ears as swearwords began flying and muttered about the inappropriateness of Stanley's recommendation. But Stanley usually got it right. Long before it won the Oscar for best picture, Stanley told us about "a little, modest, lovely British film" called *Chariots of Fire*. My father and his girls, whom he'd taught to love the Olympics and who adored Blake's "Jerusalem" (sung at Brearley's moving-up ceremonies and graduations), were enchanted. I stayed up late to watch it win the Oscar, although my father scorned such award shows.

For old movies, our father took us to the Upper West Side's revival movie houses, the Regency on Broadway and 67th Street and the Thalia thirty blocks or so uptown. During the ninety minutes or two hours we sat in the darkened theater, the films—classic Hitchcocks, *The Apartment*, *Some Like It Hot*—typically brought us into a world outside, above, and counter to the messiness, pain, and complexity of our real lives. But there was one film that shot straight through these layers of happy distraction into something truer and more revealing.

> Look, he can't be dead. He can't.
> They don't understand.
> Maybe you could let me have a baby someday, and it could be a
>   boy, so it could be just like him.
> It'd have to be me.
> Nobody else loved him like I do.
> Maybe you could do that for me.
> And if you could, he wouldn't even die.
>
> —Francie to God, of her father, Johnny,
> in the film of *A Tree Grows in Brooklyn*

In the spring of 1982, my father took me to see the 1946 Elia Kazan film version of *A Tree Grows in Brooklyn*. It was a favorite of his, he told me, and it depicted a Brooklyn immigrant experience close to the one his parents had had, although these immigrants were Irish, not Jewish. From the first frame, I was entranced—by the vital, teeming streets with the array of neighborhood stores, the boys in their knickerbockers, sweater vests, caps, and kneesocks who jostled and played and smoked (I could imagine my father in this gang), and most of all, eleven-year-old Francie, the dreamy girl who escapes the pain and loneliness of her life by voracious, tireless, ecstatic reading. Because this wasn't just a period piece to me or a way of gaining access to my grandparents' and my father's childhood worlds. Gazing up at Peggy Ann Garner's openhearted, innocent face, alternately lit up and weighed down, elated and anxious in her father's presence, I felt I was watching myself on the screen.

Unlike Francie, I was well off, well educated, a Manhattan girl. I had no squalor to rise above, no fear that I might never live a life of meaning and intellectual passion. But I nonetheless felt a deep kinship with the little girl who worried incessantly about her father, winced at her mother's harshness toward him, and needed to be the mature, adult caregiver for both of them. Francie was Priscilla without privilege, without Claire, without Brearley. But she was Priscilla all the same. Torn between a dreamy, weak, romantic parent and a hard, capable, realistic one. A little girl who was enraptured by her father's magical qualities, recognized his vulnerability and addictive tendencies, and feared his inevitable demise.

And her father, Johnny Nolan—handsome, debonair, hapless, charming, doomed Johnny—well, he was my father in so many ways. In the film, we first hear Johnny merrily singing "Molly Malone," an Irish song my father always sang to us at bedtime. Then Johnny bursts through the door with a graceful spring in his step and a supremely animated face that in its rubbery expressivity uncannily reminded me of my father. Forcefully gesticulating as he talks, his voice swooping and soaring, in his physicality, his spirit, his ardent love for his daughter, Johnny simply *was* my father.

In that first scene between them, when Johnny has just learned he landed a singing waiter gig and Francie realizes he's in a good mood, her face loses its self-contained solemnity. "Oh, Papa, you've got a job tonight! Maybe tonight will be it!" she cries, giddy with relief that he's happy and not drunk. Like Francie, there was nothing I loved more than to hear my father talk, and nothing that gave me greater relief than the realization that he wasn't depressed or angry. When he was in a happy, buoyant mood, he filled a room with zip and zest and made me almost dizzy with joy.

Like my father with me before my parents' split, Johnny is Francie's comforter. When she tells him she's sad that the tree in their yard was cut down, he immediately springs into action. "Oh no, prima donna," he reassures her, "they didn't kill it. That tree will always live—wait till spring and you'll see it." And as eager as he is to alleviate his daughter's sadness, he passionately wants to make her wishes come true (her biggest wish is that he not come home "sick," i.e., drunk). He tells her to come up with her own wish, just for her, and it's then that she exclaims, with heartbreaking sweetness, "Oh, I just love you so much, Papa!" as she hugs him fiercely, arms wrapped around his neck. That is exactly how I felt about my father.

And as the film continued, the parallels between Johnny and my father grew all the more striking. His geniality and gallantry. His gusto. The way he makes everyone he encounters feel noticed and special. His compassionate acceptance of those deemed "sinners" or "losers" by conventional society. His glowing pride in his children, his belief that they were "the best children in the world," his unconditional, pure love for them. The way he winces, even cowers, as his wife, Katie, speaks to him in "a crisp, hard way." Johnny was, like my father, at once sunny, optimistic, electric with life, and shadowed by insecurity and melancholy.

In the film, it is Johnny who comforts Francie and reassures her of the tree's ultimate survival. But it is also Johnny who cannot recover from the blow of his wife's contempt, the killing necessity of removing the veil from his daughter's eyes when his wife insists they take her out of school and send her to work, the death of his romantic aspirations, the stark reality of his failures. I wanted my father to be that tree. Resourceful, resilient, refusing to die. Even as blows were leveled, even as axes fell, couldn't the seed or essence of my father and all he meant survive?

Did my father see himself on the screen? He wasn't a drunk, he was able to hold down a steady job, but he was in the thrall of his cigarettes, he was intermittently "sick" with depression, he harbored deep insecurities about the worth of his work, he'd been rebuffed by his wife and was helplessly adored by his oldest daughter. Yes, my father worked at Yale, but I was always aware that he was an adjunct, on a year-to-year contract, never tenured, underpaid, without a graduate degree. And I was always haunted by the sense that he would leave, disappear, die before his time. That his addiction would cut him down. That his yearnings would never be realized in a way that gave him peace.

As Johnny moved inexorably toward his demise, I found my eyes welling up again and again, and ordered the tears not to fall. In this, I was like Francie, who is quiet, stoic, pulled into herself after Johnny's death from pneumonia brought on by alcoholism. Katie wonders and worries about her daughter not crying or showing any emotion. And then we see Francie alone on their tenement's roof, finally sobbing. "He can't be dead!" she cries incredulously. "Nobody else loved him like I do!" Daddy and I are gulping, sniffing, weeping. I reach out to hold his hand. Are we crying for Francie and Johnny or for ourselves?

I retain an affection for the live theater, battered though it is—perhaps because it is. I keep an openness to those occasions of pleasure—a performance, a new voice—that come along rarely but are inimitable, restorative. And I guess I have a desire, too, after so many years away from the action, to take on again that function Shaw described when he said that the critic wasn't "the partner of [the theater's] guilty joys" but its "policeman." Ah, but policemen don't only nab malefactors; they help children across streets, give directions to visitors, break up quarrels, and, occasionally, even preside over happy times for all.

—Richard Gilman, inaugural column as drama critic
for *The Nation*, April 11, 1981

During my father's tenure as *The Nation*'s drama critic, he got two seats—critic's seats—to each and every Broadway and off-Broadway show—and anything that he thought was appropriate for us, he took me or Claire to. It was exciting to enter the theaters on his arm and walk to our choice seats with the knowledge that I was not only At the Theater but also helping my father with his work. Because I wasn't just sitting by him as he judged. He cared about my reaction, valued it, made it clear that he thought I had good taste and interesting observations. He'd warn me not to say anything negative too loudly—"The woman sitting next to you could be one of the actors' aunts!" he'd chuckle—but nonetheless would solicit my "honest opinion" and ask me never to worry about "being mean" (my biggest fear) when I delivered my verdicts. He asked me questions and answered mine; we debated how hard to come down on certain actors; he contextualized the productions for me and explored his ideas about them in conversation with me. But even as he gave me this heady power, he made it clear that it was all right to be a little girl as well:

> At the end of the first segment of *The Life and Adventures of Nicholas Nickleby*, my 11-year-old daughter turned to me and said, "It's wonderful, Daddy, but I'm getting so tired." Ah, Priscilla, the spirit was willing, etc. After promising to tell her what happened, I put her in a cab, grabbed a frankfurter at a stand and went back for the evening session, which lasted four and a half hours on top of the afternoon's four.
>
> —Richard Gilman, *The Nation*, November 7, 1981

Even as I watched and listened to the productions unfolding before us, I'd be aware of him scribbling furiously in the small spiral notebook he carried. His handwriting was largely illegible, but I grew to understand what different expressions and intensities of writing meant. I'll never forget his energetically penned "Ghastly!" as *Cats'* Rum Tum Tugger was gyrating and belting out his number. I was also acutely aware of how he registered the productions in his body—I could sense by his posture, his gestures, his gaze, when he was pleased or, by contrast, recoiling. It was sometimes hard when I liked something and I could tell my father didn't. Even as he stiffened in obvious revulsion, I became teary when Grizabella the Glamour Cat sang "Memory." My father inveighed against it in his *Nation* review as "an obnoxious ballad . . . entirely out of keeping with the spirit of Old Possum." I, by contrast, performed it in a camp talent show a year or so later and never told my father how I'd succumbed to its heart-stirring sentimentality.

Sometimes I'd notice fellow theatergoers notice my father, whisper to each other while pointing to his notepad and pen, occasionally introduce themselves with a reverent attitude. He received their greetings and compliments graciously, although he preferred to lie low and not be recognized. But for me, the recognition was a boon because it meant that despite his precarious hold on stability and equanimity, in this realm, my father was still important.

The first Thanksgiving after my parents separated, Anne and Herman Roiphe, old friends of my parents' and the parents of one of my best Brearley friends, Becky, invited my father, Claire, and me to dinner at their brownstone on East 95th Street (then an unglamorous block). Their house had scuffed carpets, furniture covered in dog and cat hair, bookshelves overflowing with books, and was home to the large blended family of five girls that Herman, a child psychiatrist whose office was on the ground floor, and Anne, a writer, shared. This family was both close-knit and "different," warm and unconventional; it felt comforting to be there. While the meal preparations were underway and the grown-ups were chatting over drinks, Claire and I played with Becky and her sister Katie and their cousin Marco Roth, holding séances in an upstairs bedroom, romping around with the dogs. The dinner itself was at once literary and homey; everyone at the table received a book at their place, and everyone had to read a poem or a passage from a book aloud as a kind of grace before eating. My father, naturally, adored this. We no longer had him carving a Thanksgiving turkey at the head of our dining room table in Weston or at 44 West 77th Street, but we had him in his element, with his friends, happy, relaxed, and expansive (my mother, meanwhile, celebrated with various friends; she'd never liked the holiday and was probably relieved not to have to host a dinner).

And if Thanksgiving at the Roiphes' became a tradition, so did New Year's Day at the Kauffmanns'. Stanley and his wife, Laura, held a New Year's Day cocktail party each year in their loft in then-unfashionable Chelsea, and my father would always bring us as his dates. We'd choose our most girlish and pretty outfits to wear—prim, floral Laura Ashley dresses with tights, Mary Janes, velvet headbands, and fitted wool coats, and later Putumayo dresses—and play our role as our father's sprightly companions and the only party guests under eighteen to the hilt. Stanley and Laura had never had children; they considered me and Claire honorary nieces. Stanley would be impeccably turned out in natty tweeds, give us crushingly strong hugs, then hold court in the center of the room, his flirtatious demeanor and intense charisma drawing everyone to him. Laura, with her gray pixie-cut hair, round, rosy, cheerful face, her tinkling laugh, buzzed around offering appetizers, refilling glasses, and checking in on everyone's personal lives. Claire and I were always excited to see the current and former Yale Drama School students, many of whom we harbored little crushes on, unbeknownst to our father. It felt right to usher in a new year by making our father happy.

But no new rituals or traditions could save Christmas or preserve it as a joyful time for our father and his girls. For Christmas 1981, we stayed in New York so that we could see our father. At first, the novelty of being in New York City for the holidays was a welcome distraction. Carrie took us out on Columbus Avenue to buy a Christmas tree and one of the doormen carried it home for us. We'd never had one in our New York City apartment before, so Carrie bought strings of lights from Woolworth's and helped us hang them along with candy canes and popcorn garlands on the tree. Grammy Peg and Grampy

Merle arrived with much fanfare a few days before Christmas, along with many suitcases full of some of their Christmas ornaments and the handmade stockings (minus my father's), although not the full panoply of crèches and winter scenes we were used to in their white gingerbread house. Grammy took us to Fifth Avenue to see the department store windows and have hot chocolate with whipped cream at Rumpelmayer's on Central Park South. On Christmas Eve, Claire and I performed with Katie Anthony in the Christmas pageant at West End Collegiate Church and then had a festive supper at home with my grandparents, Mom, Katie, and her mom. Christmas morning, our grandparents did everything in their power to make stocking and present opening as special as they could, and because everything was so different, I didn't miss Daddy as much as I might have. But as the afternoon lengthened and the time approached for me and Claire to visit Daddy, I felt a sense of dread.

Bundled up in our parkas and hats and scarves crocheted by Grammy Gilman, we walked by ourselves to where Daddy was staying (a temporary crash pad in a former student's apartment). We carried a pound cake baked by Carrie, a box of Frango mints from Marshall Field's department store in Chicago to which my grandmother had attached a loving card, and a new tie Carrie had helped us pick out. My mother sent no message or gift of any kind. I don't remember the building or the block, but I vividly remember Daddy sitting in a dim room with a tiny, forlorn Christmas tree bearing a few cheap balls and two clumsily wrapped presents beneath. As soon as we stepped into the apartment, we pealed in unison: "Merry Christmas, Daddy!" and threw our arms around him. He tried, but couldn't muster much holiday cheer. He looked so sad. So lonely. Just desolate. And looking at his Charlie Brown Christmas tree, I thought: He's the tree, and I'm the blanket who can bolster him and bring him to tinselly life. So I swallowed the strange feeling in my chest and started to chatter on about gifts we'd gotten, delicious dishes we'd eaten, funny things we'd found in our stockings, but he looked as glum as ever. None of what I'd said or done was helpful; all of it was useless or worse than useless because it was only reminding him of how the Christmas he had for us fell short.

I turned to the gifts from Carrie and Grammy Peg, which buoyed him, and then he gave us some Christmas cookies another former student had dropped off for him. We opened the presents—a *Sports Illustrated* subscription for me and an art book for Claire—and Claire and I sang the safely cheerful carols "Good King Wenceslas" and "Joy to the World." I didn't want to ask how he'd filled his day, what he'd done before we came over, what he would do after we left. I didn't want the extent of his loneliness emphasized. We snuggled with him on the sofa, exclaimed over the cookies and the presents, and smiled till our cheeks hurt. We gave him high-spirited good-byes, and then, as soon as he'd shut the apartment door, Claire and I looked at each other with wide, sad eyes and gaping mouths. In the elevator, I leaned against the wall and Claire leaned her head on my shoulder. We walked home somberly, hand in hand.

n late 1981, my mother got a new television, cable, Atari, HBO, and a VCR in quick succession (my father hadn't allowed Atari, and he'd resisted our seeing even PG-rated movies). Ironically, the television and all its enticing accouterments were set up in my father's old office. Now his office was entertainment central: it's where Claire and I and our friends gathered to watch movies (R-rated movies!) on HBO, play Space Invaders and Pac-Man, and screen the movies we'd rent from the local video store. At the same time, Claire and I took over my father's private telephone line, listed under the pseudonym "Robert Donner" to protect him from the irate family members of writers, directors, and actors he'd reproached (I didn't know about this alias until we got many calls for a Robert Donner, expressed our confusion, and my mother explained the secret). My father's white desk and office chair became my go-to spot for endless, giggling phone calls with friends and brief, charged phone calls with boys. Although most of the bookshelves had been removed, my father's majestic library ladder remained, and was now used as a kind of jungle gym for my friends to clamber up and down.

Other parts of the apartment were changing too. My parents' bedroom, now only my mother's, was redecorated to reflect her new, snazzier, more glamorous—and hot single woman—status. Pale wood built-ins, sleek and modern, filled the large space. There was a huge TV on a wheeled table that pulled over the bed so you could watch from a distance or quite close up. There were drawers upon drawers for the elegant and increasingly expensive clothing she wore. There was a vanity table fit for a movie star, equipped with a three-way mirror, professional makeup lighting, glass shelf upon shelf for the pots and tubes, compacts and curlers that were proliferating by the week, it seemed.

Almost as soon as sixth grade began, I began attending boy-girl dances on Friday nights. Goddard Gaieties, Grosvenor House—these were essentially charity fund-raisers, and that's how I convinced my mother to let me start going. I primped for them like one of Beverly Cleary's heroines. I'd wear Gloria Vanderbilt, Calvin Klein, or Guess jeans (with zippers at the ankles) with an off-the-shoulder sweatshirt.

Clothing was becoming newly important to me. My friends and I began making thrilling forays downtown on the subway (our parents didn't want us to take it) to Canal Jeans or Unique Boutique for thin black rubber or asymmetrical chunky plastic bracelets, oversized vintage men's overcoats, denim jackets, cool buttons to bedeck our uniform skirts or coats. *The Official Preppy Handbook* became all the rage, and I begged my mother to buy me the important gear: Izod polo shirts, pink and green woolly Lacoste sweaters, an L.L.Bean navy blue puffer vest, L.L.Bean bluchers and moccasins (I'd had no idea they were different things), argyle socks, white Tretorn sneakers. Many of the girls in my class, who summered in Maine, went to tennis camp and dancing school, sailed, came from old Northeast money, dominated in gym class, and had hair the color of moonlight, already owned and effortlessly wore everything the rest of us coveted. Since the clothing wasn't at all flirty and my father wasn't aware that preppy was a thing, he was fine with it all. If he'd known it was a trend or fad, he would have been horrified. After all, he once wrote that "fashion is a form of tyranny as well as a sign of boredom."

When I saw my father, I was careful not to wear anything that indicated an interest in pop culture or fashion, anything that emphasized that I was growing up. I couldn't wear Izod shirts with him because they showed my budding breasts, so I'd wear my largest rugby shirts and baggiest sweatshirts (but never the cobalt blue *America's Top 10* sweatshirt Bill had given me). Before seeing Daddy, I'd remove the Rolling Stones tongue and the Police *Zenyatta Mondatta* buttons from my jean jacket, but keep the one that said "Bedtime for Ronzo" over a picture of Ronald Reagan with an *X* through his face.

But even as I became boy crazy, pop music crazy, entertainment crazy, in other ways I continued to be the innocent girl my father loved. I didn't come to dances with a face full of makeup and blue-silver hubcaps for eyes as many girls in my grade did. No tight clothes or girly jewelry for me either. I eschewed provocative clothing, wore only funky bracelets, and declined to get my ears pierced (I didn't end up doing that until well into college). I wore boyish baseball caps—a Mets hat my father gave me for my birthday, an army camouflage cap. I never painted my fingernails or toenails.

In fifth grade, I'd been ostracized by some of my peers for being a "nerd" because I didn't listen to pop music, still loved my stuffed animals, had close relationships with my teachers. But now, in sixth grade, I was breaking out of my Goody Two-shoes role in an exhilarating way. I no longer felt comfortable with my straight-arrow friends who had parents in conventional marriages, their fathers lawyers or bankers, their mothers housewives. My new friends were less prissy and more fun-loving, and their parents were more bookish, artistic, less white bread. Becky Roiphe was the only holdover.

I see now that changing friends was also a way of avoiding going deep about my parents' split. My old friends had known and adored my father. My new friends hardly knew him; with them, I could start anew. I wouldn't have to bear any more pitying looks, any more solicitous questions, any expressions of concern or of their own sadness at losing access to him. Kind and caring tenderness toward me has always made me dissolve in tears. I couldn't afford to dissolve in tears. I needed to stay strong for my parents, and to keep myself moving forward. So I tapped into my sense of humor: I entertained my new friends with funny stories and endeared myself to them with my Fozzie Bear imitation.

And I began to privilege my friendships above everything else. I went from being a devout and responsible student to the class clown, playing pranks on teachers, zipping through homework so I could get on the phone with my friends, doodling, playing MASH, and passing notes in class. In the spring of sixth grade, a letter was sent home to my mother about my cutting up in class, not handing in assignments, being unfocused and undisciplined. My report cards became littered with reproving remarks about my excessive socializing and lack of attentiveness. My father never knew about this. He wasn't contacted and I asked my mom not to tell him.

The work I *was* invested in were what I called "singing science projects"—my more academic friends did the hard research and I turned it into lyrics for fun pop confections, then sang lead when we performed a number about ecology to the tune of the Go-Go's "Our Lips Are Sealed," a project about the dangers of pot set to the soundtrack from *Chariots of Fire*, the J. Geils Band's "Centerfold," and "Coke is it!" (which I changed to "Pot is it!"). It goes without saying that I no longer shared news of my school projects with my father.

And little did he know that my friends and I were surreptitiously passing around a dog-eared copy of Judy Blume's *Forever* in sixth-grade study hall, giggling about Ralph the penis and yearning for the romantic relationship Katherine found with Ralph's owner, Michael. We were listening to Dr. Ruth Westheimer's late-night call-in show (and daring each other to call her with a concocted question). When my mother was out for the evening or in Los Angeles visiting Bill (Addie would stay with us), my friends and I would gather on her king-size bed to watch MTV or chortle at the titillating but absurd sex shows—*Ugly George* (he had actually approached Addie about posing topless for his show), *Midnight Blue*, and *Interludes after Midnight*—on Channel J. At boy-girl parties, we played kissing games like College, Seven Minutes in Heaven (the closet), Spin the Bottle, and Museum but never kissed or even held hands outside of this constructed intimacy.

One afternoon in June of 1982, our father took me and Claire to see *ET*, and there was a preview for the Rolling Stones' live concert film. I knew the second that preview began that trouble was on the way. My father wasn't a classical purist; he loved Bob Dylan, Joan Baez, and the Beatles. But he *loathed* Mick Jagger. Mick was strutting and peacocking around in large living color up on the screen, in orange and yellow crop tops or shirtless with skintight pants, suggestively wiggling his hips and puckering his R-rated lips, singing about spending the night together, satisfying his woman's every need. I could sense my father stiffen, then heard him groan in exasperation and disgust. All of a sudden he yelled: "Get this jackass off the screen! There are children here!" "Lighten up, man," one guy retorted. "Yeah, there are kids here, and you just used a swearword!" another exclaimed. Humiliated, Claire and I sank a little lower in our seats. Even the bliss of *ET* couldn't undo the shame of our father's outburst, and when we left the theater after the closing credits, I tried to walk a few steps ahead of him so other moviegoers wouldn't know we were connected. And I thought to myself how futile his misguided and embarrassing attempt at protecting us was. After all, I'd recently gone to see two R-rated movies, *Shoot the Moon* (about a wrenching divorce and featuring the Stones' "Play with Fire") and *Andy Warhol's Frankenstein*, with my friends, the Stones' *Hot Rocks* was the album of sixth grade, and

I was regularly slow-dancing with boys to "Ruby Tuesday"! Thank goodness he would never need to know about any of it.

Question: Secret Unfulfilled Ambition?
Answer: To be the cultural dictator of the world.
Question: What do you consider your worst fault?
Answer: Arrogance.
Question: What do you consider your chief virtue?
Answer: Ability to say unpleasant and disturbing truth about
what I see in the world.
—Richard Gilman, Q&A with *Glamour* magazine, October 1966,
"Do You Trust the Critics?"

Other aspects of my father that I hadn't previously questioned also began to seem problematic. One night, I had a sleepover at my new friend Sarah Towers's Upper West Side apartment. Sarah's father was the novelist and critic Bob Towers, head of the fiction department in the MFA program at Columbia, her mother magazine editor Pat Towers. We went to Video Vault on Broadway to rent a comedy and a scary movie and bought bulk packages of M&M's and Twizzlers at the local supermarket, ordered in Chinese food to eat while we curled up on the ratty pullout sofa in the apartment's tiny "maid's room" to watch the movies, and stayed up into the wee hours of the morning, laughing and giggling and gossiping.

The next morning, after breakfast, as I was packing up my small overnight bag, Sarah asked me what I was going to do that afternoon with my father, and I said we were going to Connecticut to visit some close friends, the Broyards. Her face fell.

"*Anatole* Broyard?" she asked.

"Um, yes?"

"In our family, we call him *Ayatollah* Broyard!" Sarah said indignantly. "He's a horrible, horrible man. He gave my father's novel such an incredibly mean review. My mother will never forgive him! Don't tell my parents that's where you're going!" She brushed tears from her eyes and shuddered.

After promising Sarah that I wouldn't let her parents know about our trip to the Broyards', I quickly changed the subject. But as I chattered on about cute boys and what movies we'd watch at our next sleepover, I pondered what she'd said.

To me, Anatole seemed the opposite of an Ayatollah. He was the jovial and witty father who adored his daughter Bliss. He was the lighthearted guy with a perpetual mischievous gleam in his eye. He was the guy who threw us up in the air in his swimming pool and threw balls to his dogs. He was the sly, charming, incorrigible flirt at my parents' parties. He was the stalwart, faithful friend to my father, one of the few who'd managed to remain close to both of my parents after they split. And now, he was being defined as a tyrannical, stern, humorless despot, someone who'd devastated kindly, gentle, pure-hearted Bob Towers and made Pat Towers and Sarah his enemies for life. In an instant, I grasped the power of criticism.

And as I took the elevator downstairs, I wondered how many daughters, or wives, or people felt this way about my father. Were there many Sarahs out there who considered my father a heartless, awful man?

⸻

> The brilliant bitterness between his father and his mother, a bitterness as smooth and fixed as steel.
>
> —Toni Morrison, *Song of Solomon*

My father had tried to woo back my mother for a good year after the initial announcement that they were separating, but when it became clear she was intractable, he began asking for money. It was his right under the law, which had recently been changed with the aim of helping primarily women: stay-at-home or part-time working mothers whose labor was finally being valued. Assets earned during the marriage were supposed to be shared. My father, who'd spent much more time with the children, turned down job opportunities so they could stay in New York for the sake of my mother's career, and earned far, far less than she, was taking advantage of that change. I gleaned this from reading a letter his lawyer sent her—she left it lying out on the kitchen table—and from overhearing a few of my parents' phone conversations. To me, it made sense, but my mother was outraged. She'd have her girlfriends over for dinner or drinks and they'd collectively castigate and mock my father for his "outrageous demands"—and his weakness. "What *man* asks a *woman* for money?!" one glamorously coiffed fashion magazine editor friend scoffed as she elegantly blew smoke rings. He was "pathetic!" "disgusting!" They made no effort to hide their contempt and fury from me.

I couldn't quite understand their logic. Why shouldn't a father's care for his children, a father's career sacrifices, a father's desire to have a home for his children, matter too?! I knew from reading the *New York Times* and from walking around our neighborhood that real estate on the Upper West Side was skyrocketing in price. Fancy boutiques were taking over the spaces previously inhabited by mom-and-pop joints, the streets were getting cleaner, our neighbors were no longer writers or therapists but lawyers, doctors, bankers. My father wanted to be near us so he could easily meet us for a meal and eventually have us over to sleep at his place. But he had no savings, no tenure, no way to earn much more than he already was. And setting up a new household on the Upper West Side was becoming out of reach for him. My father never spent much money on anything. Where would the money my mother gave him go? Toward a new home, where he could welcome us.

But I knew that with his financial demands, with the terse, cold letters from his attorney, the imprecations he'd utter when they spoke on the phone, my father was angering my mother, and that upset me. I was so enjoying the less tense, warmer, cozier mother she was becoming after shedding the albatross my father had been for her. I could see, in his absence, what a weight he'd been on her, how much managing his moods had drained her, what a toll it had taken having to pretend they were a happy couple.

And besides, she didn't know—didn't want to know—how much he was struggling. How desperately he and we longed for him to have a home where we could visit comfortably; how small, dingy, and uninviting the sublets were; how he clipped coupons furiously and took us to the cheapest places possible. I didn't want to embarrass my father by telling my mom about his living conditions. She never took us to or picked us up from his places, let alone set foot inside them. She never asked us what our meals with him or the apartments were like, how we felt seeing him. She probably didn't want to know about his precarious economic position because she might then have to admit that he did in fact need money, and she was livid that he was asking for it. And I didn't want to complain about anything, so I never told her how he was late, how he rushed us through the meals, how spartan and depressing his living situation was. How he'd get irritated or teary or despairing. I wanted to protect him from her judgment, and I wanted to protect her from guilt.

In 1981 or 1982, soon after its publication, my mother read Alice Miller's *The Drama of the Gifted Child*. She devoured the book, discussed it endlessly with her friends, and scribbled notes in the margins. One evening she urgently called me into her bedroom and told me she needed to share it with me. "It explains so much about your father," she said, "and about his relationship with you and Claire! It will help you understand why his love for you isn't real." I was stunned, but I stayed calm and attentive, not betraying at all how that last sentence had lacerated me. She showed me a passage:

> The grandiose person is never really free; first because he is excessively dependent on admiration from others, and second, because his self-respect is dependent on qualities, functions, and achievements that can suddenly fail.

"This is your father!" she exclaimed. "It's why I felt so drained with him. I could never give him enough praise. And Claire refused to cater to him so he rejected her." I thought to myself, But he didn't *reject* Claire. She tried his patience. He yelled at her on occasion. He definitely favored me. But did he reject her? Never.

"Look at this, sweetheart!" my mother cried, pointing out these passages:

> Narcissistic cathexis of the child by the mother does not exclude emotional devotion. On the contrary, she loves the child as her self-object, excessively, though not in the manner that he needs, and always on the condition that he presents his "false self." This is no obstacle to the development of intellectual abilities, but it is one to the unfolding of an authentic emotional life.

> If a person is able to experience the reality that he was never loved as a child for what he was but was instead needed and exploited for his achievements, success, and good qualities— and that he sacrificed his childhood for this form of love—he will be very deeply shaken, but one day he will feel the desire to end these efforts. He will discover in himself a need to

live according to his true self and no longer be forced to earn "love" that always leaves him empty-handed, since it is given to his false self.

"This," my mother said to me, "is how your father 'loved' you. He was devoted to you, yes. But he loved your false self. That's so much pressure to put on you! He needed and exploited you, Sid!" she said tenderly, protectively, and with a sense of being aggrieved and affronted on my behalf. "He relied on you to bolster his own self-image."

I stood there nodding. But I didn't agree. I had never felt that my father loved me for any kind of false self. In fact, I thought, he was the one who had always seen and nurtured my true self: my playful, creative, loving, exuberant self. I'd tamped myself down around my mother, who had no interest in playing, no patience for loud voices, and who wasn't romantic like my father, me, and Claire. My father was the parent I would bring worries and fears to, never my mother, because she was herself anxious and not as good at comforting. But after the split, I'd had to put on a strained front of competence and maturity in order to hold him together. He'd become my primary worry rather than the one who dissolved worries and took the best care of me. I'd had to spring into action to save him and in the process suppress my own fear and anxiety and sadness. And now I had to do the same thing vis-à-vis my mother. I pushed down my emotions about how problematic it was that my mother had shared this with me, about how misguided I thought she was about my relationship with my father. I knew I needed to agree with her. It was vital to her that I accept her version of the past. I knew she thought she was doing me a service, but that didn't undo the harm she had inflicted unwittingly.

That night as I lay in bed, lines from one of my favorite books, *The Velveteen Rabbit*, came to my mind as I turned over and over my mother's claim that my father's love for me wasn't "real."

Real isn't how you are made," said the Skin Horse. "It's a thing that happens to you. When a child loves you for a long, long time, not just to play with, but REALLY loves you, then you become Real.

Daddy and I had been that child to each other. What could my mother possibly mean? Wasn't our love the most real thing I'd ever known? "Once you are Real you can't become unreal again. It lasts for always," the Skin Horse had said. But now that my father was gone, now that his double life had been exposed, could I really trust that anything would last for always?

In the spring of my sixth-grade year, my father secured a sublet in an apartment on West 67th Street, a ritzy block now, but then a sleepy, unglamorous one. The apartment was awkwardly laid out, with the front door opening right into a tiny triangular kitchen, and most of its windows looked onto air shafts. But it was a place we could stay over!

The visits soon fell into a predictable pattern. Every Saturday afternoon we would walk the ten blocks downtown and our father would buzz us up. We were allowed to split a can of Coke, poured over ice cubes into familiar glasses. We remembered those glasses in different hands, in different circumstances, filled with my mother's Tab or Grampy Merle's Diet Rite soda in Weston. We had to be careful with the glasses because our father only had four, and they always had dishwashing spots on them. We scorned those superficial women in the commercials who cared about spots on their glasses and sang the praises of the dishwashing powders that didn't leave spots, but we always noticed with a sinking heart the spots on Daddy's glasses. Along with the Coke, we were each given ten to fifteen Fritos, carefully counted out and allotted, on green plastic plates (the same plates we'd had snacks on in Weston). This was not about minding our health, not about the sugar content of the Coke or the high sodium or fat content of the Fritos—it was strictly about conserving money.

We'd play the Mad Magazine Game, Life, or Clue, and the conviviality distracted us from the peeling paint on the apartment's bare walls, the uneven floorboards, the sight of our father's familiar typewriter on an unfamiliar desk. Daddy would order pizza or Chinese food, and after dinner we'd watch classic black-and-white movies or *Diff'rent Strokes* and *Silver Spoons*. My father loved Gary Coleman but only begrudgingly allowed us to continue with *Silver Spoons*—we never told him of our crushes on both Ricky Schroder (to whom a Brearley friend and I wrote a fan love letter) and Jason Bateman. At some point, the "treat" would be brought out: an Entenmann's chocolate or cinnamon donut, a butter almond ice cream soda with ginger ale, a sliver of chocolate cake from Cafe Éclair on 72nd Street. The "dud treat" was a Jell-O chocolate pudding—a small serving from a plastic six-pack and not as good as the homemade pudding we were cooking up often now at our mother's. There was a forced gaiety to those evenings, punctuated by occasional teariness from Claire or irritability from my father.

This apartment had a bedroom for us, but it was unfurnished, so Carrie took us to buy sleeping bags at Morris Brothers, a camp outfitter on Broadway. We lugged them over and gingerly spread them out on the small bedroom's hardwood floor. "See, this is fun!" Daddy exclaimed. "It's like you're camping out together!" Claire and I were less certain that this was going to be fun in any way. We'd toss and turn restlessly, Claire would wake up scared in the unfamiliar, empty room, and I'd soothe her back to sleep. We'd often take our arms out of the sleeping bags, reach out across the floor toward

each other, and grab hands. We were allies, bunkmates, compatriots always. We were in a unit of two. No one else knew what we did.

About a year in, Daddy bought a bunk bed for us. It had no bedding, so we still slept in our sleeping bags, and even though we didn't
miss the stiff surface and the aches and pains we'd get in our backs,
we missed sleeping closer to each other and would try for as long
as we could to hold hands—with me straining my arm down toward
Claire's reaching up. For breakfast the next morning Daddy would
make us French toast or Eggo toaster waffles before rushing us off to
Sunday school at the church near our mother's apartment.

When I was in my early thirties, and trying out a novel, I wrote
the following of the father character and his two young daughters on
sleepover night:

> He forced them to be his audience, and the show wasn't very
> successful. They smiled till their mouths and jaws ached,
> they forced their voices into an unnatural high pitch to say
> "It's good," "It's nice," "I love you," they called him affection-
> ate names like "Doodlebird" when they felt hatred and rage
> toward him in their heart.
>
> But how could they hate him? They had to love him, or he
> would fall apart.

I remember the horror I felt at learning that he'd violated our
family with his affairs; the anxiety, the frustration, the anger I'd
feel when he would snap harshly at Claire. But I don't remember ever
hating him. I suppose, though, at some point I did. In those first
years after my father left my daily life, I detached from him emotionally even as I was always warm, loving, effusive in his presence.
I put my hopes for intimate connection and love in my friendships
and in boys. My father wasn't the locus of my love anymore. I loved

him, of course, but I came to accept my mother's narrative about him: that he was deceptive and dark, that he was cruel to Claire, that he loved me so much because I reflected so well on him. My father never spoke about my mother at all, never said a negative word about her, never tried to explain the split from his perspective. My mother revealed everything and had a narrative, a story, an agenda. My father revealed nothing and had no narrative, no story, no agenda. And so my mother's version won, at least temporarily. And believing in my mother's story helped me to muffle the thrum of worry about my father, my grief in losing him.

I know that my friends would have been understanding had I shared with them the story of my parents' split and my worries about my father, but I didn't want to talk about any of it with them. I didn't feel comfortable in the role of a person to be comforted. I didn't want to be pitied. My friends were people I could be vivacious and hopeful with. In seventh grade, I became "Cil the Gil," a nickname created by a classmate; my friends would write Cil the Gil alongside a drawing of a fish with a beaming smile. I liked being the cheerful, strong, energizing one—the rock—for my friends. I wore a yellow smiley face button on the lapel of my jean jacket, I ended notes to my friends "Keep Smiling!" and wrote "Keep Smiling!" and "*Ridet!*" (after beginning Latin) on my desks, lockers, notebooks.

My Cil the Gil persona, my role as the one who bucked up those who were faltering, sad, struggling with insecurity, the one who dispensed sage counsel, brought humor and warmth to my friends, was largely true to who I was. My father would often recount how every morning when I was a baby, he'd hear a tinkling music and come into my bedroom to find me awake and smiling, contentedly playing with my mobile. An iconic story in our family was of the time an old man came up to Carrie in Central Park as she sat on a bench beside my pram to tell her: "That's the happiest baby I have ever seen!

Heck, that's the happiest *person* I've ever seen!" According to all the grown-ups who knew me, I almost never cried as a baby, and was never moody or irritable as a little girl. I didn't whine or pout, sulk or melt down. It's true that I was blessed with a happy temperament, a natural optimism and sunniness, but it's also the case that I studiously avoided giving in to darker feelings or problematic actions of any kind. That kind of behavior was simply not tolerated by my parents or by Carrie. Claire, of course, didn't get the memo in full, and I'd watched, in trepidation and sadness, how her talking back or tantrums brought on my father's frustration, my mother's babying her, Carrie's quiet refusal to indulge her. In fact, my mother had told me, "One of the reasons your father preferred you is that you were so much more cheerful than Claire."

I defined myself as that wide-smiled Cil the Gil. I was fun. Adventurous. Buoyantly joyful. And I was all of those things, but I was also confused, sad, racked with anxiety about my father. One way of minimizing the anxiety and sadness was accepting my mother's narrative about him and surrendering to the new life that adolescence offered.

Did my mother give us a gift by removing my father from our daily orbit so we could have a relatively normal, joyful, unfettered adolescence? The split both allowed my freedom from and preserved my closeness to my father. There were no fraught confrontations, no slammed doors, no curfews or groundings or sullen silences. I didn't tell him about movies I'd seen or dances I'd gone to or conversations I'd had that he might not approve of. He never came to our apartment—ever—after his relationship with my mother became venomous, so he didn't have to see the David Bowie, Tom Cruise, and Harrison Ford pictures tacked to my bulletin board. He didn't need to know about the sleepovers and slumber parties where we debated which of the Go-Go's was prettiest, made prank phone calls, played Truth or Dare, gorged on Orville Redenbacher microwave popcorn and Double Stuff Oreos, watched horror movies like *Friday the 13th* or *The Howling* followed by raunchy comedies (*Stripes*, *Fast Times at Ridgemont High*, *Risky Business*, *The Last American Virgin*). He didn't know about the shopping trips with my friends to Bloomingdale's, Fiorucci, Liberty House. He didn't see the cute, flouncy Betsy Johnson minidresses, Guess pink denim miniskirt, or the strapless vintage prom dresses bought at Alice Underground and Unique Boutique now hanging in my closet. I never brought friends to any of his various apartments, he never picked me up from a party or dance. When I was at his house and I had my period, I'd cover the Tampax and pads in layers and layers of toilet paper and put them in my overnight bag so I could dispose of them in the garbage at our apartment. I didn't want him to have to confront the visible signs of my impending womanhood. Because he didn't know or see any of this, my position as an innocent sprite and his ideal being could be preserved.

> Only in Anna's company was he truly at ease. She was his secret treasure, his one, pure, unspoiled source of joy.
>
> —Jennifer Egan, *Manhattan Beach*, of a father and his daughter

I relished my role as my father's secret treasure. I was his beautiful secret, not one of his sordid or painful or shameful ones. He was truly at ease with me. And yet, there was pressure involved in remaining pure and unspoiled for him, in knowing that I was his greatest source of joy. I directed my appearance, my behavior, my life trajectory in ways that would bring him the most joy, sometimes at the cost of suppressing vital aspects of my being.

And Claire and I protected our father from any negative thoughts or feelings we might have had about him. Every summer, my father would do teaching or lecturing stints in South America, Europe, or Asia to supplement his income. He'd be gone for two, three, even four weeks, but would keep in touch with witty, tender notes scribbled in his spidery handwriting on picture postcards (when we were at camp and he in New York City, he'd send us letters on Yale Drama School stationary, typed with the exception of a scribbled "Daddy" at the bottom). On his return, he'd always present us with gifts specific to the country he'd visited. There were painted wooden birds from Korea (with a string around the beak of the female bird to keep it quiet!), thin, chintzy "peasant" blouses with puffed sleeves from Russia, brightly dressed dolls with baskets of fruit on their heads from Brazil. He picked things out carefully and presented them proudly. We oohed and aahed and thanked him effusively, then shoved the clothes to the back of our drawers and never wore them, put the dolls, trinkets, and objects on shelves and never played with them.

One night, Claire and I were hanging out in her room with a school friend, and Claire was laughingly showing us a recent gift from Daddy—a piece of clothing he'd bought for her on one of his travels. "How could he think I'd like this?!" she snorted. "You'd look ridiculous in that!" our friend giggled. Then, with no word or warning, Claire suddenly got up, ran to the phone, and dialed a number. "Hi Daddy," I heard her say, "I just called to say I love you." She'd had a ping of guilt, a pang of tenderness, a streak of love. I knew exactly how she felt.

———

On Friday nights and Sunday afternoons of my seventh-grade year, sandwiched between my visits with my father, I was spending time with a boy I still consider my first love. That fall, I met Josh at an interschool dance where we won the dance contest—our prize, Men at Work's *Business as Usual*—and we quickly became "boyfriend and girlfriend." Josh had recently moved to New York from Los Angeles with his mother and sister; his father was a big special effects guy in Hollywood. Josh was tall, skinny, quiet, and adorable—with his freckles, sandy hair, intelligent yet playful hazel eyes, he reminded me of what I'd imagined Tom Sawyer would look like. But along with his charisma, there was a sadness to him that I was instantly drawn to. His best friend was my first friend from babyhood and 333 Central Park West, Nicky Seaver.

I decorated my Latin textbook with band names and "Cil and Josh" in hearts—I wrote with glittery silver or purple pens. My mother never looked at my schoolwork, and I never brought that Latin notebook to my father's. Inside, Caecilius and Metella were having dinner in the kitchen, but on the back and front covers I was exuberantly proclaiming my love for bands and singers and a certain freckle-faced laconic boy with whom I won dance contest after dance contest (an achievement I didn't tell my father about). He and I danced with abandon and elaborate moves to everything from "Hungry Like the Wolf" to "Rock Lobster," and then I'd rest my head on his shoulder and feel him hold me close as we slow-danced to current hits like "Hard to Say I'm Sorry" and "Open Arms," or FM radio classics like "Free Bird" and "Stairway to Heaven." Those dances were sheer bliss—a total escape from the pressures of school and the sadness of my father's life. But I did sometimes feel my heart sink when I thought about having to go to Daddy's the next night, or wondered how he was spending his Friday night, or realized just how little he knew about my new, adolescent life.

When Nicky Seaver began dating my friend Chrissy, Josh and I did some double dates with them. It was great to be back in regular touch with an old buddy from 333 Central Park West. But now Nicky and I weren't toddling around while our parents discussed avant-garde literature; we were going to the movies on Sunday afternoons with our respective girlfriend and boyfriend and holding a joint boy-girl birthday party at my apartment (the boys spiked the Red Cheek apple juice). About a month later, at Sarah Towers's end-of-the-school-year boy-girl party, Josh and I finally kissed in her bedroom. And after our next date, seeing *WarGames* together at a big run-down theater on Broadway, followed by a lingering kiss outside my apartment's front door, he left for a summer in Los Angeles with his father. We wrote weekly letters to each other, his on pale blue stationary in surprisingly elegant handwriting. The first letters were signed "Love, Josh," but over time he dropped a "Lots of love," then went to "Much love," and finally "All my love, Josh." I lived for the escalation of affection in those sign-offs.

In late August, a few days after I'd received the "All my love" Josh epistle, Mom, Claire, and I went to stay for a week with my grandparents in Illinois. My grandmother was pulling out all the stops as always—nightly expeditions to Dairy Queen for Buster Bars, treasure hunts, and gifts under our pillows—but I was counting down the days until school started because that would mean Josh was back in New York City. One afternoon my mother got a phone call from Jeannette Seaver. After hanging up the phone, Mom came to find me in the living room, where I was curled up reading.

"Sweetheart," she told me, "you know your friend Josh? Well, Nicky told Jeannette to let you know that Josh decided to stay in California with his father. He isn't coming back to New York."

I blanched and felt as if I might throw up. As soon as my mother had left the room, I ran through the house and down the narrow, steep stairs into my grandparents' basement. Once I got to the bottom, I collapsed on the cold, dank cement floor and sobbed, wildly, shudderingly.

I never cried for my father the way I did for Josh. I somehow couldn't let go and cry about Daddy. It would have been a betrayal of my mother. It would have felt wrong and bad and shameful. It would have been a surrender to feelings I needed to suppress.

When I was in seventh or eighth grade, Jill Krementz, who'd taken our photos many times and who was the author of the *A Very Young* books we loved, asked me and Claire if we'd like to be included in a book she was working on called *How It Feels When Parents Divorce.* We'd be photographed and interviewed in the service of helping other children in similar situations. My mother made it clear that she thought it a bad idea. "This is private," she said. "You don't want to talk about this publicly!" I didn't want to, really. But I did want to talk about it with someone, and Jill had always struck me as an especially empathetic and sensitive listener. Still, I told my mother to tell Jill no for us.

I pushed it out of my mind and forgot about it until a year or so later when an advance copy of the book addressed to me and Claire arrived in the mail. I took it to my room, sat down at my white desk, and began reading. In the second sentence of her introduction, Jill referred to "the shattering displacement of divorce," and something inside me unclenched.

My mother didn't want us to see the divorce as shattering or as entailing displacement. But what she didn't see, couldn't see, didn't want to see, was that my father's shattering and displacement had shattered me, in imperceptible and unacknowledged ways. And that with the illusion of our happy family shattered and my parents locked in litigation, Claire and I would always be in some sense displaced, caught between two parents we dearly loved, one of whom hated the other.

I kept reading:

It took courage for [these children] to talk openly about their
fears, their sorrows, their confusions, knowing full well that
what they were revealing about themselves would not only be
read by strangers but by the very people whose actions had
caused much of their pain.

I didn't have the courage to talk openly about my fears, my sorrows,
my confusions. Or rather, I wasn't given permission to do so. I knew
that to participate in this book would have been an act of rebellion
against my mother and a betrayal of my father. It would have meant
defying my mother's wishes and exposing my father in all his vulnerability to the world's scrutiny. It would also have been to own emotions we weren't supposed to have. We were not to be sad. We were not
to be afraid or confused. It was my *father* who was sad, fearful, confused. My mother had contempt for his dissolution. She insisted on
positivity. This split was a good thing, a positive step. My father relied
on my positivity to keep him from shattering into fragments that
could never be reassembled. And with both of them, my being cheerful and energizing, understanding and accepting, was what made
them happy. I was an effervescent girl with a great gaggle of friends
and a zest for life. But there were breaks, cracks, gulfs of sorrow deep
inside me that my parents and my friends knew nothing of.

Some girls in my class met with therapists, but Claire and I didn't
get any therapy until many years later, when we demanded it. In
those months and years after the separation, my mother, as always,
was in pragmatic survival mode, moving on, getting on with it. Chin
up, girls, there's no time to waste, no point in wallowing, was the
message we got. The second summer after my parents' split, when
Claire and I were at sleepaway camp in Maine and the apartment
was being renovated, my mother threw out most of our dolls and
stuffed animals, donated our children's books to the church, gave

our dollhouse away to a friend with young children. It's true that it had been a year or so since we'd actively played with them. It's true that she thought she was clearing the way for our new adolescent lives in the cool new teenage girl rooms she was providing for us. But the sudden loss of all the paraphernalia of our childhood left a deep hole that I tried to fill with wild adolescent fun even as it left me vulnerable to a wistful nostalgia that tinged my present life with a barely stifled sadness.

In the fall of my eighth-grade year, my father took a one-year sublet in the apartment of his close friend and Yale Drama School colleague Gordon Rogoff, the man who'd introduced my parents in 1964. Gordon and his partner, Mort, were spending the year in Ireland, and they'd generously offered their two-bedroom rent-controlled Upper West Side apartment to my father. Rent-controlled apartments were less and less available in New York City, and this one, on West 96th between Central Park West and Columbus, was a godsend. Filled with books and plants, the floors covered in faded Oriental rugs, the walls festooned with Mort's colorful abstract paintings and framed theatrical posters, with light streaming in through the large old windows, the apartment had character and warmth and space. It felt like someone else's home, yes, but at least it felt like a home, and the home of artistic, congenial people. Claire and I got the second bedroom—we'd take turns sleeping in the single bed or on the heavily carpeted floor in a sleeping bag—and for the first time, we had our own desk to work at and an en suite bathroom.

Just around the time my father moved into the apartment, the Mets began to do well, and I became almost as hooked on baseball as I was on football. On sticky summer evenings, my father and I would turn on the air conditioner, dish up the ice cream, and luxuriate in the sheer, unadulterated joy of rooting for a young, on-the-rise baseball team. And our fandom connected us even when we weren't together—we'd speak on the phone before and after each game (and often many times during the games), clip articles and photos for each other, fill each other in when one of us wasn't able to watch. We were both emotional fans, prone to shouting with happiness, groaning in dismay, trembling expectantly, leaping up to exclaim. And I was even more emotional than my father—I'd cover my eyes, or put my fingers in my ears, or leave the room during crucial at-bats. I'd get teary at especially devastating losses. But this greater vulnerability to the strong feeling that accompanied ardent fandom meant that my father could once again be the father—the one who reassured, comforted, and stayed strong for me.

But even as I relied on him to shepherd me through the ups and downs, what he once called the "euphoria or heartbreak" of being a rabid sports fan, I kept other emotionally turbulent things from him. I never wanted my father to feel that he couldn't handle anything we brought to him, but I also never wanted to bring him anything he couldn't handle. So I kept things from him. Worries, illnesses, doubts, and fears. Anything that could unsettle him or make me less of a beacon in his eyes.

One winter Saturday night at Gordon's, soon after a pepperoni and onion pizza dinner, I began feeling queasy. We were all sitting in the living room reading, and I got up, said something about going to get some homework, and ran into the bathroom inside our bedroom to throw up. I so didn't want my father to think he'd given me something that had made me sick. After a few minutes of violent vomiting, I felt a small hand on my shoulder.

"Siddee, you look green. We need to call Mommy."

"No, please don't, Clairey, I promise I'm"—I was overcome by another bout of nausea.

Moments later, I heard her whispering frantically into the phone: "Mommy, Siddee's sick. What should I do?"

I turned around to see her glancing over her shoulder to make sure our father wasn't coming. But it was too late.

"What's going on here?" he shouted.

"Siddee's throwing up," Claire whimpered.

"Don't you think I know how to handle this, Claire??"

He snatched the phone out of Claire's hand and began yelling into it. "Lynn, she's fine, I can take care of this!"

I was crouched in front of the toilet, shaking with nausea and fear, Claire was crying, and my father was screaming. He slammed down the phone and turned to Claire, who was cowering near the bathroom door.

"Don't you *ever* call your mother again like this. If something is wrong, you come to ME. I can take care of you girls. You don't need to get her involved!"

"Yes, you can, Daddy, I know," I reassured him. "I didn't think we needed to call Mommy, but Clairey was worried about me. Please forgive her. I'll tell Mommy it's all fine and you did a great job taking care of me, OK?"

"I'm sorry, Daddy, I got scared," Claire added, sniffling and wiping her eyes with the backs of her fists.

My father's shoulders came down and his voice softened. "OK, Swanee, let's get Sid a glass of ginger ale. Hopefully she's through the worst of it now."

He brought me the drink and some oyster crackers wrapped in plastic he'd taken from a restaurant (he hoarded these as well), wiped my mouth with a stiff and pilly washcloth, ran his hand over my head. Whether it was the shock of the scene or that I'd already gotten everything out, I didn't throw up again. And I forgave my father, quickly, for his outburst. I knew that Claire had triggered his feelings of insecurity and inadequacy. He wanted his parenting validated and valued.

I first saw *Kramer vs. Kramer* when I was about eleven years old. I stumbled onto it one afternoon on HBO and was instantly drawn in. A movie about divorce? Set in contemporary New York City? And one featuring my father's adored former student Meryl Streep, whom I'd met several times when she'd come to my parents' parties? I was riveted (a word my father hated, but one that accurately describes the sensation I felt).

At the start of the film, Ted and Joanna Kramer couldn't have been less like my parents (with the exception of the Jewish-guy-with-the-shiksa thing). Ted is a savvy, glib Madison Avenue advertising man, a rainmaker and schmoozer, the family provider, disconnected from his son; Joanna a conventional stay-at-home mother. Ted Kramer has stayed late at his corporate office, laughed with his smarmy boss about spending money on a Burberry coat, and comes swaggering into the Upper East Side apartment he shares with Joanna and their little boy, Billy, exulting in having landed a major account. But as Joanna briskly announces that she is leaving him, takes her suitcase, and gets on the elevator despite his protestations and pleas, Ted and Joanna's connection to my parents began to emerge. There was nothing Ted could do to keep Joanna in the marriage. She was dead set on getting out. Her cold certainty cut through Ted's bravado and rendered him bewildered and powerless.

And as the movie proceeds, Ted Kramer evolves into the man my father had always been: a passionately devoted father. It was our father or Carrie, never our mother, who had taken us to and picked us up from school, the park, birthday parties. The scene where Dustin Hoffman runs with a bleeding Billy in his arms to the emergency room had me sobbing (reminding me as it did of my father taking me to the ER for my broken wrist), as did the final breakfast scene where father and son silently demonstrate the deep bond they've forged in the wake of Joanna's departure. Largely culinarily impaired, my father had always made a mean French toast.

Kramer vs. Kramer. My mother had dropped the Gilman from her name as soon as my parents separated, but the divorce battle was still Gilman vs. Gilman. I saw that phrase or versions of it on documents my mother left lying out. What venom and vitriol, contention and animosity, resided in that vs.! Joanna and Ted were fighting over Billy and my parents were fighting over money, but my father's request for money had always been essentially a request for an apartment that would enable his involved parenting. In both cases, the children uneasily inhabited the space of that vs.

But even at the height of his feelings of anger and betrayal, Ted is able to honor Billy's relationship to his mother. He's painstakingly removed any trace of Joanna from the apartment—we see all her clothes, jewelry, and knickknacks and any and all photos or mementos of her go into boxes that are then forcibly sealed with lots and lots of tape. But when he finds a large framed photo of Joanna hidden in one of Billy's drawers, Ted sets it gently but firmly by his son's bedside. Neither of my parents would ever have done that.

I was a passionate believer in the importance of fathers, in their ability to love and nurture just as successfully as mothers. So when the decision comes down in Joanna's favor, I let out a disbelieving sob. "No! No!" I murmured, and I never stopped crying from that point on. Joanna's eleventh-hour admission that Ted could in fact give Billy what he needed made me gasp in relief and turned my tears to happy ones. And then seeing Ted and Joanna reach a fragile but tender, appreciative rapprochement in the film's final scene, I thought to myself: Why can't my parents put aside their animosity and value each other again? If the Kramers could do it, surely my parents could too??

I watched *Kramer vs. Kramer* over and over again in the months and years that followed. I never mentioned it to my mother, my sister, or my father. It was a kind of sacred text that I studied, immersed myself in, for solace, catharsis, wisdom, validation.

In the late 1980s, my father watched all of Dustin Hoffman's movies in preparation for writing a *New York Times* profile of him. Hoffman was appearing as Shylock in *The Merchant of Venice* on Broadway, and my father took me as his date to that production. As he worked on the piece, we watched many of Hoffman's films together: we wept over Ratso Rizzo, we laughed about Benjamin Braddock, we marveled at Raymond Babbitt. But we never watched or spoke of *Kramer vs. Kramer*. In the piece, my father praised Hoffman's "long speech on the witness stand in *Kramer vs. Kramer* . . . [as] a masterpiece of rhythm and timing, alternating passion and reflection, memory and desire." But never did he suggest that we watch the film together or bring it up in conversation with me. Perhaps my father felt, as I did, that there was something too painful, too incendiary, too risky in that film for the two of us to confront.

In his piece, "Short, Nasal, Unhandsome, and a Star," my father described Hoffman in a way that eerily resonated with my own sense of my father: "Impotence, debility, affliction of the body or spirit: these have been conditions into which Mr. Hoffman has moved as an actor, with a boldness and indifference to his 'aura' that very few of his contemporaries can match." My father's impotence, debility, afflictions of the spirit—I had seen them on the screen in Ted Kramer, and Ted Kramer had also given me my father at his best: warm, funny, ferociously protective, charismatic, quiveringly alive.

ACT 3

THE WOUNDED GIANT
REGAINS HIS DIGNITY

The wounded giant is on his feet now, the despised colossus
has regained, in one small but resonant area, his strength and
dignity.

—Richard Gilman, "The Wounded Giant Regains His Dignity,"
New York Times, January 25, 1987

Around the time I entered high school, my father was at last able to secure his own, "permanent" home. The Weston house had finally sold for about $100,000, and he had a chunk of cash to make a down payment on an apartment. The Roiphes told him about a new development in a converted monastery on West 108th between Riverside and Broadway. They had already bought and combined two apartments in the building; they vouched for my father with the co-op board. The area was considered somewhat sketchy at that time, his apartment looked out onto brick walls, had very little natural light, and only one bedroom. But it was a duplex with enormously high ceilings in the living room, which allowed for floor-to-gloriously-high-ceiling bookshelves and a ladder again like he'd had at 44 West 77th Street. It also had a wood-burning fireplace plus a tiny balcony on which he could put a grill; he could make fires and cook out again as he had during the Weston days! And it was his! His to decorate, his to keep! He could bring all of his books out of storage. He could set up a real home.

But even though he'd come into a bit of money (he was still locked in litigation with my mother over the assets gained during the course of their marriage), he didn't buy any new furniture or bedding or homeware/tableware. Frugal—cheap?—as ever, my father repurposed, reused, and restored to life items and objects that had been shoved into storage. Virtually every single thing he used to furnish and outfit his new place was from the Weston house. Suddenly pieces of furniture, sheets, plates I hadn't seen in years reappeared. A sofa from the Weston guesthouse now had the place of honor in front of the television, which may have been the only new thing he bought. The Weston coffee table (a shoemaker's bench my mother had bought at a local antiques store) now held my father's glasses of whiskey and ashtrays again. The fireplace set from Weston sat beside the large brick fireplace. Colorful ceramic figures my parents had acquired during our summers in Italy and framed photos of me and Claire returned to the walls. The mahogany dining room table around which festive, voluble gatherings of friends and family had debated, laughed, and chatted convivially, where we'd celebrated Thanksgivings and Claire's summer birthday, now never had more than a few people sitting at it, so the leaves were folded under, which made it difficult to fit one's legs comfortably. Adorned with the same earth-toned quilted oval placemats, the same yellow plastic-topped honey dispenser, the same green-and-orange plastic salt and pepper shakers (oh so seventies!), the table felt disconcertingly familiar. In our Weston bedroom, Claire and I had had a fire-engine red wooden play table with two tiny backless benches. That table and one bench were now my father's telephone table and seat; the other bench sat atop the table and served as a stand for the telephone book. Claire's and my childhood drinking cups—plastic pink and yellow—were now the toothpaste and toiletry cups in the bathroom.

Since the apartment only had one bedroom, my father would give me and Claire his bedroom to sleep in (on our sleepover nights, he'd sleep in a narrow single bed in the loft space above the living room and use the blue-and-white sheets from our Weston bedroom). His bedroom had all of the white wicker furniture from my parents' country bedroom—the vanity, the stool, the rocking chair. It had the very same bed my parents had slept in in Connecticut, with the very same white floral sheets and quilt. But where that bed had once seemed huge and inviting, where it had once been a place to romp and read, it now appeared unkempt, with a lumpy mattress gaping foam out of the sheets and a quilt reeking of cigarette smoke (my mother had never allowed smoking in bedrooms). It was a California king so we had plenty of room, but Claire was a fitful sleeper, and she'd thrash around in the night, waking me up with her kicks and sighs.

Despite the apartment's oddities and limitations, despite the strange sadness emanating from the Weston furnishings, what an enormous relief it was to have Daddy in his own home at last! He was no longer a nomad, a transient, an interloper in someone else's home or someone else's neighborhood. He was no longer consumed with anxiety that he'd be priced out of Manhattan entirely. He was a homeowner, at home.

He was also hard at work on a viable book project, a memoir about his conversion. Since his split from my mother, there'd been a number of book ideas that had gone nowhere. He never complained about his work travails to us—ever—but from overheard conversations between him and his friends and a rejection note I saw from an editor, I gathered that he was frustrated and stymied. Now, with a contract to write the memoir under the editorship of the legendary Alice Mayhew (a barely five-foot dynamo who smoked as much as he did and whose throaty chuckle had been part of the music of my childhood) and ideas, sentences, paragraphs pouring forth after being long pent up, the typewriter was once again a place of exhilarating production rather than a looming reminder of his own shortcomings.

And with him settled in his own apartment, more emotionally steady and professionally secure, Claire and I began to actually look forward to our time with our father. We'd take the Broadway bus and then walk down beautiful, quiet 108th Street to his building almost at Riverside Drive. With its bay windows, white columns, and terra-cotta brick, the building had a classic New York City look that in and of itself relaxed me. His doormen would beam at us—they loved our father and knew how much he loved us—and wave us to the eleva-tor. Ringing his doorbell, I never had that nervous feeling or that pain around my heart anymore, but rather a happy sense of antic-ipation. He'd open the door in a T-shirt or a denim shirt and jeans and cry "Sidda! Swanee!" as he threw his arms around us. Then, his voice rising and falling in joyful animation, he'd usher us into the apartment.

In high school, sleepover night shifted from Saturday to Sun-day. I'd spend Friday and Saturday nights at smoky parties kissing boys, or at nightclubs like Area, Limelight, and Nell's dancing in a drugged-out sea of people (I never smoked or took the drugs myself), or going to the movies in a gang of teenage girls, and then Sundays—midday or mid-afternoon depending on whether there was a 1 or 4 p.m. Giants game—I would go to my father's. We'd watch the game, I'd discuss books or politics with him, and we'd have dinner, our takeout options expanding from pizza and Chinese to tandoori chicken from Indian Cafe or garlic chicken, beans, and rice from the Cuban restaurant. Our father also began to alternate takeout with meals he'd cook—if by "cook" you mean cutting up scallions, cucumbers, radishes, and carrots for a salad (no lettuce), or strew-ing chunks of onion through raw hamburger meat before shaping them into patties and pan-frying them. Being able to provide us with "home-cooked dinners" gave him such satisfaction. And after dinner, every Sunday night, at 8 p.m., my father and his mystery-loving girls would watch Angela Lansbury in the eminently satisfy-ing *Murder, She Wrote*.

On Saturdays or days we didn't have school, Claire and I would often go uptown for solo lunches with our father. For Claire, a red meat and deli food lover like him, he'd make a pastrami or ham sandwich on rye with a pickle on the side; they'd talk about art—she was a talented artist and loved the same painters he did (Matisse, Rembrandt, Cézanne)—and Agatha Christie mysteries. For me, he'd make Lipton chicken noodle soup or a bowl of Wheatena or Cream of Wheat cereal (he and I always liked eating hot cereal for lunch). It took him little time or effort to prepare these lunches, but watching him do so, in his own kitchen, made me feel happy and peaceful. We'd sit at the dining room table and eat and talk. About books, movies, sports, politics. He was proud of me for working on leftwing political campaigns—Jesse Jackson's, Mark Green's, Walter Mondale's, Gary Hart's—for going to marches for a nuclear freeze, abortion rights, and gay rights, and volunteering for Planned Parenthood. We were excited that our Giants were actually a decent, and improving, team with talented players to root for and exult in.

In the months and years after my parents' separation, I'd often wondered if I would ever be able to relax into being loved by him again, into needing him, relying on him, seeking help and solace from him. Now, as his mood improved and his life became more stable, as my intellectual curiosity and artistic predilections blossomed, our relationship took on new and nourishing forms.

In the fall of ninth grade, we Brearley girls had begun hanging out with Collegiate boys, and I spent the first few months giddy with the fun of our new social life, drinking for the first time—straight gin or vodka or peach schnapps nicked from parents' liquor cabinets—staying out late at parties or gatherings. I had never been a hard worker or an especially disciplined or well-organized student, and now I was even more scattershot and doing the bare minimum required. My grades dropped, and various teachers were continually lecturing me about my "goofing off" and "putting fun over studies." My father didn't get my report cards—the noncustodial parent didn't at that time—but my mother, who hadn't paid much attention to my schoolwork till then, gave me a stern upbraiding. "Don't you want to be able to pick your college rather than having them pick you?!" she admonished me. "Why are you wasting your brain?" I didn't stop my weekend socializing, but I did cut back on my phone time and recommit myself to my academics. And once I buckled down and applied myself, I began to do extremely well; both of my parents were immensely proud.

It soon became clear that excelling academically was the most effective way to please my parents individually and bring them together; the one thing I'd ever overhear them discussing in a semifriendly tone of voice was my academic success. My A's became a tenuous bridge between my parents, and getting them quickly became addictive for me. Each top grade felt like a means of uniting my mother and father in mutual happiness. My report cards were now sent to both parents, at my request.

My mother told me that no one she'd ever known was more brilliant about literature than my father; she encouraged me to ask him for suggestions and converse with him about everything I read. Now, rather than taking me to the Weston and Westport libraries or reading aloud to me, Daddy recommended books and authors, lent me volumes from his vast collection, discussed them with me. There was *Middlemarch*: he adored ardent, questing, noble-souled Dorothea and had a soft spot for the gifted but quixotic and late-blooming Will Ladislaw, who always reminded me of him. *The Magic Mountain, Anna Karenina, Go Tell It on the Mountain*: reading these masterpieces in conversation with him was intoxicating even as it laid down the sturdiest intellectual foundation for all my subsequent work in literature. *Pride and Prejudice*'s Elizabeth Bennet was one of his favorite heroines; he loved her feisty irreverence, her disdain for snobs and hypocrites, her refusal to court approval and ingratiate herself with undeserving people, her unconventional beauty, the intelligent gleam in her "fine eyes." He loved the way she won over Mr. Darcy, who at first looked at her "only to criticize," and the way she herself changed as a result of being loved by him. Their love affair, he told me, was between two equals, only possible once both had been humbled, both had learned their limitations, both were able to be at once passionate and playful, romantic and wry. I could hear admiration and yearning in his voice as he spoke these words. He wanted his own Lizzy, but would he ever find her?

In the spring of tenth grade, I was assigned an essay on Faulkner's *Light in August*; I found Faulkner difficult and the assignment daunting, but my father made the process exhilarating. He coaxed me through a patient close reading of a scene where eight-year-old Joe Christmas is beaten by his foster father, McEachern, because Joe has failed to learn his catechism satisfactorily. My father showed me how tiny details could be illustrative of larger themes; he made noticing and exploring such details a pleasure—the word "clean" appears six times in the first paragraph alone!—and he got me excited about an assignment I'd dreaded. Together we traced how McEachern's dehumanizing violence, his "rigid ethical sense, which allows no room for compassion or forgiveness," gave Joe Christmas a warped idea of manhood: repressing emotions, being stoic, using violence as a means of asserting power and control (this, of course, was the opposite of the kind of man my father was).

Working on this essay together taught me a lot about my father's loathing of religious fanatics and intolerant, rigid, dogmatic people, his search for a more accepting, humane, and compassionate spirituality. In an introduction he wrote to C. S. Lewis's *The Screwtape Letters* just a year later, he castigates "foolish preachers," evangelists, and fundamentalists including Jerry Falwell, Jim Bakker, and Oral Roberts, who, he said, hawked and peddled Christianity as a "patent medicine." Their judgmental, holier-than-thou attitudes, their cruel condemnation of AIDS patients, their misogyny and condescension, simply enraged him. For even as my father was a mighty judge, someone who wielded a great deal of cultural power and to some extent reveled in that power, he felt very strongly about what he regarded as unfair judgments of people's personal lives. This was an irony central to his self-positioning: he was arrogating to himself the authority to judge Falwell et al. for being cruelly judgmental. The contradiction was patent but embraced in the name of a higher humanity: he would defend the idea of art against any impostors, and also the ordinary human being oppressed by bigotry and ignorant rejection.

Edmund White once wrote to me: "I admired your father, who was such a brilliant man and one of the first truly tolerant heterosexuals who befriended me." My father always identified with the outcasts, the ostracized, the subversives, those who felt shut out of or condemned by conventional society.

At the same time that my father and I were bonding via my academic work, an ever-deepening point of connection was my growing passion for theater, singing, and performing. When I was cast in an interschool production of *Anything Goes* as one of Reno Sweeney's Angels, my father, a huge Cole Porter fan, was delighted. He had me run through all the classic songs for him, sinking back into his worn armchair with a sigh of pleasure as I regaled him with "I Get a Kick out of You," "You're the Top," and "Take Me back to Manhattan." He lovingly called me his "young Ethel Merman." Claire and I knew something that most people didn't: Richard Gilman, the formidable drama critic who favored anything avant-garde, radical, and strange, also had a passion for classic musicals. That I was developing as a musical theater singer thrilled him.

We ran my lines for the many plays I appeared in, with my father in a whole range of other roles, and he instructed me in production history and possible interpretations—I had in him my own personal dramaturge! He was especially excited when I was cast in his student Chris Durang's *The Actor's Nightmare*—as a trash-can-dwelling woman named Beckette no less!—and when I got major parts in *The Threepenny Opera*, *Marat-Sade*, and André Gregory's *Alice in Wonderland*. These experimental productions were directed by a chain-smoking, brooding, Collegiate School drama teacher who kept my father's books on a shelf in his office (he hadn't known I was my father's daughter until I noticed the books one afternoon). Although I worried about my father seeing me in my Reno Sweeney's Angel costume (a cropped tank top and short shorts) and my Brechtian hooker costume (a black corset and purple velvet miniskirt with spike heels and fishnets), I loved having him come to see the shows. My mother's appearances were perfunctory—she came because she loved me, not because she had any interest whatsoever in the shows—and I could sometimes see her stifling a yawn. My father, on the other hand, was an especially enthusiastic and knowledgeable audience member who took the time after the shows to individually praise various performers, commend the directors, and comment incisively on everything he'd seen.

I never felt as happy, free, and expansive as when I was performing. I loved being part of a community of singers or actors, learning and creating together, enacting an artistic vision. But my father remained adamant that I should not take voice or acting lessons, study drama in college, or take any steps toward becoming a professional singer or actress. My mother, who had been in the acting program at Northwestern before switching to the Oral Interpretation of Literature after being horrified by the ruthlessness of the drama division, wholeheartedly agreed. My friends and peers who did theater and sang had vocal coaches, attended performing arts summer camps or Acting Shakespeare programs in England. I was simply performing and singing, with no training at all, and I was developing bad vocal habits that left me hoarse.

Nonetheless, my parents continued to insist that I should not be given any training and that I should abandon any dream of being a performer. My mother would cite my father to back her up, he'd cite her to back him up. It was the only time they used each other as support, and that really made an impression on me. They both told me that acting was a brutal profession, that it was incompatible with having children, that I needed to deliver on my academic promise. This was one of the very few things they agreed on after their split. So by forgoing a career in the arts, I could please them both and somehow bring them together, which made giving up dreams of acting and singing professionally a superficially easy decision. And of course growing up with a man who sits in the audience and takes copious notes with an aggressive, pointed pen, writing things like "oh no," "dreadful," "sentimental schlock," who relishes the prospect of coming up with stinging put-downs and eviscerating remarks about theatrical productions, made the world of theater seem threatening, judgmental, exposed, even as it underscored just how much was at stake in theater, how much it could matter.

The same was true of creative writing. As a young girl, I'd written poems, plays, even two novels, but I stopped writing, abruptly, just around the time my parents split up. In eleventh grade, I became the editor of Brearley's literary magazine and contributed to it, but only my creative writing assignments for English class, never anything done on my own time. When Brearley offered a Creative Writing elective, I bypassed it for the more hard-core, academic Modern British Fiction (Woolf, Joyce, Hardy). I had internalized my parents' injunction that my best self was a critic—a scholar and writer of analytic prose—not a performer or a creative writer.

Succeeding academically was easier for me, less risky. A 98 was a 98. An A was an A. I knew how to get those. Writing something imaginative or personal, performing professionally—these were much more fraught endeavors, their outcome much more uncertain, vulnerable to criticism. A's, accolades, prizes were clear cut, and most of all they were gifts to my parents. Beginning in tenth grade and continuing through graduate school, I gave my parents bound books of my essays for Christmas each year, complete with the grade and the teacher's or professor's comments. It was the only present both would cherish.

n late 1986, my father's memoir, *Faith, Sex, Mystery*, was published. It was a book about his conversion from Judaism to Catholicism in his late twenties, but also about the sexual predilections and worldly ambitions that led to his falling away from the church. Rife with details about his masochism, visits to prostitutes, and infidelity in his first marriage, the book was improbably dedicated to Claire and me: "For my daughters, Claire and Priscilla, who will understand some of this book now and the rest of it in time." My father didn't tell Claire and me what it contained, other than to say that it was about his conversion, and he didn't encourage us to read it. Claire told me she'd decided she didn't want to read it; I was curious but hesitant.

Then, on a plane ride home from Christmas in Illinois, I looked over to see Claire sobbing as she thrust a copy of *Vogue* magazine with Cindy Crawford on the cover at me, crying: "Siddee, I can't read this! It makes Daddy sound disgusting. And it's so *mean*!" The piece in question was a review of *Faith, Sex, Mystery* by Francine Prose called "Spiritual Striptease." The review's tone immediately struck me as arch and contemptuous. Prose scorned the book's conceit of spiritual questing and especially lingered on the taboo-titillating— the subject of my father's masochistic fantasies. The extensive confessions I knew it had wrenched him to make were dismissed as so much moral exhibitionism. I read the piece through quickly, felt my stomach flip over, then ripped the page out of the magazine, balled it up, and placed it in the seat pocket in front of me. "Don't worry, Clairey," I comforted her. "That reviewer doesn't understand Daddy at all, and he doesn't read *Vogue* so he'll never know about this!" She smiled through tears and took the magazine back.

A few weeks later, the book received a rapturous front-page review in the *New York Times Book Review* by Mary Gordon; she declared it "deserving of all honor for its dark honesty, its fierce, reflective intellectuality, the lambent constancy of both its vision and its style." A short, reverent piece about my father and his "book-intoxicated" life ran with the review. More raves followed. But while I was happy and relieved, oh so relieved, that my father had finally published his first book since the separation and that it was being heaped with accolades, the book's success—and attendant notoriety—made for a tense, difficult time. My mother was mortified on both her own and our behalf. She grimaced every time *Faith, Sex, Mystery* was mentioned, and refused to buy or read it. When she read a review that mentioned my father's persistent fantasies of "amazonian women wrapping their powerful thighs around my head . . . imprisonments from which I could only be released if I accepted my fate as these women's sexual slave," she hastened to remind me that she had never indulged those fantasies herself. During those months when the book was being reviewed and discussed in every major publication, I lived in terror of my Brearley teachers, my conservative grandparents, and upright, Baptist Carrie reading about my father's "sins" and struggles. When my boyfriend told me that his parents had listened to an NPR *Fresh Air* interview with my father and were buying his book, my heart sank.

But what bothered me weren't the revelations about my father's sexual being, his past lapses, his erotic urges. No, the confession that undid me was one about his current life. About a month after the book was published, I finally opened it, but could only bring myself to read the last section, a summary of my father's life and "spiritual condition" after leaving the Catholic Church. After enumerating all of the things he was grateful for—his children, his health, his job at Yale—he wrote: "And so I have lived, multiplied and, as they say, made something of myself, and am far from being happy (the pursuit of happiness is all we're entitled to, boy!)." Even as I winced at the admission of his unhappiness, I smiled at the characteristically wry humor of that parenthetical. And then, I read this:

> There are moments when I like living alone but more when I yearn for the presence of a mate and when, most often on days when my daughters stay over and I'm inserted temporarily and, yes, it's not too strong a word, achingly into their lives again, I long for the fullness of a family, its continuity and volatile, encompassing reality, all blessings and oppressions.

"I have plans for several more books . . . I have friends, a place in the world, an identity," he went on, "but I'm not happy." That simple confession devastated me. "I've less happiness than I once had," he wrote, "I haven't been pursuing it in the right way. And the thought has come to me more than once of late that I may have lost my chance." The title of Mary Gordon's review, "What He Found, What He Lost," seemed all the more apropos. The happy father of my childhood seemed lost forever. Even with his own apartment, even with professional success, even with all the love and adoration I heaped upon him, he wasn't happy.

But thankfully there was one area of his life in which he'd never been happier, and that was as a sports fan. The fall of 1986 had been a magical time for our Mets and Giants, both of whom were blazing trails toward their respective championships. During Game 6 of the World Series, when the ball went through Red Sox Bill Buckner's legs and the Mets pulled off the win, I was the only girl in a bathroom of boys huddled around a transistor radio listening. It was a Saturday night and I was at a party in some loft downtown, but I didn't care about anything other than reaching my father, so I ran outside and called him from a pay phone. We watched Game 7 separately since it was a Monday night, but we made frequent calls to each other, and at the triumphant end were almost delirious with joy.

The Giants' miraculous season brought us even greater fulfillment. It was almost unbelievable, but the Giants, our poor, struggling, ill-starred Giants, were finally dominant, impressive, mighty, winning fourteen out of their sixteen regular-season games. My father no longer bet on games. He'd made that promise to my mother in the early days of their separation, seemingly as a bargaining tactic, but he'd made good on it. He'd realized that betting turned the enterprise into something he didn't want it to be. Now he was watching for the pure love of the team, the game, the sport. And without the stress of beating the spread, my father was able to protect and support me in my own fandom. I sometimes couldn't bear the exquisitely tense moments—third down and four, going for it on fourth down, field goals for either our team (please please make it!) or the other team (miss, miss, miss!). I'd closet myself in the tiny bathroom just a few feet away from the television, turn the sink on, and hum loudly until the play was over. When I emerged, my father would oh-so-gently break the bad news of a dropped pass or missed field goal to me, or the light in his eyes and grin on his face would tell me that we'd been successful. Together, we lived through all the moments and all the emotions as the Giants won all their playoff games and made it to their first Super Bowl!

After its admiring coverage of *Faith, Sex, Mystery*, the *New York Times* invited my father to write a piece on anything he wanted, for any section he wanted. It didn't take him long to choose his subject. "I'm going to write an article for the Sports section, Sidda," he told me, "and it's going to be about our Giants." That's all I knew. Until I opened the paper that Sunday morning in January of 1987 to see his byline under a huge picture of a girl at a desk writing a letter with a photo of a football player taped to the wall. I began to read:

THE WOUNDED GIANT REGAINS HIS DIGNITY

BY RICHARD GILMAN: Richard Gilman's
latest book, *Faith, Sex, Mystery: A Memoir*, has
just been published by Simon and Schuster.

On a darkening afternoon seven or eight years ago, I sat with my small daughter in Giants Stadium watching Roger Staubach drive the Cowboys 60 or 70 yards for a winning field goal in the last few seconds. As Rafael Septién's kick went through the uprights, my daughter burst into tears. The next day, she saw a photo in The Times of Harry Carson sitting in dejection on the Giants' bench and told me she wanted to write to him. I remember the words of the letter because we worked on it together hoping to relieve both our broken hearts. Or rather, I simply helped out with some editorial advice, for the sentiments, which I endorsed, came directly from her. "You mustn't be sad," she told the Giant linebacker. "You're a great player and a wonderful man. We'll all be happy again. I love you. Priscilla Gilman, age 9."

Three or four weeks later a large photo arrived showing Carson zeroing in on a ball carrier. Across it was written in graceful calligraphy: "To Priscilla. May God bless you always. Old 53. Harry." She's had it on her bedroom wall over her desk ever since.

And she's remained a football fan, a Giants zealot (my younger daughter Claire, hasn't been hooked yet, but I expect it to happen). She hasn't been to another game, for I depend on the largesse of friends for my own very occasional ticket, but

together we've watched more than a hundred Giants games on
television. Two weeks ago, when the victory over the Redskins
was assured, this lovely young woman, now nearly 17 and with
a strong intellectual bent, suddenly jumped up and shrieked:
"I don't believe it! The Giants are in the Super Bowl! Can you
believe it, Daddy?" I felt like quoting a line from her letter to
Carson, the one about the eventual happiness of us all.

That being a fan can induce either euphoria or heartbreak
is, of course, from a sober responsible point of view, nothing
less than an absurdity. Why were my daughter and I so often
depressed during the Giants' losing years? . . . And why are we
so elated now? . . .

My former wife, an extremely rational person and a greatly
competent businesswoman, was driven nearly wild by my, and
our daughter's, ritual Sundays in front of the TV set, and our
living and dying with the Giants. Once she said to me: "If I'd
wanted to marry a Midwestern jock, I would have!" Well, to
be sure, I wasn't from the Midwest, having been born in mid-
Manhattan and raised in Brooklyn. And I wasn't a jock either.
But I knew what she meant. I was a writer, so what was I doing
wasting my time in such gross frivolity, so passive and undig-
nified an activity?

I despaired of trying to explain to her that being a sports
fan is a complex matter, in part irrational, I'll admit, but not
unworthy. For me—and I think I'm fairly representative—it's
an amalgam of many things, chiefly perhaps, a relief from the
seriousness of the real world, with its unending pressures and
often grave obligations. It's also a playing out of the drama of
fate, the roles in all our destinies of skill, chance, risk and
will, with a saving grace that it has nonfatal consequences.

Being a fan means practicing a form of sympathetic magic,
by which you suffer with, draw strength from and generally

share in the vicissitudes and personas of modern-day champions and heroes . . . And there's an appreciation, not unlike that for dancers or tightrope walkers, of the body undergoing tests and coming through them by courage and technique; a desire for "clean" results—there's no ambiguity about winning or losing; and, finally, in the special case of the Giants or Mets fan (my daughter and I love them both), pride, restored now in this annus mirabilis, in those teams as incarnations of aspects of the spirit of New York.

The pride may be partly illogical; after all, few if any of the Giants come from New York and, as Mayor Koch so graciously said, the team doesn't even play in the city. But the geography of rooting isn't bound by such facts. The Giants will always represent New York, the part of our idea of the city, a component of its ongoing history. But surely one element of our present satisfaction is the sort of in-your-face move that being in the Super Bowl presents to the way the rest of the country mostly thinks of us: huge, cold, rich, conceited, unnatural, deserving therefore of all our misfortunes. Well, the wounded giant is on his feet now, the despised colossus has regained, in one small but resonant area, his strength and dignity.

We all know that like the World Series the Super Bowl has far more significance as a symbolic event than an actual one. Nothing will change in the real world if the Giants win or the Broncos do. We'll still have our rent to pay, our children to guide and cope with, term papers to write; our egos will continue to be buffeted. But I think of a pertinent phrase that's had much currency lately—quality of life. The quality of some of our lives will change if the Giants win, has already changed because they're in Pasadena, Calif. It's fragile, temporary and rather irrational. But it exists. So this afternoon several of us will gather in my apartment to eat Mexican food and drink

Carta Blanca . . . Priscilla will of course be there . . . She'll
be on edge, agog, scared sometimes, but finally, I predict,
ecstatic. Tomorrow she may even want to write another letter
to Harry Carson, saying some such thing as this: "Didn't I tell
you? I still love you. More than ever."

I don't think I've ever read anything in my life that brought me such
deep happiness. I sat at the kitchen table, shaking my head, in a kind
of dazed glow. Then I jumped up and ran to the phone to call him,
lowering my voice so my mother, whose bedroom was down the hall,
wouldn't hear. His backhanded compliment of her—"a greatly competent businesswoman"—was the only jarring note in the piece—we
all knew what he thought of businesspeople! Thankfully, I knew
she'd never read the Sports section.

"Oh, Daddy!!!!" I cried as soon as he picked up. "It's the best thing
I've ever read. It's soooooo wonderful!! THANK YOU!" I didn't have
the heart to tell him that that signed photo of Harry Carson was
no longer on my bedroom wall over my desk. Like so many other
precious things from my childhood, it had been lost or thrown out
when the apartment had been renovated a few summers earlier,
another casualty of my "extremely rational" mother's relentless
need to redo, update, move on. But I didn't need the physical photo
anymore. My father had preserved for all time the nature and shape
and quality of our fandom. He'd captured the essence of our bond.

The Giants of course did win that night. I didn't write the second
letter to Harry Carson, but my father and I were certainly ecstatic.
And somehow the Giants' victory seemed to represent my father's
climb back from dejection, his fragile hold on happiness.

"You mustn't be sad. You're a great player and a wonderful man,"
I had written as a nine-year-old. "We'll all be happy again. I love
you." Only one year after I'd tenderly reassured my favorite Giants
player that despair wouldn't be permanent, that better days would

follow, I'd uttered much the same words to my father. And I'd been speaking versions of them ever since. With his own home, the success of his latest book, and a renewed bond with his children, the wounded giant of my childhood, the one I had always rooted for most ardently, had finally, precariously, regained his dignity. But his confession of fundamental unhappiness in *Faith, Sex, Mystery* still haunted me. Would he ever be truly happy, or had he indeed, as he feared, lost his chance?

That spring of my eleventh-grade year, my father and I took a trip to New Haven to look at Yale for college. Although he'd had his issues with various Drama School administrators, he loved Yale wholeheartedly. He'd wanted to go to Yale as an undergraduate, but there were strict quotas for Jews then, and he'd ended up at the University of Wisconsin. Getting hired by Yale in his mid-forties, with no advanced degree, was a huge triumph. But while my father spent three days and two nights a week at Yale from 1967 on, for me and Claire, Yale was the letterhead on his stationary, the impressive logo on the T-shirts and sweatshirts my parents dressed me in as a baby and toddler, the locus of our father's power, a magical place we never visited. Not only had I never been to New Haven before, I had never seen my father teach or even lecture.

One brisk April morning, I met my father on the train platform at 125th Street for the trip to New Haven. On the train, we sat in companionable silence as I did my Brearley homework while he edited student work. This was the same train route Claire, Mom, and I had taken to Westport every Friday, but now I was continuing on, going all the way to the end of the line with my father. I was at last experiencing what he'd done every Wednesday morning since before I was born.

I remember the shock of how dirty and gritty and sketchy the

New Haven train station and some of the streets were (they made New York City seem safe and clean!), the beauty of Yale's Gothic spires silhouetted against a brilliant blue sky, the busy din of the Yale Co-Op. This was a store I'd known only from a logo on the bag that held what my father would call the "ark animals" he'd present me and Claire with each week—"A hippo for you and one for you!" he'd laughingly say as he handed them to us. I couldn't find any ark animals in the store, but I did revel in the row after row of books for courses that sounded fascinating. While my father was teaching or in meetings, one of his students gave me a tour of the campus. That night, my father took me to dinner with a group of students. I remember a dark, smoky room, a group of intense, witty students around a convivial table, explosive laughter, talk of baseball and off-Broadway. I hadn't seen him surrounded by a crowd of students since those old Weston parties. He was in his element here, but even more so because I was with him.

I slept in his hotel room bed—he used the pullout sofa—and the next morning, after a breakfast of croissants and scrambled eggs at the hotel's restaurant, we walked together to his Modern Drama seminar. I'd never read the play, Pirandello's *Six Characters in Search of an Author*, so much of the discussion went over my head, but I was caught up in the exhilaration of watching him command the room with an inimitable combination of rigor and warmth, penetrating insight and jocularity. The students revered him, it was clear, they wanted to please him, impress him, wow him, but they also had a tender affection for him. I saw myself in them.

After class was over, many of the students lingered so they could be introduced to me. They treated me like a visiting celebrity or a mystical being whose physical presence felt to them almost miraculous. It was clear from what they told me that Claire and I were the central dramatis personae of the personal life he shared snippets of with them. They watched, smiling, as he and I bantered together, as he put a protective and proud hand on my shoulder, as he tenderly tucked his arm through mine. And seeing how they loved him made me feel he had a whole flock of surrogate children at Yale who were doing some of the buffering and bolstering Claire and I had always done, and also giving him an opportunity to be the paternal sage. There was no whiff of impropriety I could sense in any of these relationships; romantic entanglements with students seemed to be a thing of the past.

And for these students, as for his daughters, my father was Grover. Three students told me how his Grover imitation, which he apparently used often in class, had humanized him. By turns goofy and wistful, silly and vulnerable, Grover is the opposite of an intimidating, stern, imperious critic. By being Grover for his students, my father showed them his childlike enthusiasm, his sense of humor and humility, his undefended self.

———————

During the first seven years after my parents split up, my father had never had any steady girlfriend whom we knew about or were introduced to. In part, he was protecting us from the vagaries of his dating life, and I was grateful to him for that, especially against the example of my friend's father trotting out new women every month. But it was also the case that he simply hadn't met a woman with whom he could enter into the great and lasting love affair he longed for.

In the summer of 1987, my father departed on another of his overseas teaching stints; this time he'd spend two weeks as a lecturer at the Kyoto American Studies Seminar. He'd been to Japan a few years earlier, as the American delegate to the International PEN Congress, but this was his first time in Kyoto. He came back with red and blue happi coats for us, and tremulous with hope. He'd met a woman, he told us, a remarkable woman. A professor in the English Department at Doshisha University, Yasuko Shiojiri Oku had been his assigned guide during his time in Japan. She had done some graduate work in the US on a Fulbright and specialized, improbably for a Japanese woman, in Oscar Wilde. She and my father had spent two weeks together as she helped him navigate the intricacies of Japanese culture, drove him around, translated for him. They had parted with an expression of deep intellectual and emotional kinship, a confession of mutual attraction, and a kiss.

Yasuko was wonderful, marvelous! my father exclaimed, a glow on his face I'd never seen before. In his elation, his boyish rapture, he reminded me of one of his and my favorite actors, Gene Kelly, whom my father had taught me to love—*An American in Paris* was the first film he ever took me to, and shortly thereafter he'd introduced me to *Singin' in the Rain*. What a glorious feeling, he was happy again!

But the obstacles to their happiness were formidable. Yasuko was in a miserable marriage, arranged when she was in her late twenties. Told she would have to accept this dour, unromantic chemist because she was washed up and no one else would take her, Yasuko was nonetheless encouraged by the fact that her prospective husband didn't insist she give up her work after marriage. She was that rarity, a female academic in Japan, and worked a double shift as a professor and at home—cooking, cleaning, doing laundry and dishes for her unyielding, dictatorial husband and their two young children, a boy, ten, and a girl, fourteen.

My father and Yasuko were terrified of succumbing fully to their feelings. Years later, my father wrote: "We fought against falling in love—she because she feared losing her children or injuring them; I because I didn't want to be the agent of that and dreaded being an interloper in so fixed and hierarchic a culture." But for now, the romantic in him won out. He planned to stay in touch with Yasuko and hope that somehow she'd be able to extricate from her soul-killing marriage.

In December 1987, early-action college decisions were coming in. I'd submitted an early application to Yale, so during my lunch period I put on my coat and slipped out of school, walking through the gray air to a pay phone on the corner of 83rd and East End Avenue; I put a quarter in and called Carrie at home. I asked her to see if the mail had arrived, and Carrie told me there was a thin envelope from Yale addressed to me. I asked her to open it and read me the letter inside. " 'Congratulations on your acceptance'—Sid! You did it!" she cried. "I'm so proud of you!" After telling her I loved her and couldn't wait to celebrate with her when I got home, I fished two more quarters out of my bag and called my father, then my mother. My mother's reaction was as it always was to news of my accomplishments: a smiling "Well, of course!" She'd been pushing Harvard for me—"Who wants to live in or visit New Haven?" she'd said—and had begrudgingly accepted my preference for Yale. But my father was overcome. "Sidda! I can't believe it! You're going to be a Yale girl!! Well, I can believe it, of course, but still, it's just going to be so *wonderful*!" That we would be at Yale together seemed like the realization of an impossible and beautiful dream.

High school graduation was looming, and I was consumed with anxiety about how to handle my parents at the same event. I hadn't seen them in a room together since that *Barnum* night when my father had taken his ignominious fall and wept, to my mother's disdain. And while that night had been painful, their relationship had grown dramatically more acrimonious since. Throughout my adolescence, I'd had a recurring dream about just this situation. In a college creative writing class, I wrote about that dream from the perspective of eleven-year-old me:

> In the dream I was standing on the stage in the auditorium at school dressed in my costume and reciting my big speech. All of a sudden, I heard screaming coming from the audience and I looked out and saw Mommy and Daddy standing on top of their seats waving their arms in the air and yelling at the top of their lungs. All my teachers and friends were looking at them like they were crazy and then Daddy started crying and they both started calling my name and then I forgot my lines and I started panicking and then I woke up. I can't stop thinking about it. And what's going to happen at my high school graduation and my wedding? I don't understand why all of a sudden after fourteen years they don't get along anymore. I guess you can't really trust that anything will stay the same. Since Daddy left, it seems anything is possible.

In middle school and high school, at camps and in churches, I'd performed in countless assemblies, pageants, concerts, and shows, but my parents always came on different nights or one bowed out. But now, there was no escape.

When, at graduation rehearsal, I learned I'd be receiving three academic prizes—the outstanding student awards for English, history, and French literature—my first feeling was not joy or pride but overwhelming relief. My winning these prizes would be my protection against bitterness, chill, animosity between my parents, the means of smoothing over any strangeness or conflict that might arise when they saw each other for the first time in many years.

On a hot Friday in June, after the graduation ceremony was over, I went first to find my father, and was relieved when I spotted him in a jovial conversation with my grandparents and Carrie. My mother was nowhere to be seen. My father gave me one of his wonderfully hearty hugs, I showed him the books I'd won as prizes, and he told me he'd gotten a little teary during the singing of "Jerusalem." Even as I basked in his loving attention, I maintained a vigilance about my mother—where was she? I hugged him again, he bid a fond farewell to my grandparents and Carrie, and then my father went home. I eventually saw my mother, beautifully coiffed and made up, dressed in a stylish skirt suit and pointed-toe heels, and ran to receive her congratulations. Then we all went off for a celebratory lunch Mom had organized at Petaluma, a fashionable upscale Italian restaurant on the Upper East Side. It was a fun event, but I couldn't help thinking about my father. He was the one who'd been so invested in my education all along, who'd taught me more and educated me better than even my stellar Brearley teachers. And he was relegated to a five-minute post-ceremony conversation. It didn't seem right. I called him as soon as I walked in our apartment door from the party. He was leaving soon for Japan to see Yasuko, but their relationship was tenuous. She was still in her marriage and mustering the courage to leave her husband; my father was trying to temper his optimism. I hoped and prayed that this mystery woman whom my father adored would come through for him.

———

I'd been waiting my entire life, it seemed, to go to Yale. But the beginning of my freshman year was a rude awakening. My roommate was a soccer recruit who set the alarm for 6 a.m. every morning, then hit snooze every ten minutes for an hour or so, and who typed her papers at her desk with the light on at 2 a.m. or staggered into the room in the wee hours of the morning. As a result, I wasn't sleeping much, and I needed sleep more than ever. I'd enrolled in a freshman honors program, Directed Studies—or DS—an intensive series of seminars in the history of literature, philosophy, and political thought from the Greeks to the present. I loved the interdisciplinary work, the intimate relationships with fellow students and faculty, and the immersion in intellectual history. But it was a lot of work and stress: DS was referred to as "Don't Sleep" and "Directed Suicide." Some of the kids were much more openly competitive than the girls I'd gone to school with at Brearley, where we never compared grades. I got a B+ on two of my first three essays and had the wind knocked out of my once-confident sails. I wasn't getting enough sleep, and I struggled with colds and sinus infections.

Eventually things got so bad with my roommate that I slept in my father's hotel room three Wednesday nights in a row—he took the couch. We'd have dinner at the Chinese restaurant across the street from the hotel, and I'd think about those dinners at the Chinese restaurant on West 79th Street in the early days of his separation from my mother—the tension, the need to coddle him, the agony of being torn between Claire, with her outspoken complaints, and my father, with his fragility and irritability. Now, my father was my rock again. He made me laugh, he did his Grover imitation—"Hello dere, this is your old pal Grover!"—to lighten discussions of how to handle my roommate, he helped me problem-solve. He urged me to advocate for myself with the housing office, and to my great relief I was assigned a new roommate, a close friend from Sweden (the former roommate was given a single where she could hit snooze and burn the 2 a.m. oil to her heart's content).

And all along my weekly lunches with my father were a respite. Every Thursday, after my philosophy seminar ended at 12:45, I walked over to meet him for a 1 p.m. lunch before my 2:30 literature seminar. I'd see him standing outside the restaurant, and my heart would leap up. He always wore a London Fog trench coat (with warm lining in the winter), a suit jacket with pants, a button-down shirt, sometimes a sweater, no tie, often a handkerchief in his pocket. He had oversized glasses, thinning, graying hair, and a neutral, unsmiling expression until he caught sight of me—then his face would light up. "Sidda!" I'd often run toward him and into his waiting arms.

We'd eat at Kavanagh's or the Old Heidelberg, old-timey pub-style restaurants near his hotel on Chapel Street. He'd order beef stew or meat loaf with mashed potatoes and gravy or some other similarly heavy, unhealthy dish; I'd get a salad and soup. I tried to get him to order chicken dishes rather than beef or to lay off the butter, but it was futile. I shoved the worry about his expanding belly, his increasingly intrusive and ugly-sounding cough, the arthritis he was developing in his hands as he approached his mid-sixties, out of my mind. Because in general there was so much less to worry about! These lunches were so different from those anxious meals we'd had when he and my mother had first split. Now there were no worries about what to say or how to act. If anything, it was he who had to calm and uplift me. If I was worried about roommate issues or a difficult paper assignment, he instantly defused the worry. He'd prepare me to bang out my weekly DS essay with a much sharper argument and original take; we'd catch up on sports news. And after lunch, I'd walk him to the Drama School; there was a coziness and comfort just strolling arm in arm with him. We were both aware of how lucky we were to have this opportunity—to have him there at my college.

And it seemed my father's luck was finally turning in matters of love as well. Yasuko had left her husband and was coming to New York for two weeks over the Christmas break. Claire and I would meet her at last!

The day after Yasuko's arrival in New York City, my father threw a welcome party for her. My father never threw parties! He got help from a kind neighbor couple, from Gordon Rogoff, and from us. Claire and I baked brownies and brought them in large pans up to 108th Street; Nicky made Mexican hors d'oeuvres. We all hoped we would love Yasuko and that she would not turn out to be some idealized fantasy figure.

But the instant I saw Yasuko, I knew she was right for my father. She wore a calf-length print dress and low-heeled shoes, an outfit that might have been considered dowdy had she not worn it with such grace and natural elegance. She had a pretty, wise, serene face and "a figure neither slim nor bulky," as my father once put it. Immediately, I thought: She's calm, kind, and smart—a good combination for Daddy. Despite her nerves at meeting my father's children for the first time, not to mention many of his friends, she was present, open, generous with her enthusiasms. She was both childlike— she had a purity of expression and intention, a sweet, spontaneous giggle—and deeply intelligent. She took my hands in hers and pressed them tenderly, gazing at me with empathetic understanding. "I know you want so much for your daddy to be happy," she told me, "and that it must have been so hard for you not to know me. And to worry about him, his feelings, his heart. But now I am here!"

Watching my father and Yasuko together, I knew this was love, the kind of love I'd always wanted for my father. She got him. She was patient with him. She accepted and adored him without reservation. And while they were clearly on that high of new love, there was also a peaceful solidity about them. When my father toasted to her, his voice breaking, all of us at that party, from my father's friend and Yale Drama School dean Lloyd Richards to his old buddy, the painter Sherman Drexler, knew that this was It. There she was, standing there, loving him. At last he had something good.

During the meals we had with them over the next two weeks, my father rhapsodized over her cooking skills, tucking into the delicious food with gusto and turning to stroke her hand or her cheek every few minutes. As we sat around the Weston dining table, I learned that Yasuko was no shrinking violet; she could hold her own in intellectual debate, offer idiosyncratic opinions, disagree, fondly, with my father when necessary. She was reverent of him but also tender, spirited, and silly with him. They joked, teased each other, bantered with clear affection. He doted on her but didn't worship her blindly, called her "darling" as he gazed at her with unbedazzled adoration. She brought out his natural sunniness of temperament, his childlike enthusiasm, his good humor and great sense of fun. He gave her the admiration and affection, respect and esteem, and ardent romantic love she had never before experienced. In each other's presence, they seemed to feel what my father once described as "an extraordinary ease, as well as a sense of relief from . . . fundamental discontent." My father at his best, my father's most essential self, the father of my childhood—all of these were reappearing before my eyes as I watched him with Yasuko. It felt almost miraculous.

My father had worried that Yasuko might find New York City overwhelming, but she loved his unpretentious Upper West Side neighborhood and the low-key life he led. They went to independent films, bookstores, and museums together, cozied up at home to watch movies and read side by side, spent time with friends and family. Aunt Edith came for one lunch; she was a sharp-talking, smart, brassy woman who smoked even more than my father and took no prisoners. As we were bringing plates into the kitchen, Edith turned to me and said: "Dick's found her."

But there were so many hurdles still to be cleared, so many questions without obvious answers. Now that she had left the family home, would she be able to see her children? Win custody of them? Her husband had threatened to kill himself if the children contacted her. How many years and thousands of dollars would it take for her to formally extricate herself from her marriage? The divorce process in Japan made *Kramer vs. Kramer* seem benign and uncomplicated. How would she and my father maintain a connection and a romance given their commitment to their teaching jobs and over six thousand miles between them most of the year?

The second semester of my freshman year at Yale went much more smoothly than the first, and late in May I received a letter announcing that I was a co-winner of the impressively named E. Francis Riggs Memorial Prize, awarded to the outstanding student in Directed Studies. My father was thrilled by the news of my award; I was momentarily proud, but the boost proved ephemeral. A few weeks later, my mother took me and Claire, who had just graduated from Brearley and would attend Carleton College that fall, on a vacation to Paris and Madrid. It should have been a carefree trip, but instead I was preoccupied with what courses I was going to take in the fall, how I was going to top myself after making it through freshman year with seven A's, one A–, and a major prize.

And when I arrived at Yale for my sophomore year, I felt both adrift and burnt out. A few weeks in, I became sick with yet another sinus infection, listless and unmotivated in my classes, overwhelmed by a sense of malaise and exhaustion. I called my parents and said I needed time off. This was a huge step for me. Acknowledging— especially to them—that I wasn't OK. Stepping off the academic treadmill and leaving the world of gold stars and A grades. I was terrified of disappointing them, but both were so supportive, especially my father. He took my major-declaration form in for me—I declared as a history major—he handled all the administrative issues involved in taking a leave of absence, and most of all, he reassured me that not only was he not upset with me, he was proud of me for identifying what I needed to do and not soldiering on in an unquestioning way. Perhaps it was the bohemian bum in him that enabled him to welcome the opportunity for me to slow down.

My mother tackled my year off with all the fixing and solving drive she brought to any important endeavor. She got me in to see a top ear, nose, and throat doctor (he confirmed that my sinuses were riddled with infection and put me on a dairy-free diet and an extensive regimen of prescription medications) and finally found me a therapist. She didn't look far. Within a month of arriving home, I was in three-times-a-week, heavy-duty Freudian analysis with my mother's psychiatrist. Dr. T was world renowned, in his late seventies; my mother had recommended him to numerous friends and clients and thought of him as the best of the best. Sometimes I'd bump into one of my mother's illustrious authors in his waiting room.

Dr. T's office near Grand Central had a portrait of Moses on one wall and Freud on the other. He was wise and kind, with a grandfatherly presence. He understood me, he knew that I needed hugs as well as dispassionate analysis, and he helped me to see that by "dropping out," I was sending a message to my parents that I was not as strong or perfect as they'd thought. I had played the role of "the good girl," "the mature one," able to handle anything, who could be told everything bad my dad ever did and still be OK. Dr. T was struck by the fact that I'd never complained or cried or told my father how he scared me, hurt me, disgusted me. I'd never told my mother that I needed more nurturing and less pressure put on me. Being sick, he helped me to see, was in some way a cry for help and support from parents who had depended too much on me and had not given me the empathetic understanding I needed.

But even as Dr. T nurtured me in ways my parents hadn't, he himself needed nurturing. His wife was dying of breast cancer, and he was flying down to Florida, where they lived, for long weekends. He often fell asleep during our sessions; he'd call me "Patricia" at least fifty percent of the time. I never corrected him and sometimes found myself going along with whatever he said even if I disagreed with it, because I wanted to be a good, easy patient. I wanted to minimize his stress and make him feel good about the work he was doing. My father had trained me well.

During that year I worked at a furniture store called the Bombay Company, at Endicott Books on Columbus, and finally as an aerobics teacher for Body Design by Gilda. Part of a chain that was the Equinox of its day, housed on two levels of a brownstone on West 70th between Central Park West and Columbus, the studio became a refuge for me, a place where my positive energy, enthusiasm, and warmth were valued (in the pressure cookers of Brearley and Yale, I'd often felt it was only my brain and grades/scores that mattered). I taught high-impact, low-impact, step aerobics, body sculpting, Stretch and Firm to students including Elisabeth Shue, Mary Stuart Masterson, Connie Chung, Mary Tyler Moore, Peter Yarrow of Peter, Paul and Mary, and many ABC-TV anchors and reporters. My co-teachers included Annabella Sciorra, Erin O'Brien, and Connie Britton, and an eclectic cast of dancers, actresses, and singers. I didn't share much about this job with my father, who scorned health nuts and what he considered the vanity of "exercise fiends," and I certainly didn't ever wear my workout gear—brightly colored spandex thong leotards over sports bras with bike shorts or capri leggings (think Jane Fonda in her eponymous videos or Jamie Lee Curtis in *Perfect*)—in his presence. My mother, on the other hand, often took my class!

One day I glanced at the sign-in sheet for my step aerobics class and saw the name Wendy Wasserstein. My heart dropped to the floor. Wendy had been one of my father's Yale Drama School students, and he'd often mocked the way she'd show up to class wearing pajamas and eating Mallomars. More recently, he'd inveighed against her as overhyped and overrated; he found her plays vapid, pandering, the dreaded "middle-brow." I knew how cruel and contemptuous he could be! After taking a number of my classes, Wendy did figure out that I was Richard Gilman's daughter, but she couldn't have been lovelier. Years later, she became a client of my mother's.

My mother's life was in upheaval that year. She had left the large talent agency where she'd worked for most of her career and formed her own literary agency with a partner; a few clients had balked at her commission going up from 10 to 15 percent and had jumped ship. She'd lost her boyfriend of two years, a man she thought she might marry. She'd also lost a lot of money as a result of relying too heavily on her business manager, and this loss revived her fury at my father and intensified her resentment that she'd recently had to pay him a lump sum settlement when the divorce, after almost nine years of litigation, finally went through.

In the summer of 1989, fifty-eight-year-old Donald Barthelme's death from cancers related to his heavy smoking and drinking had brought up a lot of submerged grief for her. I'd found her sobbing—and my mother almost never cried—as she went through old telegrams, letters, and memorabilia. Over that year I was home, bits and pieces of the fuller story of her relationship with Don emerged. He'd been one of her first clients and her first great love, separated from his second wife when she and he had embarked on their love affair. A year or so in, he'd gone off to Europe, ostensibly to work. A few months later, my mother received a telegram from Don that read: GIRL PREGNANT. NEED MONEY. STILL LOVE YOU. Eventually, Don decided to marry his European girlfriend so he could be an involved father to their baby. My mother had met and married my father on the rebound from her heartbreaking loss.

"Dick liked Don's work and Don greatly admired him. I think in a strange way I was holding on to Don through Dick," she told me. "I was never in love with your father, you know. When he first mentioned getting married, I told him, 'I'm not really in love with you,' and he said: 'Passion passes, and companionship is what survives.' And I believed him. My experience with Don prepared me to buy into what Dick was selling. I suppose I had given up on passionate love after what happened with Don."

She'd never been in love with my father. Even as this information thudded into my heart, I had always somehow known it. What was new was seeing how wounded my typically steely mother had been, understanding how a shattering loss had precipitated her marriage to someone she wasn't romantically suited to. My empathy for her grew even as her difference from me became more evident; I couldn't imagine ever marrying someone I didn't passionately love.

My father's affairs also appeared in a different light. Now they seemed not so much flagrant violations of a strong romantic and marital bond, as fumblings toward the connection and love that my mother had denied him. How awful must it have been for my father to marry a woman he knew loved another man, a woman who disapproved of his sexual tendencies, a woman with whom he would perpetually be at a disadvantage. Barthelme had blurbed *The Making of Modern Drama*. He and my father had served on PEN judging panels together. And all along my father knew that a writer he admired immensely was the one my mother had really wanted.

Like me, my mother was on a journey of self-discovery that year, in search of greater equanimity and meaning beyond conventional markers of achievement. She was reading books on Indian meditation and Ayurvedic medicine, taking classes at NYU in philosophy, religion, and literature. She loved having me around to help edit her essays, eat dinner with, make a pan of popcorn to nibble on while we watched TV, see movies with.

At the same time, I was furthering my literary and cinematic education, with my father as my mentor. Under his tutelage, I continued to work my way through all the great European novels I'd never read and watched a movie or two a day. Now it was foreign films he introduced me to—Kurosawa, Bergman, Rohmer, Fellini, Ozu. He'd also tell me which actors I needed to bone up on, and I eagerly hunted down every movie I could find starring Robert Duvall, Katharine Hepburn, Richard Burton, Paul Scofield, Laurence Olivier, Dirk Bogarde, and Glenda Jackson.

There was one thing I did with both of my parents that year: discuss Proust's *Remembrance of Things Past*, which I was reading for the first time. My parents had always connected over their shared love of Proust; now, in talks about *Swann's Way*, my mother would even say something vaguely complimentary about my father: "Dick always did know how to open up Proust for me," she'd murmur. Talking about Proust with my mother and my father somehow felt like a tenuous way of reconnecting them.

Happy with his beloved Yasuko and happily at work on a book about his beloved Chekhov, my father was finally stable, content, productive. Those chilling sentences from *Faith, Sex, Mystery* about his not being happy were no longer operative. I hadn't seen him get angry or even irritable in several years. He had been my Super Grover during my turbulent freshman year at Yale. And he would be the one who smoothed my transition back to Yale.

I went back to college in the fall of 1990, with my sinus issues relatively under control and my zest for learning restored. Now, in addition to Thursday lunches, my father and I would often meet for Wednesday afternoon conferences in his Drama School office to brainstorm ideas or go over rough drafts of my essays. My classmates and friends took their ideas or papers to tutors at Yale's Writing Center or their professors; I had Richard Gilman as my personal writing mentor! Despite his reputation as a punishing critic of writing, I never felt afraid to show him my work. He was the one I could talk to when things were in a muddle, when I didn't know what my main point or thesis was, when sentences were clunky and thoughts half formed. I never felt one ounce of insecurity or nervousness about his reaction. There was a baseline of respect and recognition of worth that made our conversations about writing egoless and all about clarifying, honing, and improving. He was rigorous, but he was never unduly harsh. He helped me untangle knotty problems, elucidate complex ideas, achieve clarity and precision. And he did it deftly, empathetically. He never wasted time on empty praise. If I'd read any outside criticism, he gently nudged me to use it only as a springboard for my own original ideas. Our conversations were leavened with humor and a genuine sense of discovery, and when I left him to return to my dorm room or meet my friends for dinner, I invariably felt lighter, clearer. Once again, I could bring my problems and worries to my father and relax into letting him help me.

Nonetheless, my health issues continued, and in the spring of 1991, after classes ended, my mother sent me to a Center for Complementary Medicine on West 57th Street. A battery of blood tests revealed that I'd had a severe case of mono at some point, had all sorts of vitamin and mineral deficiencies, and my immune system was shot. I was diagnosed with chronic fatigue immune dysfunction syndrome and began intensive treatments: IV vitamin C and B12 drips, chelation therapy for lead and aluminum, a profusion of vitamin and herbal supplements. I was enjoined to give up sugar, dairy, and alcohol. After a few months on the regimen, and especially with the addition of transcendental meditation to my healing arsenal, my health improved dramatically. My father would have found most of this ludicrous, my complementary medicine doctor a charlatan, and the maharishi at the helm of TM the worst kind of fraudulent guru. The mind-body connection was something he had no belief in whatsoever. For him, it was an absolute schism between mind and body, and even as he neglected his body, he considered his mind a monument of unageing intellect.

ACT 4

WHAT TO MAKE OF
A DIMINISHED THING

The chief change in me of attitude or morale after my faith
left was that I stopped thinking about death, or rather, I
only thought about it when it somehow managed to get my
attention, as a matter of palpable threat . . . Which is to say that
I didn't really think about it; I denied it by refusing any longer
to consider it as within my life, with all the consequences of
that for my spirit, my soul.

—Richard Gilman, *Faith, Sex, Mystery*

The question that he frames in all but words
Is what to make of a diminished thing.

—Robert Frost, "The Oven-Bird"

Toward the end of *Faith, Sex, Mystery*, my father begins a section: "I shall probably live long." Both of his parents lived into their nineties in good health, his mother dying at something like ninety-eight of old age. Of his health and longevity, my father was supremely confident, nonchalant, thinking he had all the time in the world. "My father smoked and he was fine!" he'd always tell us. "I'll quit at sixty-five like he did." But sixty-five came and went and he kept smoking.

Despite his impeccable genes, I'd always feared losing my father—to his depression, anger, and frustration. To his cigarettes and his stiff drinks and his red meat. To his writer's block, his professional insecurity. I'd known that as omnipotent and formidable as he seemed, he was not secure, and that I couldn't ever stop worrying or something terrible would happen. I believed that worrying was in fact the right thing to do, that vigilance was required.

But finally, now, in the summer of 1992, I thought that I could relax my watch. After years of high drama in their bicontinental love affair, including threats by Yasuko's ex-husband to send men with samurai swords to kill my father, my father's furtive stays in hotels under an assumed name—he chose "Michael Howard," to sound like a British actor from the 1940s—and her bitterly contested divorce, which required my father to pay Yasuko's ex-husband about twenty-five thousand dollars for "breaking up a family," they were at last free to marry. That July, they had a civil ceremony in Japan, followed by a small lunch at a good French restaurant for a dozen or so friends, and were planning a party in New York City after their arrival in late August. Knowing that he would have a happy-at-last third marriage, domestic tranquillity, someone who truly understood and cherished him, I was filled with relief and joy.

Every few years, my mom, Claire, and I took trips to Canyon Ranch, a health spa in the Berkshires, where we learned how to control our stress with meditation, biofeedback, and hypnotherapy, ate even more healthfully than we already did, took vigorous hikes, got massages. I didn't tell my father much about the experience, as he would have scorned it as self-indulgent, quackish, pampered.

One afternoon a student of my father's who was subletting his NYC apartment while he was in Japan left a series of urgent messages with the spa's front desk. I finally got the student on the phone. My father had had a very serious heart attack. Yasuko had waited to let anyone in the US know until he was stable and out of danger. Claire and I were stunned. This had happened several weeks ago? We hadn't known a thing? It didn't seem real.

In the next few days, I managed to get through to Yasuko. She told me the symptoms had been vague—nausea, some arm pain—that he hadn't gone to the hospital for about twenty hours, and by the time he'd gotten there, he'd lost a major artery. But, she rushed to assure me, he would be OK. Finally, he'd lost his cockiness about his good genes. He'd been told he had to quit smoking, and was sternly advised to lose thirty pounds and get his cholesterol and blood pressure under control, dramatically change his diet. And he seemed committed to doing so, shocked into finally getting healthy.

My father and Yasuko came to New York a few weeks later, but soon she had to return to Japan to teach (she'd come back around Christmastime). She felt safe leaving him alone because he would have me. Fortuitously, I'd already planned to spend the academic year in New York. In the fall, I had a volunteer position in the Upper West Side office of Bill Clinton's campaign and was going to fill out applications to PhD programs in English literature; in the spring, I'd commute up to Yale for my final semester.

Armed with the validation of a life-threatening incident, a brush with mortality, I tried to become my father's mentor and ally in good health. I went with him to his cardiologist appointments and, ever the good student, took assiduous notes, then typed them up and faxed them to Yasuko. I went shopping with him at neighborhood health food stores, where I found healthy substitutes for his favorites—baked pretzels for Fritos, lentil soup for Chunky Sirloin Burger soup. I helped him modify his orders from neighborhood takeout places. I cooked him pots of black bean chili and chickpea stew and baked him low-fat muffins. At Yasuko's and my urging, he bought an exercise bike and began to bike thirty minutes a day. My mother had nagged my father mercilessly about the need to exercise; when my father and mother broke up, exercise fell by the wayside. Now he was determined again.

That fall, we watched every Giants game together, we walked arm in arm in Riverside Park, we exulted when Clinton broke the Republican stronghold on the presidency. And the next February, when I made the decision to attend graduate school at Yale, my father was elated.

In the fall of 1993, just a few months after graduating with a BA in English, I went back to Yale to begin the PhD program in English literature. And in graduate school, I met someone whose twin passions for literature and family matched my own in their intensity and purity. Richard had been two years ahead of me at Yale as an undergraduate, but I'd never met him until we were part of the same cohort in our graduate school year. Richard came trailing clouds of glory—I knew he'd won several of the most prestigious undergraduate prizes in the Yale English Department, some of the department's most esteemed professors made it clear they considered him a cut above the rest, and the book review he wrote for Renaissance Lyric Poetry class stunned all of us into jealous, admiring silence. But he wasn't aggressive or bombastic with his brilliance; he didn't make comments to impress or intimidate; he didn't ostentatiously throw out references to chic theorists like so many of our graduate school classmates. With his tall, thin, lanky frame, serious, somewhat forbidding expression, and jet black hair and eyebrows, he looked like a combination of Abraham Lincoln and W. B. Yeats, but he seemed completely unaware of his own attractiveness. His hair was long and shaggy, he wore faded flannel shirts, worn-in jeans, Adidas sneakers, and oversized, unstylish glasses. Most important, the way he prioritized family above all else endeared him to me. I heard from a mutual friend that his fifty-four-year-old father had died six months earlier after a twenty-five-year battle with multiple sclerosis, and that his mother had advanced breast cancer. Richard, the oldest son, had done much of the caretaking. He didn't come to the colloquia and gatherings flocked to by assiduous, on-the-make students; instead he took his mom to chemo or visited his dying grandfather. I was overcome with admiration and tenderness.

Richard was reserved and shy, but I soon drew him out. During coffee dates and talks after class, he opened up to me and it became clear that our values were shared. Although we were intellectually ambitious, we wanted more than anything else to have a large, happy family with many children. We had both been camp counselors in Maine, we were both passionate about poetry, football, the

Olympics, nature. We understood each other's sense of longing for a magical family, each other's nostalgia for a time when our parents were strong, healthy, united, and each other's identity as a caregiver for frail or flawed parents. The day after I told him about my parents' separation and all the losses that ensued (our puppy, the Weston house, my father's regular presence in my life), Richard left a photocopied page in my department box. It was Elizabeth Bishop's "One Art," a poem about "the art of losing." Across the top he had written: "For P—In Solidarity—R."

Richard's supple and sophisticated intellect, his unpretentiousness, down-to-earth coziness, his love of dogs and babies, his idealizing of fatherhood—all this reminded me in wonderful ways of my father. But many of my father's most problematic qualities— his neediness, his relentless desire to prove himself, his compulsive smoking, his tendency toward infidelity, his temper—were completely absent in Richard. He was emotionally steady, patient, even-tempered, not at all volatile or irritable. He didn't drink, had never smoked a cigarette or done a single drug, had had very few girlfriends. He was someone who would never cheat, never sink into addiction, never keep secrets or tell lies. And he had suffered so much trauma, so much loss. With him, I could be the light-giver, the one who made his life better, richer, more filled with love. That was a familiar and fulfilling role.

Four and a half months after we met and three months after our first kiss, he proposed to me by asking me to be the mother of his children.

The fear of my wedding day that had stalked me since my parents' split was now largely allayed. Happily remarried, my father had no impetus to be anything but pleasant and detached with my mother.

There would be no needy pleas, no bumbling or fumbling around to woo or win her, no need for me to protect him from her judgment. And my mother was happy that my father had found a wife to take care of him (thus relieving the burden on her daughters). She was thriving professionally, had exciting plans to build a country home in Connecticut, and was thrilled by the chance to throw an elegant party to which she could invite many of her friends. Both of my parents were so pleased by my stellar academic record in graduate school and by my choice of brilliant, handsome, and lovely Richard as a husband. Again, my "successes" were a means of uniting them.

And yet of course some anxiety lingered. I told my parents I wanted to walk down the aisle by myself as a kind of feminist statement. In truth, I did it to keep my parents separate during the leadup to the ceremony and to avoid upsetting either one of them. Given that he hadn't paid for my or Claire's expenses since the split, my mother would have been furious had I walked down the aisle with my father. And choosing my mother over my father would have felt to everyone present like a deliberate rebuke to him.

I worried also about my father's reaction to the formality and fanciness of the event. My wedding dress was purchased at Vera Wang's store on Madison Avenue (although it was by an obscure British designer), and the groomsmen were to wear morning jackets with tails. I dreaded informing my father of this development. What if he refused to wear a tux, as he had at a Brearley Father-Daughter Dance my senior year? He and Herman Roiphe (thank god for Herman) had been the only two fathers there in suits, and my father had grumbled about how preppy and stodgy and snobby the event was. Fortunately, Nicky took him off my hands: breaking the news to him, taking him to get fitted for the ensemble, and following up the fitting with pastrami sandwiches at the Carnegie Deli.

The wedding was held at Wave Hill, a historic house on the Hudson River in Riverdale, New York. This venue had been recommended to my mom by the Lehmann-Haupts, but despite it having the imprimatur of my parents' friends from the old days, the event must have intensified my father's sense of the gap between what had been and what my mother had become. Besides, he and the Lehmann-Haupts had fallen out a bit since Christopher's *New York Times* review of *Faith, Sex, Mystery*, which, while being strongly positive, had rankled my father. Christopher's not offering him Giants tickets had also contributed to the cooling-off between them.

The wedding really was my mother's show, and she certainly did it in high style. A top florist who produced gorgeous arrangements of white, pink, and tan roses, a society photographer, and Peter Duchin's band playing standards made the event feel glamorous yet tasteful. Many of Mom's newer, wealthier friends were there, people whose glistening, highlighted hair, tanned and taut flesh, Prada and Armani dresses, screamed health, wealth, leisure. My mother herself was ravishing in an apple-green Scaasi couture dress, her long shapely limbs flashing around the dance floor as one man after another spun or dipped her. My father, jet-lagged and ill at ease, seemed terribly out of place, although putting him at a table where he'd be buffered by old friends like the poet John Hollander (my graduate school professor), Jill Robinson and Stuart Shaw, the Kauffmanns, and Sandy Broyard (Anatole had died a few years earlier) gave him a circle of support. He was thrilled to see my grandparents and Carrie, all of whom gave him affectionate hugs and sought him out for conversation even as my mother pointedly avoided him.

And he took on his role as my new mother-in-law's escort with touching gravity and grace: gallantly walking her down the aisle and leading her onto the dance floor with a charming joie de vivre. Sarah was a warm, fun-loving, down-to-earth drama teacher for children. She'd wanted to be an actress and had been the bohemian spirit in her staid Richmond, Virginia, family. She dressed in purple and teal and bright floral patterns, carried woven or fringe-festooned bags, was studying to be a bodywork therapist. Undergoing chemo and wearing a teal turban to cover her bald head, she nonetheless danced with abandon and utterly delighted in the festivities. She saw and appreciated my father's sweetness and "coziness," as she called it. They had fun together.

And then it came time for my father's toast. He shared all the Priscilla anecdotes he'd always trot out:

> When Priscilla was a little over six, floating on her back in a pool behind the house we'd rented in Italy, she suddenly intoned in a portentous voice: "Coming this summer, a film so frightening you'll never go back in the water again. More terrifying than *Jaws* . . . *Toes*!" As she spoke that last, dramatic word, she wiggled her toes ominously in my direction.

> How about the time I asked Priscilla to name all twenty-eight NFL starting quarterbacks for a group of my buddies? She got twenty-seven right instantly, and the one she missed had recently been injured and she hadn't caught up on who they'd named as his replacement. She was seven at the time.

> In seventh grade at Brearley, twelve-year-old Priscilla was cast as Julius Caesar in an abridged version of Shakespeare's play. One day as she was rehearsing her role, walking around, learning her lines, she suddenly turned to me and said: "Daddy, I know I'm supposed to say 'Et tu, Brute?' But isn't Caesar really saying, 'And *even* you, Brutus?'"

Sometimes it embarrassed me, the way my father would rhapsodize about me to his friends or my teachers, tell stories about my doing things that didn't seem all that spectacular but to him were the most magnificent feats imaginable. Tonight, however, it felt right and loving and true. Richard enjoyed my mischievous sense of humor. Richard loved sports as much as my father and I did. Richard and I had fallen in love in an English class, charmed by each other's sensitive interpretations of lines from literature.

My father's toast concluded with a celebration of all three of his children:

> My dear son Nicholas is an artist. My dear daughter Claire is studying art history. Priscilla and Richard are getting their PhDs in literature. They are all pursuing what we used to call, without embarrassment, "the life of the mind." That way is wide and expansive, and I wish them joy as they wander in its precincts.

Warm applause filled the room. I was incredibly relieved. He hadn't teared up or broken down. He'd spoken eloquently about values Richard and I shared. He'd taken the opportunity to celebrate not only me but also Nick and Claire. But as he walked back to his table, I heard my mother mutter, in an arch tone: "And who's paying for that life of the mind?" I wasn't even sure what she meant. Claire and I had received substantial discounts on our college tuition as a benefit of our father's Yale affiliation. Richard, Claire, and I all had our graduate school tuitions covered in full and received living stipends. Yes, she had just paid for the wedding, but it wasn't a large one and the cost was something she was easily able to bear. Besides, miserly Daddy had given me and Richard a check for five thousand dollars that afternoon, slipping an envelope unobtrusively into Richard's pocket. And didn't the life of the mind matter? Wasn't there something beautiful and true in my father's words? I made my way to his table, hugged him, thanked him. He left shortly after. One of Richard's aunts had heard my mother's remark too. She gave me an extra-long hug and whispered in my ear: "Your father gave a beautiful toast." This was the only time that day when I got teary.

Three weeks after our wedding, Richard and I learned that Sarah's breast cancer had spread to her brain. We immediately decided we needed to take the next year off from graduate school so that we could spend as much time with her as possible. Richard's two younger brothers came home to join us. That summer and fall, we spent weeks in Maine at the small cottage Richard's father had built when he was still a healthy, vigorous architect. We traveled to visit family and cozied up at Sarah's apartment in West Hartford, Connecticut, to order in food and watch movies. Even as she underwent grueling whole-brain radiation therapy and her face swelled and reddened so that she was almost unrecognizable, Sarah's spirits stayed buoyant and her sense of adventure undimmed; she made it easier for all of us. Nonetheless, she was the first person close to me who'd ever been gravely ill, and it was almost unbearable for me to think of the sadness involved in a mother's leaving her three boys. I comforted myself with the knowledge that Richard and I would build a loving, intact family. Watching him care for his mother tenderly and devotedly, hearing her contentedly murmur, "It always makes me feel better to have Ricko here, because he's just so reassuring," I knew I had chosen the right father for the children we both so looked forward to having. And Sarah repeatedly told me that Richard's marrying me had relieved any anxiety she might have about leaving her oldest son. "He has you," she'd say, "so I don't have to worry about him at all." That felt good to me. It reminded me of what I had been for my father during his times of stress and sadness, his mourning and grieving.

> The elusiveness of Chekhov's plays, their amplitude, their temper, have always been invoked by critics, but only a critic with this kind of affinity could so lovingly, so adoringly demonstrate them.
>
> —Ross Wetzsteon, *Village Voice*, review of Richard Gilman,
> *Chekhov's Plays: An Opening into Eternity*

In January 1996, Yale University Press held a publication party for my father's long-awaited Chekhov book. Its completion had been threatened by the heart attack, but now it was out, and it was receiving some of the greatest acclaim of anything my father ever wrote. I think in part as a result of his and Yasuko's mutual adoration, my father's critical work had become warmer. In his younger days, when he was less secure in work and in love, he was more concerned to dazzle, to woo and win my mother with his fearless intellect, to make a name for himself, to command respect and inspire admiration—and a little fear! Later, he was able to be more vulnerable on the page. Writing *Faith, Sex, Mystery*, he came to terms with the enormous shame and guilt he'd carried about his sexual makeup, and hoped that the book would help others who'd struggled as he had. Having done that work, he was still sad and sorry about his infidelity, but no longer ashamed of who he essentially was. And *Chekhov's Plays*, the book he wrote as he fell in love with and settled blissfully down with Yasuko, was at its heart an expression of what my father called his "extravagant admiration" for his favorite playwright and his desire to "protect his art from all the reductive uses people sought to make of it." From the "destructive" critic of polemical zeal, my father had become more the appreciator, clearing away the interpretive debris, the false ideas and conventions, in order to let the plays shine and Chekhov speak. In the *New York Times Book Review*, D. M. Thomas claimed that my father wrote of Chekhov like "an obsessed lover." The *Los Angeles Times* called *Chekhov's Plays* "his most ardent study," exemplifying "his lifelong passion for a writer who grew only more estimable to him over time." The only anger in the Chekhov book is directed at misinterpretations of his beloved. The book is suffused with wonder, awe, joy, and yes, love.

On the night we came together to celebrate its publication, the mood was jubilant. I vividly remember the crowded, loving atmosphere in the wonderful Drama Book Shop, the oldest performing arts bookshop in the United States, then on Seventh Avenue and 48th Street. I remember the shelves lined with script after script, the palpable feeling in the air that theater and criticism, actors and playwrights and dramaturgs, mattered. I remember rumpled tweed jackets and sweaters with patches on the elbows, my father at his most genial, gesticulating enthusiastically, greeting former students, old friends, and colleagues with his usual wit and warmth, Yasuko's serene happiness in his success. And I remember him reading a passage from a Chekhov letter he'd used as an organizing principle of his book:

> I would like to be a free artist and nothing else . . . I hate lies and violence in all of their forms . . . I look upon tags and labels as prejudices. My holy of holies is the human body, health, intelligence, talent, inspiration, love, and the most absolute freedom imaginable—freedom from violence and lies, no matter what form [they] . . . take.

As he read, I felt his own intake of breath at the word "health." He knew his body had almost given out. He was grateful for and respectful of his human body in a way he never had been before. He sent me and Richard back to Connecticut with an inscribed copy of the book for Sarah, whom he wished to comfort during her last months.

Richard's and my year out of graduate school was for a sad purpose—to help care for a dying woman—but it was studded with moments of incandescent beauty, profound connection, and reminders of the primacy of love and family. With his brothers and his mother, Richard and I had cozy meals, played board games, took walks in nature. Sarah saw and celebrated my essence. She lamented that I hadn't pursued a career as a performer, she encouraged me to write children's books, she snuggled up with me while we watched figure skating, Christmas specials, and the Olympics on TV. Thankfully she was cogent and comfortable until almost the end; she died at home a little over a year after the discovery of the brain metastases. Losing Sarah, a vibrantly alive maternal figure who had helped remind me of my most cherished values, filled me with sorrow, but I was certain that I could hold on to those values in the family I was creating with Richard.

Three weeks after Sarah's death, Richard and I returned to Yale for our third year of graduate school. I went back into the hyper-competitive arena of academia both armed with a deeper sense of what really mattered and troubled by doubts over whether a PhD program was where I was meant to be. I'd been increasingly bothered by the cutthroat environment of academia, its petty politics, its infection by the worst kinds of hazy theorizing and irrelevant, pompous, or inane arguments—all things my father had decried even as he urged me to get credentialed in ways he had never been. But as I began teaching for the first time as a teaching assistant for a lecture class on Modern Poetry, my anxiety and frustration were somewhat eased. The professor was a brilliant humanist, and the literature we were reading—Frost's "The Oven-Bird," about what to make of a diminished thing, Yeats's poetry of loss and disenchantment—helped me in my grieving. I fell in love with teaching, and that love—for the poems, the students, the act of instruction—sustained me through my disaffection with academia.

And my father was also a major source of sustenance. He'd take me and Richard out for Chinese dinners and share his own loving impressions of Richard's mom. He and I continued our nourishing Thursday lunches; now, rather than hammering out arguments for my essays, we'd talk about what approach I'd take in my discussion section for Modern Poetry or The Victorian Novel later that afternoon.

After that intense third year of grad school, during which we took our oral exams and wrote dissertation prospectuses in addition to teaching for the first time, Richard and I moved from New Haven into Sarah's condo in West Hartford. The first month was spent in a happy daze of boxes and the glow of setting up our own domestic life for the first time outside New Haven and the undergrad- and grad-student-filled apartment building we'd lived in for the past three years. Here in bucolic West Hartford, in Richard's family home, we felt like we'd attained a wider view, a broader perspective.

A week or so after the move, I learned I'd won the Yale Graduate School Prize Teaching Fellowship. I would now be able to teach my very own undergraduate classes. My heart leapt up at the prospect of a successful life as a teacher, and even more at the prospect of bringing great happiness to my parents with this exciting news.

My father was also intrigued by my dissertation topic. I'd called the dissertation " 'Beyond the Power of Criticism': Authorial Invul-

nerability in Later Eighteenth-Century and Romantic Literature."
I took the phrase "Beyond the Power of Criticism" from the literary
critic Francis Jeffrey's scathing review of William Wordsworth's *The
Excursion*, in which Jeffrey summarizes his judgment by pronounc-
ing his patient the author terminally ill: "The case of Mr. Wordsworth, we perceive, is now manifestly hopeless, and we give him
up as altogether incurable, and beyond the power of criticism." But
while Jeffrey meant to specify the worst possible fate a writer could
suffer, he unwittingly identified what I took to be a strong aim of
Wordsworth and his contemporaries. My plan was to examine the
rise of literary criticism in England in the second half of the eigh-
teenth century and explore authors' resistance to the encroach-
ing power of critics as well as the ways in which criticism, whether
anticipated or actual, both cowed and galvanized, inhibited and
inspired them. The research I'd done had given me a new appreciation for the withering power of the critic's glare and the generative
force of the critical gaze.

Was this dissertation a way of mediating between my parents, my
mother the fierce advocate of authors, my father the ruthless arbiter
of their worth? Many of the themes I would explore—the nature of
the critical act and the role of the critic; the artist's strategies and
defenses, aggressions and evasions; criticism as diagnosis, advocacy, evaluation, execution; criticism and creativity, psychology,
spirituality; what lies beyond criticism—resonated with their professional lives and with my experience growing up in their literary
and critical milieus. Were there also ways in which the dissertation
resonated with my own status as a daughter who attempted to avoid
or skirt their judgment, to win their approval, to put myself in an
invulnerable position where love could not be withdrawn and my
father would not fall apart?

But now, my father was strong. That summer would mark both his
and Yasuko's fifth wedding anniversary and the fifth anniversary

of his heart attack. Once he'd passed that marker, he'd be at a much lower risk of future heart issues. And he was so much healthier. He'd kept the weight off, lowered his cholesterol and blood pressure significantly, and not smoked one cigarette or cigar since the heart attack. And my father had love—sustaining, mature, reliable love—with Yasuko. Because they both had teaching jobs they couldn't afford to give up, their marriage was a long-distance one, but they'd fallen into a workable rhythm: she came for six weeks in late summer through early fall and a few weeks at Christmas; he spent mid-May to the end of July in Japan. When apart, they racked up a small fortune in fax and phone bills; when together, they enjoyed a cozy domesticity: watching movies and British comedies like *Are You Being Served?*, *Keeping Up Appearances*, and *Fawlty Towers*, or mystery series like Sir Peter Wimsey, Poirot, and Miss Marple, having lunch at local Chinese and Italian restaurants and quiet dinners at home, reading side by side or to each other, sharing their writing with each other. Their apartment building didn't allow dogs, so Yasuko pleaded with him to get a cat, and Koko, a lithe, orange beauty, became my father's constant companion. That June I received a postcard from my father with a scribbled note about how much he was enjoying planting flowers on their apartment's balcony. My father gardening? A devoted cat owner? Happy and peaceful in love? It felt almost too good to be true. He had what the poet Jane Kenyon once called "ordinary contentment."

t began with an innocuous blinking light on our answering machine. Then, a voice message from Yasuko—that alone was odd. She spoke slowly, carefully, in a strangely detached way as she unfurled a saga we hadn't been privy to until now. A few weeks earlier, a routine chest X-ray to check on my father's heart had revealed an ominous shadow on his right lung. Was it the remnant of a bout of TB or pneumonia he hadn't known he'd had? Tests had been run. An infection had been detected. Medication had failed to clear up the spot. Further tests had determined that it was lung cancer.

As I stood in the kitchen, frozen in place, I felt overcome by nausea. Cancer had always been my biggest fear, even though no one in my family had ever had it. Both of my grandfathers had smoked, and lived long, healthy lives. Even as I'd worried about my father's smoking, however, I never really believed that he would get cancer from it.

My father had begun smoking at age twelve or thirteen. In virtually every photo from his teenage years, he has a cigarette dangling between his long, graceful fingers. And as a young intellectual, a writer, the "cool professor" (as one of his favorite students, David Alan Grier, always referred to him), his cigarette was his talisman, his goad, his wand, his signifier. Cigarettes littered the eulogies and remembrances people later wrote for him. In a tribute to my father, a former student wrote: "I don't think I ever saw him without a cigarette." Another once told me: "Dick smoked to think, and he certainly smoked to write." Writing was always a heroic struggle for him; cigarettes had been one of his most trusted weapons in his battle to get words onto the page.

For his children, our father's raspy, hacking cough and pallor and awful-smelling study and later apartments had made smoking entirely unappealing. Despite being a theater girl and having many friends who smoked compulsively, I'd never smoked a cigarette in my life. Neither had Nicky. Claire only smoked a cigarette here and there at college parties. We all three saw smoking not as cool or glamorous but rather as a sad, constraining addiction.

Yasuko went on: He has a good doctor, they believe the cancer is contained and can be removed surgically. Stage I. Localized. Treatable. Curable. I almost collapsed in relief onto the kitchen floor.

And then, since it was morning in Japan, I called them immediately. They sounded so good I instantly felt better. The prevailing sentiment on their end was gratitude: thank goodness he'd had his heart checked or the cancer might not have been found before it spread! This way, it had been caught early, and the surgery to remove one lobe of one lung was relatively straightforward. After a short recovery period, he should be able to return to New York City as planned at the end of July. There was no reason to believe that this would be anything other than a minor incident, with no repercussions for his longevity or quality of life.

My father's courage and optimism steadied me. Besides, this was Daddy, he of the nine lives! After all, he'd already had so many near misses, so many brushes with and escapes from disaster and death. We laughed about this spot on the lung taking its place alongside the jagged milk bottle, the hungry shark, the coconut-hurling monkey, and the Korean airline as threats that couldn't take him down. And before giving up smoking five years earlier, he had smoked for almost sixty years, a pack to a pack and a half a day plus cigars. It made sense that he hadn't escaped scot-free; a minuscule and manageable tumor, with no spread, was just about the best we could ask for!

And then, just a week or so later, a shocking reversal. The cancer was not Stage I, or Stage II, or Stage III. A tumor had been detected in his brain. The worst possible diagnosis. Stage IV cancer with metastasis to the brain. Terminal lung cancer. Incurable.

I have no memory of how I learned this news. It must have been a phone call from Yasuko, because I have no email, no fax, no voice message. All I remember is how utterly and completely heartbroken and stunned we all were. We had been assured that the cancer was at the earliest stage of Stage I, that all tests showed no spread, that a simple surgery was all that would be needed to extirpate it. "Minimally invasive," "no spread," "tiny"—these were the words the doctors and Yasuko had been using, and they'd echoed through my days as chimes of relief. But a more sophisticated test had now revealed what all the others had not, and with its verdict, my father was consigned to death.

The diagnosis had a striking intersection with both my personal and professional lives. Sarah had died ten months earlier of breast cancer with first lung and then brain metastasis; my father's lung cancer had metastasized to his brain in much the same way and to the same devastating effect. Richard and I had just begun to emerge from the grief and make progress with our graduate work, and now here we were in an uncannily parallel situation. And I felt guilty bringing more sadness, strain, and stress into Richard's life. He had been coping with seriously ill parents for the past ten years, and my role had been to lighten his load, brighten his existence, and usher in a new, happier future for him. But now we would be plunged back into an overwhelming onslaught of doctors, treatments, worried friends, insurance companies, and prognoses.

At the time of my father's diagnosis, I was working on a dissertation chapter about how metaphors of health and illness, doctors and patients, are rife in the discourse of criticism and in authors' meditations on the power of criticism. In the eighteenth- and early nineteenth-century critical discourse I was studying, criticism is often compared to evaluation, diagnosis, and prescription; authors become patients. Critics have the power to save authors by giving them medicinal or salubrious advice, or to kill them (as Shelley thought critics had done to Keats), allow them to expire, consign them to oblivion. Like Wordsworth for Jeffrey, my father had been judged a hopeless case. No longer the powerful doctor/critic, my father was now the vulnerable patient/author. The doctors had given him up as "altogether incurable" and beyond the power of medicine. No hope, no possibility of a cure.

Becoming a professional patient radically altered the nature of my father's being in the world. He was no longer the powerful one doing the assessing, the judging, the evaluating. He was dependent on others to deliver judgments, render verdicts, make assessments. And he wasn't used to being the passive one subject to others' scrutiny and analysis. He felt especially exposed. During one phone conversation, he said of the CAT scans, the MRIs, all the tests: "Sidda, it's so hard to lie on that table or in that tube and know that someone somewhere is appraising and evaluating me and I have no control over what they'll say! I feel like all those people I reviewed!" Did he make this connection because of my dissertation prospectus, which he'd read just a month or so before his diagnosis? Or was he thinking of what he once called one of the drama critic's "hardiest clichés"—the theater as "a perennial invalid"? "These doctors sum me up with phrases and pronouncements, and I'm so much more than that!" he added. "Of course you are, Daddy, of course you are," I murmured.

The brain operation had to happen first. The tumor was pressing on a nerve, and if they waited he could lose his sight. Nicky wanted to go immediately to Japan, and Claire and I asked if we could come too, but Yasuko insisted that our coming would only make things more stressful for her. News came mostly via faxes, often sent in the middle of the night (phone calls were extremely expensive—fifty dollars or so for fifteen minutes). I'd lie awake, trembling, tears slipping out of my eyes, as I thought about my father's terror, the inexorable diagnosis of terminal cancer, the prospect of losing him soon. When I heard a fax come in, I'd jump up, approach the fax machine with trepidation, then frantically scan the page for news of his condition.

But in my emails, faxes, and phone calls with my father and Yasuko, my goal was always to be calm, rational, a fount of advice, reassurance, and soothing, buoying love. Reading through the reams of correspondence now, I'm struck by how preternaturally serene I was. Not wanting to be anything but a source of sustenance, I dismissed my sadness as unworthy of consideration. When Yasuko wrote that she sometimes avoided or put off sharing the worst news with me because she feared how sad it would make me, I immediately wrote this back:

> Thank you for your concern and love! I want to reassure you that I can stand anything and am standing strong for Daddy. So please let me know of any and all developments. Though this past month and a half has been one of the most painful and scary times in my life, I have never felt totally overwhelmed or despairing. I am blessed beyond all measure that I have such a wonderful daddy who has given me such love and guidance and support over the years that I am now a grown-up who can handle even the worst news. Whether

Daddy lives only a few months or a few years, I was blessed with his love for twenty-seven years and I will continue to be so even after he dies. I *know* this, Yasuko, because of our experience with Richard's mother. Even though we miss her terribly and cry often, we also feel her around us often and talk about her all the time and know that she continues to love us and support us.

What I didn't share with her was that I spent my days in a teary fever of research, combing the internet for articles on drug trials and treatments, ordering books about lung cancer, participating in message boards organized by the families of lung cancer patients. I pulled myself together to write emails or make phone calls to the thirty or so "important people" I'd been assigned to keep informed. My dissertation fell by the wayside. And even as I kept my sadness from my father and Yasuko, I protected my husband from it as well. Richard was sympathetic and comforting, but I was determined not to impose too much on him since he had been through so much suffering and loss himself.

One day my father asked me to share the news of his diagnosis with my mother. His tone was oddly hopeful. Would she reach out to him at last? Would she be warm, kind, sympathetic? I think he and I both wondered this. But my mother's response was a clipped "Alas, but it was bound to happen sooner rather than later! Dick never took care of himself." Referring to his insouciant unconcern for diet, nutrition, or exercise, my supremely health-conscious mother had often remarked: "Your father lives his life from the neck up. It's all about what's inside his head." I agreed with her assessment, but not with the critical tone in which she uttered it. It both shocked and didn't surprise me that she had expressed no sadness upon learning that her former husband was dying. But my heart was oppressed with so much sadness for him and Yasuko, who had found a great love only to be faced with its imminent demise.

> I told her that I was in the same perilous condition as she, that I'd fallen alongside her; the two of us having bounced together into the pit . . . I said: I'm in love with you too; I've tried hard to suppress it and thought I had; I can't believe you feel the same; I'm astonished, elated, overwhelmed . . .
>
> —Richard Gilman, of Yasuko, "To the Noodle Shop," *American Scholar*, Summer 2002

During those first bewildering days after learning that my father had terminal cancer and being reminded of the seemingly unbridgeable divide that remained between my parents, songs from my favorite musical, *West Side Story*, ran through my head on an almost continuous loop. I'd seen the movie for the first time when I was about eight years old. My father noticed that it was going to be on television and told me and Claire that he thought we were ready for it.

"Stanley Kauffmann called it 'the best film musical ever made,'" he said.

"Didn't Pauline Kael give *West Side Story* a terrible review?" my mother asked.

My father snorted in disgust. "Pauline Kael was nastily dismissive in order to promote herself! Her review was a piece of pretentious nonsense!"

Then his face softened as he turned again to his little girls. "What a joy awaits you, Sidda and Swanee!"

The next afternoon, Claire and I curled up in our father's Eames armchair, in his large book-lined office, and the film began. From the first shot of a New York City cityscape, from the first scenes filmed just blocks from where we lived on the Upper West Side, we were mesmerized. Other than Disney romances with vacuous princes, I don't think I'd seen a love story play out on-screen before. An hour and a half in, my father discreetly dropped a Kleenex box onto the ottoman, and soon we were making good use of it. Maria and Tony's star-crossed love was a bewitching attraction, a profound passion, an unshakable devotion I'd never seen even a glimpse of in my parents' relationship. A romantic even as a young child, I was bowled over by the idea of love that cast aside all boundaries and barriers. What critic Brooks Atkinson in his *New York Times* review called *West Side Story*'s "total impression of wildness, ecstasy and anguish" never left me. And the idea of my father as *West Side Story*'s Tony, always latent, now took shape.

Both Tony and my father were dreamy idealists whose optimism teetered on the verge of delusion. Tony was a former gang member with a tender side, my father a formerly pugilistic critic with a romantic soul. Like Tony, my father was capable of being suddenly swept away, taken over by passion, obsessed and obsessive about who and what he loved. How wonderful a sound could be! My father felt that, knew it, lived it.

The pure part of my father was Tony. And he had become more of a Tony as he grew older. That was one of the most astonishing things to me about my father's life. After a conversion that began with ardent hope, then "failed" in a way that left him oppressed by shame and guilt; two marriages that broke apart, the second in spectacular fashion; and many romances and book projects that went nowhere, he could so easily have become cynical, hardened, impervious to romanticism or idealism. But he had retained his optimism, his sense that something was coming, if only he could wait. "The drama critic lives on hope," he once wrote. "From week to week and season to season he feeds off the possibilities of things not yet seen and makes whatever peace he can with actuality," he wrote. In his personal life as well, my father had lived on hope.

At sixty-four years old, after so much heartbreak and disappointment, he had found grand love in the most unpropitious circumstances. Across an ocean, across a yawning cultural divide, across a vast difference of experience, he and Yasuko seemed to me a late-in-life Tony and Maria, with literal and figurative Jets and Sharks ranged against them. Warning voices, punishing laws—all the hurdles that made their eventual union so improbable. A man who had fought in World War II against her people and her country, a woman who had been cautioned against loving this *gaijin*, they were One Hand, One Heart. Only death could part them now . . .

Tony falls in love and into danger at one and the same moment. So it was with my father, who stumbled into danger when he fell in love with Yasuko: a married woman with a controlling husband, a Japanese woman whose country would punish her and him severely for their transgression. Boundaries of geography, age, and situation were no obstacle in his mind. "I'm not afraid!" Tony cries when Maria warns him that her parents and her culture won't approve. Maria evokes what my father once described as Yasuko's "anguished struggle between duty and yearning." And Tony's certainty that things will work out, though it has an endearing appeal, also echoed for me my father's certainty that Yasuko would be able to keep her children. He was, of course, proven tragically wrong: choosing him had resulted in her losing them. After their father had told them he'd kill himself if they ever contacted her, they'd remained silent and she hadn't seen them in almost ten years. The Japanese legal system favored the father, especially in cases of "adultery," and she had no recourse. Now she was faced with the loss of her new husband as well.

Tony's reckless nonchalance reminded me of my father's repeated assurances that despite the risk he was taking in smoking, he would be all right. That the cigarettes he craved and counted on wouldn't harm him. "I'm not afraid," he'd tell us children when we begged him to quit or cut down. But he—and Tony—should have been afraid. From his first cigarette as a young boy in the streets of Brooklyn to his last dying day, my father's addiction would shadow his life.

As he runs toward his beloved, Tony is gunned down by Chino, Maria's arranged fiancé: Yasuko's marriage had been arranged; her husband had threatened to kill my father many times. But it was not the estranged husband who would kill my father. Chino's bullet was my mother's undermining the innocence of my love for him. Chino's bullet was my father's double life. Chino's bullet was my mother telling me about my father's double life. Chino's bullet was my father's addiction. Chino's bullet was the cancer caused by his addiction. All of these bullets would kill him.

Maria's groans of anguish as she holds Tony's body in her arms and her snarling "Don't you TOUCH HIM!"—they were mine as well. My helpless anguish as my mother desecrated my perception of my father. My heartsickness when my father snapped at Claire, undermined himself, acted poorly. My moral passion that refused to reduce my father to his worst self.

My parents' relationship had been filled with barbs and blistering attacks, distrust and disapproval. They couldn't see the casualties of their war. I'd always wanted peace and quiet and open air for our family. Not the poisonous air of resentment and disappointment and contempt. If only I, like Maria with the warring gangs, had screamed out, rebuked them for their animosity, pleaded with them to confront the consequences of the war they'd begun!

Despite his errors, his crimes, his sins, Tony is wholly loved by his Maria in the last moments of his life, and forgiven by his enemies after his death. Maria's sorrow pierces the hearts of all present, uniting the Jets and the Sharks in a mutual procession of mourning. Tony is honored, paid homage to, remembered with gravity and respect. Would my father attain this? Would my mother find a way of forgiving?

My father got through the brain surgery quite well, but the lung surgery had to be delayed because he'd developed a lung infection. And every day, tests revealed new issues, problems, diagnoses. His arteries were in terrible shape. He had multiple aneurysms. He was found to have hepatitis C (my mother and Yasuko, Nick, Claire, and I all had to be tested since the doctors said he might have infected his wives via sexual activity and us as children while bandaging our cuts). His lung infection was a type sometimes seen in AIDS patients, so he was tested for HIV; given his sexual history, there was good reason to believe he could be positive, and our relief was immense when at least one piece of news was good.

The doctors finally got the infection under control and performed surgery to remove a lobe of his right lung. Initial reports were promising: the surgery had been successful, and our father was recovering well. But three days later, a frightening missive written in Yasuko's cramped, curly handwriting came through the fax machine. Our father had had a mild stroke. What would this mean? Lasting brain damage? A day or so later, another fax arrived announcing a change of heart about our visiting: "Daddy is having a successful but very painful and uncomfortable recovery from the lung surgery, so he is in quite bad spirits now. Therefore, we both think that this will be a good time for you and Nicky to come here. Your presence will cheer him up and you could be a practical help." None of us had ever been to Japan before, in part because my father was only there about two and a half months out of the year, in part because traveling there was astronomically expensive. Now, Yasuko would cover the plane fare for all of us. Nicky would fly from Mexico, where he'd moved permanently in 1991 after being priced out of the Upper West Side, Richard and I from New York, and Claire from Italy, where she was doing research for her Columbia University dissertation in art history.

The trip was about twenty-seven hours door-to-door. After two planes, a train, and two subways, Richard and I arrived, blinking and sleepy, in Shiga, the small suburb of Kyoto where Yasuko and my father had recently bought an apartment. Nicky, who'd arrived a few days earlier, met us in the subway station and helped carry our huge suitcases, weighed down with all the comfort items I'd brought at my father's request: soft T-shirts from the Gap, boxes of Lipton chicken noodle soup, Cream of Wheat and Wheatena cereal, Jell-O chocolate and tapioca pudding mix. The very lunches and "treats" he'd prepared for me and Claire were now what he wanted most from us.

We followed Nicky as he confidently wove through the hectic, impeccably clean streets. It was a blazingly sunny day, and walking past pachinko parlors and restaurants with shiny plastic models of food displayed in their front window, with unfamiliar signs and characters everywhere, we felt we were in an utterly foreign land. This was my father's neighborhood? It was an odd combination of garish and sterile, cutesy and anodyne. On every corner, it seemed, smiley women in uniforms were cheerfully handing out packs of Kleenex to passersby. The architecture was nondescript at best, ugly at worst, the streets crowded and confusing, with awkwardly situated buildings looming up seemingly out of nowhere and others jutting out at odd angles. There was nothing beautiful, or orderly, or tranquil about it. It wasn't at all the Japan I'd been expecting. How could our father, a native New Yorker, someone who prized the gritty, diverse, artistic, soulful Upper West Side, survive here? When we got to my father's apartment building, Richard remarked that it looked like a Disney World hotel.

We took the elevator to the twenty-third floor and arrived to a compact but pleasant, modern apartment with floor-to-ceiling glass in most rooms, a huge wheel of fresh sushi from a neighborhood store, and a steady, calm, loving Yasuko, who was clearly so relieved to have us there. Evidence of my father and Yasuko's happy domestic life was everywhere. Stacks of VCR tapes of British mystery and comedy series, their small offices side by side, the purple and pink flowers they'd planted on the balcony, Koko the cat, framed photos from their wedding, my father beaming in a spiffy blue suit and tie, gazing at Yasuko with unabashed love.

Claire and I slept on the floor in the tatami room, a traditional space with straw mat flooring and sliding paper doors, Richard on the futon in the living room, Nicky on an inflatable mattress in my father's study. And the next morning after breakfast, Claire and I took the subway to see my father in the hospital. Bare-bones, with dark hallways down which coughing or masked men trundled laboriously, it felt like something out of a fifties movie. Walking through the door into the room where he lay, separated by a curtain from another ailing patient, I summoned all the equanimity I could muster. But when I parted the curtain and saw him in the bed, his head completely bald and scored with a fresh scar, my self-possession vanished. "Daddy!" We ran to him and took his hands, gnarled by arthritis, the skin paper-thin and pale, in ours. He exclaimed, in a high, hoarse voice: "Sidda! Swanee! You're here!!" His "Sidda!" had lost its happy lilt. It was feeble, labored, with a question mark rather than an exclamation point at the end. Yasuko had warned us that the stroke had affected his mouth, which now drooped on one side. As we talked with him, it became clear that he'd lost the range of intonation that had always made his voice—once described by a student as variously "deep, flat, musical, dry, skeptical, droll"—such a marvelously expressive instrument.

Yasuko had done what she could to make his area cheerful. A

stuffed dog I'd sent lay beside him on the bed; Super Grover, whom Claire had retrieved from the New York apartment and mailed before leaving for Italy, hung from one of the metal bedposts. The standard hospital bedding had been replaced with the blue sheets with white polka dots and cheery red trim that Claire and I had had on our childhood beds in Weston. Seeing these talismans of our childhood, this reminder of my father as worry-soother rather than source of worry, I felt at once dizzy, disoriented, and determined. I took a deep breath and began chattering away in an effort to dispel sadness and heaviness. I addressed Grover with a joking remark about the long trip and jet lag, and my father attempted to do his famous Grover imitation in response, but his now-limited voice failed him. Claire took a seat in the wheelchair next to his bed so she could hold his hand, I at the foot of the bed with my hand comfortingly resting on his wizened legs. We rhapsodized about the apartment and Yasuko, Koko the cat and the sushi we'd eaten, we boosted and bolstered him. And when, after a half hour or so, he began yawning and dozing off, we left our father, a gaunt, frail figure, alone in a hospital where no one spoke his language, in a country that seemed all the more foreign and forbidding the more we got to know it.

Every morning thereafter and throughout our stay, Yasuko pressed Japanese money into our hands and sent us out on sightseeing expeditions led by her graduate students, who were fascinated by Americans, eager to please, and longing for as much conversation in English as possible. Richard and I answered their earnest questions about English PhD programs in the US, Claire and I their wide-eyed queries about New York City. We listened to them expatiate on the history of various structures and places, the significance of various features of the landscape and cityscape, the traditions and customs underlying our meals. With them as our companions and our guides, we climbed mountains and took boat rides, attended tea ceremonies and visited temples, ate traditional Japanese dishes and ambled through historic districts. We oohed and aahed at the deer running up to us and the giant bronze Buddha in Nara, the beautiful zen rock gardens, famous paintings in important museums. Our experience was so novel that at times it carried me out of my sadness. But mostly it felt strange—and somehow wrong—to be playing the role of excited, admiring tourists and carrying out the rituals of mind-expanding travel when our father lay dying.

It was a blisteringly hot summer in Japan that year, and photos show us glistening with sweat, with large rings under our eyes but insouciant smiles plastered on our faces, as we stand in front of temples and immense Buddhas with paper parasols posed flirtatiously in our hands. But there are also a few unguarded photos, of Claire leaning her head on my shoulder with her eyes closed, Claire and me walking with our arms around each other. I don't remember crying once. There was nowhere to do it. And I feared that if I gave in to the sadness that prickled behind my eyes and pushed up in my throat, I would lose control and my ability to be the comforter. I was in Japan to raise my father's spirits. I was in Japan to be a steady rock of support for Yasuko. Those were my parts and I would perform them well.

One afternoon when Yasuko had gone to the hospital, Nicky summoned me to our father's study. The expression on his face was both gleeful and flabbergasted as he handed me a sheaf of papers and urged me to read. The papers seemed to be a draft of a book proposal about my father and Yasuko's cross-cultural relationship. The first page contained a dramatic statement: "My wife and I couldn't be more different. She has slept with two men, her ex-husband and me. I have slept with several hundred women, and a few men."

Several hundred women—strangely, that didn't really surprise us. But a few men?! That was a complete shock, and not for the reasons one might think. More than half of my father's closest male friends were gay or bisexual. He was a fervent supporter of gay rights. When Nicky had come out to him, he'd been entirely supportive, his only concern that he'd wanted Nicky to experience fatherhood, and then later he'd worried about AIDS. But there had never been any hint that he himself had had gay experiences or was anything other than inveterately heterosexual. We'd never ever suspected this. Why wouldn't he have written about this? We wondered: When? Where? With whom? Harold Brodkey? A fellow marine? W. H. Auden, with whom my father had been friendly as a young man and who, we'd been told, had hit on him several times?

The pages disappeared a few days later, and we never asked either our father or Yasuko about them. No difficult topics could be broached, no challenging conversations initiated. Because virtually every single interaction with my father now was difficult and challenging, and adding a controversial subject to the mix would have taken too much out of us and him.

About a week after we arrived in Japan, my father was allowed to leave the hospital, but that privilege came with a grim prognosis: seven months to live, at most. My father once described himself post-heart attack as having a "slow, ghostly gait and hollow spectral appearance"; now, he was even more specter-like. Observing my father after his cancer diagnosis, the surgeries, the stroke, which all had happened in the span of just a few weeks, I felt as if he had aged twenty years. He was old and stooped; he moved slowly, gingerly, nervously. The droop in his mouth gave him a perpetually peevish expression. It was as if the stroke had literalized, actualized in his expression the sneering, downcast, contemptuous attitude that had always threatened to overwhelm the sunny side of him. Whatever could go wrong, whatever could fail, had gone wrong, had failed. He was no longer the cool bohemian, the spry Great Finder. We had lost his gallant stride, his warm embraces, his nimble grace.

My father had become more relaxed and joyous, like the father of my childhood, in his older age and his marriage to Yasuko, but illness and a grave prognosis sent him hurtling backwards. He was disconsolate, bitter, more irritable than I'd ever seen him. He sniped at Nicky's well-meaning questions about his biography: which regiment he'd been in during the war, his early jobs in journalism. He criticized Yasuko for misremembering or misinterpreting details of movies. And despite his reduced condition, his striking vulnerability, he repeatedly rejected or foiled our attempts to coddle or protect him. Every time Nicky tried to help him out of or into a chair, he'd angrily push his hand away. If Yasuko cheered him on when he took several shaky steps, he'd retort: "It wasn't so great!" If Claire exclaimed, "You look much better today, Daddy!" he'd brusquely reply: "Well, I don't feel better." When we looked for tiny signs of progress—a few more bites of food eaten, a few more steps taken than the day before—he was having none of it. "You're being patronizing," he'd say. "Stop it." He pushed back when I reminded him that people often outlived their prognoses. "It's seven months, Sidda—seven months—and nothing you say can change that!" he snapped. " 'Nothing makes me more pessimistic than the obligation to be optimistic,' " he told me another day. "Ionesco said that, and he was right!" For me, whose relationship with him had always been predicated on my capacity to bring him reassurance and happiness, his unwavering despair was crushing. There was nothing I could do, nothing I could say, to improve his mood or lighten the situation for him. Helplessness broke over me in waves.

There were spots of nourishing time—visits from Yasuko's lovely older sister, two nieces, and adorable great-nephews and -nieces, choosing Japanese characters to put on scrolls Yasuko wanted to buy us, trying on Yasuko's family kimonos for Daddy. Any activity that increased our connection to Yasuko and her culture gratified and pleased him. But even as he appreciated our learning about Japan, he lashed out at the country in full critic mode. He spluttered angrily about the garish game shows and manic talk shows on television. He hated fish and wasn't a fan of teriyaki seasoning, so found most Japanese cuisine unpalatable (thank goodness Yasuko could cook anything). He considered much of Japanese popular culture revolting and rebarbative, unbearably cutesy and kitschy. At the same time, however, he craved the wise serenity of Japan's zen gardens, admired the austerity and dignity of its war memorials and museums, and told us he wanted to be buried in Yasuko's family plot in a cemetery adjoining one of its most famous temples. He loved Japanese art, literature, and film. Sometimes after dinner, we'd watch classic films by Kurosawa and Ozu. My father had first introduced me to Japanese films during my year off from Yale; one we both especially loved was *Ikiru*. *Ikiru*, or "To Live," tells the story of a terminally ill man who vows to make his final days rich and meaningful, to push through the constraints of his limited emotional palette and do something good for others before he dies. But this, of course, was a film we never would have watched now: the parallels with my father's situation would have been too striking and painful. Still, I thought of *Ikiru* and how that dying man became better as a result of his diagnosis. All signs pointed in the opposite direction for my father.

On the innumerable subways and trains we took during our stay in Japan, I carried a volume of the eighteenth-century poet William Cowper's letters, dutifully underlining and annotating all of his references to critics and criticism in order to create the illusion (to myself) that I was making progress on the first chapter of my dissertation. Cowper's consuming preoccupation with criticism pervades his letters, which gave him a space both to express his anxiety about criticism and to experiment with ways of overcoming it. "The frown of a critic freezes my poetical powers," Cowper wrote in a letter to his cousin, and elsewhere he refers to the "formidable" critics who reduce him to a "shivering" petitioner, describes a positive review of his poem *The Task* as "my handsome escape . . . out of the paws of the Critics," and tells his best friend he will write again only "if the Critics do not set their feet upon this first Egg that I have laid, and crush it." I couldn't help juxtaposing the image of critics as all-powerful, terrifying beings that emerges in those letters with the image of my weak, struggling, terrified father. And it wasn't just his diminution in the wake of diagnoses and surgeries. Even as my father had displayed himself in print and presented himself in public as virtually omnipotent, even as he had struck terror into the hearts of scores of playwrights, actors, and directors, in his private life he had always been insecure, self-doubting, beset by anxiety. And just when he'd finally achieved a romantic relationship in which he was accepted in all his complexity, for both his strength and his weakness, illness had brought out his very worst qualities and was undermining much of the progress he'd made. The psychic defenses—all there already but latent, coiled, lying in wait—erected themselves over his body like quills, like spines, like shields, even as the body itself had no physical defenses against the cancer that was ravaging it.

Yasuko believed that cancer cells in his brain or residual effects of the stroke were the cause of his irritability and outbursts; she seemed to see this behavior as an aberration She rationalized his prickly temperament and explosive behavior as both an understandable response to a dire prognosis and an uncontrollable manifestation of the illness. But for Nicky, Claire, and me, far from representing some strange new expression of his illness, this moodiness and volatility were sickeningly familiar. The pinched and crabby nature seemed a more pervasive and intense version of what we'd experienced intermittently during our childhoods.

One afternoon Claire and I were finishing lunch with my father and Yasuko when Koko scampered across the table and knocked over a bottle of water. "What the hell are you are doing?! Get out of here!" my father yelled. She jumped off the table, and as she landed on the floor he gave her a feeble kick and angrily scolded her: "Is this how you repay us for giving you a good home?!" She skittered away and fled the room; at almost the same moment, Claire jumped up and ran away too. I got up in a deliberately slow way so as not to add to the scene's drama, and walked down the hall to find Claire. She was huddled on the floor in my father's study, sobbing.

"Oh Siddee," she cried when she saw me, "I felt like we were back in our childhood, and Koko was me when I'd spill my milk!"

"Clairey, we have to go back in there," I urged, stroking her hair. "We don't want them to think we're upset."

She reluctantly stood up and, arm in arm, we walked back to the living room, where we found Yasuko and my father quietly talking at the table. The outburst was never mentioned again.

Eventually, after Nicky left, Yasuko sent Claire, Richard, and me to a nearby hotel. It was a relief to be able to leave the apartment when my father's mood began tilting toward black, to sleep in a bed, to have some time to decompress and laugh together. Now when we visited, he was able to muster enough equanimity to watch a *Sesame Street* episode with us, share thoughts on Yasuko's students, listen to our impressions of the tourist attractions we'd seen, and tell us about his own favorite places in and around Kyoto.

As our departure date approached, there was a slew of good news. Scans showed that the brain and lung surgeries had completely removed the tumors and my father needed no further treatment at the moment. He had been cleared to travel to New York in a few weeks. There, he'd be seen by a top lung cancer specialist who'd agreed to collaborate with the Japanese doctors and who suspected the prognosis might have been too bleak. He was hopeful he might even be able to teach his second-semester classes at Yale in January! So we left with a sense of relief and tempered optimism. And a few weeks later, he and Yasuko flew to New York, on the day Princess Diana was killed; her death was the first thing he mentioned when he called to say they'd landed safely. I think it enhanced his sense of luck; at least he'd had seventy-two good years.

Soon after their arrival, Claire and I accompanied our father and Yasuko to the second-opinion consultation at Columbia-Presbyterian. Dr. S was an expert in the field, and his assessment was that the Japanese doctors had been too pessimistic. "Given that there are no visible tumors and they seem to have removed the two small ones successfully, there's reason to believe you could have up to five years to live," he said in a dry, clinical, and therefore all-the-more-believable tone. The happiness this news inspired was slightly muddied by a strange moment. When Dr. S asked my father how old he was, he answered, with little hesitation but a slight, odd break in his voice, "Seventy-four." Seventy-four? He was seventy-two. He was born in 1925; it was 1997. Nineteen twenty-five was a year he'd referred to countless times. It was his birth year in *Who's Who in America*, he had gone to college at sixteen because he was precocious. At that "seventy-four," Claire and I, sitting behind him, stared at each other incredulously and reached out to hold hands. Later, while he was resting at home, we mentioned the age discrepancy to Yasuko, fearful the stroke had addled his brain. "Nineteen twenty-three is right," she said in a calm yet forceful voice. It was clear that she wasn't open to a conversation about a lie. It was clear she'd known all along that he had deceived the rest of us.

He had lied to Nicky's mother, to my mother, to publications and employers, Yale, his three children, but for what purpose? To lessen the shame of graduating from college late (or perhaps not graduating at all—we were never sure) and spending his twenties as "an intellectual hobo"? To shrink the large age difference between him and my mother? But why only knock off two years? We never asked him why.

Any questions would have to wait or be tabled indefinitely, because devastating news had rendered them beside the point. New scans ordered by Dr. S revealed multiple tiny tumors scattered throughout my father's brain. They'd appeared in just a month's time and were unreachable via surgery. The prognosis now was a fifty-fifty chance of living just ten months more. His situation eerily reminiscent of Sarah's just two years earlier, my father was put on steroids and began receiving whole-brain radiation.

> The thing I wanted was simply—simply!—not to be obliterated, not to have to come down to a day, a moment, when there would be nothing more I would be allowed to do or say or see or think . . . Beneath the imperviousness of my youthful energy and the vein of optimism based on an incalculably long future, I always knew that I *would* die and I couldn't bear knowing it.
>
> —Richard Gilman on himself as a young man, *Faith, Sex, Mystery*

One afternoon in September, on a day off from teaching, Richard drove me down from Connecticut to spend time with my father. He was lying on the sofa in the living room, his bald head propped up on pillows, his body covered by a colorful crocheted afghan his mother had made for me and Claire when we were children. That morning he'd had a session of whole-brain radiation; his face was flushed and starting to swell in much the same way Sarah's had. It felt like a surreal nightmare. I sat next to him, holding his hand, and he gazed up at me with imploring eyes.

"Please, Sidda, will you make me two promises? If I die soon, and it looks like I will—"

"Daddy, we don't know that," I interrupted.

"Yes, Sidda, we do." There was a hint of rebuke in his tone, and I felt the sting of failing to boost him, as I so desperately wanted to do. I was bringing my youthful energy and vein of optimism to him in a way that ignored his mood and his need for directness. I couldn't bear knowing he would die, but he was confronting the reality with clarity and urgency.

"So, first, will you try to collect my unpublished pieces into a book? There are so many I want to have a permanent home."

"Yes, Daddy, I promise, I will try," I said, gripping his hand and biting the inside of my cheek to keep from crying.

And then he made me promise that Claire, Nick, and I would always love and cherish Yasuko and keep her from being too lonely.

"I'm so afraid of leaving her alone," he murmured, tears rolling down his puffy red cheeks. "Please, please, Sidda, never desert her!"

"Of course we won't, Daddy!"

What remained unspoken, and a huge source of his anxiety, was that Yasuko no longer had her children. Even if we stayed in touch, we couldn't replace them or him.

> What matters most is to break out of the rut. Everything else
> is unimportant.
>
> —Chekhov, quoted at the end of chapter one of Richard Gilman's
> *Chekhov's Plays: An Opening into Eternity*

I n late September, after the course of radiation was complete, my
father and Yasuko returned to Japan, where Yasuko had to resume
her teaching job (her excellent health insurance would cover visiting nurses while she was at work). Once there, my father sank into a
deep melancholic rut. The depression that had always shadowed him,
sometimes enveloping him but recently held at bay, now settled on
his frail shoulders like a thick blanket of fog. He desperately missed
New York City and fall in the Northeast United States—the leaves
changing colors in Riverside and Central Parks, bagels on Sunday
mornings, the *New York Times*, football games, the back-to-school
energy, his students, colleagues, friends. After the hep C diagnosis, he had been ordered not to drink alcohol, but he craved his late-
afternoon stiff drink and Yasuko was loath to deny him (although
she agonized over having given in later). When all he would agree
to eat was steak or bacon, she fretted over his cholesterol and didn't
know if she should relent. When he'd refuse to get out of his chair

or out of bed, she'd wonder whether to indulge him or insist he try. She was also struggling with his ferocious independence: when she would tend to him too quickly or without his requesting it, he'd flare up: "Let me be!" One day she told me, "I want to convey how much I love him, and now I don't think I can do it by being critical or severe toward him. He is like a child now and seems to find it more satisfying to have me gentle and undemanding." She didn't think he could stand anything that might be construed as criticism.

That first year after my father was diagnosed, I spent a small fortune on phone bills, faxes, postage, gifts. I have a file half a drawer thick of the emails and faxes I sent him and Yasuko in one year alone. My emails to Yasuko, filled with loving support for her and ideas for improving my father's mood, were many pages long. Those to my father were shorter, cheerier, funnier, containing exciting sports news and reminders that Harry Teelock, Paddington, and Michelle G were rooting him on. Sensing that he was in need of reminders of his critical power—the ability to be the mentor and dispense advice rather than receive judgments—I nudged former students to write and call. I taped every single *New York Times* article about the Giants to a piece of typing paper, then sent it through the fax machine. I express-mailed him videotaped Giants games so he wouldn't have to wait too long to watch them (if they lost, I wouldn't mail the tape), tapes of *Murder, She Wrote*, *Matlock*, and *Columbo* movies, ginger candy and seasickness bands for his nausea, boxes of pudding and Lipton soup mix to tempt his appetite. That Christmas, Claire and I bought a lifelike stuffed dog from FAO Schwarz and sent it to Japan in an enormous Christmas box filled with gifts and treats: a stuffed Pooh for my father and a Kanga for Yasuko, comfy Lands' End pajamas, peppermint sticks, a set of Gilbert and Sullivan operettas on VHS tape. We sprinkled red and green chocolate kisses throughout the box.

That fall, I had my own class of Yale freshmen, and every minute I wasn't preparing to teach, grading, or interacting with them, I spent helping to support and guide Yasuko and my father. I put my dissertation aside, instead becoming a scholar of and expert on lung cancer. I furiously and relentlessly researched treatments and their side effects, nutritional supplements, prognoses. I dealt with CIGNA for my father's disability insurance, Yale for his health insurance, his bank, his friends. Doing doing doing kept me from feeling. I numbed myself to fear and sadness by focusing on practicalities and by playing the roles of counselor, nurturer, and pragmatic doer to the hilt.

> I have this morning such a Lethargy that I cannot write—the reason of my delaying is oftentimes from this feeling—I wait for a proper temper . . . —However I am now so depressed that I have not an Idea to put to paper—my hand feels like lead—and yet it is an unpleasant numbness it does not take away the pain of existence—
>
> —John Keats, dying of tuberculosis, 1818

It soon became clear that the most intransigent source of my father's depression was his inability to think clearly enough to write. Overcome by lethargy and an unpleasant numbness, his hands felt heavy as lead. He was rereading the acclaimed memoirs of illness and dying by his friends Harold Brodkey and Anatole Broyard, and yearned to make his own contribution to that literature. Anatole had turned his Stage IV prostate cancer diagnosis into an occasion for opening himself to what he called "the wonder, terror, and exaltation of being on the edge of being." My father's approach to his illness had none of the acerbic wit and insouciant charm, none of the crackling energy and ecstatic sense of transport Anatole had brought to *Intoxicated by My Illness*. He wasn't galvanized by his illness, let alone intoxicated by it. In the early 1990s, Harold had disclosed his AIDS diagnosis in the pages of *The New Yorker*, then published what *New*

York Times critic Michiko Kakutani called "the most chiseled and potent of Brodkey's books," in which he chronicled his "passage into nonexistence." My father's perspective on illness and death had none of the extravagant romanticism, savage intensity, or performative flair of Harold's *This Wild Darkness: The Story of My Death.* If, as Anatole had written, "being ill and dying is largely, to a great degree, a matter of style," then my father could not find or fashion a style that suited him. He couldn't turn his diagnosis into a wellspring, his illness into a story.

Yasuko reported to me that when she'd reminded him of his prodigious output and his many accolades, he told her: "But I haven't yet written my life-work. I have published several books, but nothing I can call my life-work." This felt heartrendingly sad. If *The Making of Modern Drama*, nominated for the National Book Award and used in countless Introduction to Theater classes, or his *New York Times Book Review* front-page-reviewed memoir, or his gorgeous book on Chekhov weren't Life-Works, what would be? What could ever fill the hole inside him? What would ever assuage his fear that he didn't measure up, hadn't accomplished enough, was inferior, lacking, incomplete? He had three devoted children and a remarkable wife who adored him. Shouldn't he use his remaining days to love and be loved? But even as he frustrated me, even as I saw his meager self-worth, even as I increasingly understood how different I was becoming from him, that he was caught up in ego and marks of accomplishment even as I was moving away from them, I never let on to him that I found his outlook not just sad but troubling.

I hastened to reassure him and reorient him toward what was most important:

> My Dearest Doodlebird, if you never wrote another word, it would not change anything about who you are. You are a writer whether or not you write now. You have accomplished

more with your writing than most people ever dream of, and your books will survive you. I will make sure that your uncollected pieces get published; I will edit them and write an introduction if need be. So don't worry about that for a minute. If you find that you can write, and I think it is highly possible that you will, that will be wonderful, but don't decide that if you can't, it is the end of the world . . .

Whatever happens, the most important thing to remember is that you are not defined by your ability to write, Daddy. You are defined by who you are: a brilliant, funny, imaginative, stubborn, scampish, adorable!, complex person. You will always be that person, whether or not you write. Remember that I am always here to help in any way I can and that I absolutely adore you!

I felt so grateful for Yasuko—for her patience, her indefatigable efforts to comfort and support him, and her ability to see his essence even through the scrim of his irritability. "We laugh a lot. Joke a lot. He's really, unbearably, CUTE AND SWEET," she once wrote in the midst of an email about how depressed and difficult he was. She saw this about him. My mother never had.

In December 1997, just after we found out that the radiation therapy had eradicated the brain tumors, scans showed that the cancer had metastasized to the other lung. He would need chemotherapy. The first chemo session fell on the first day of my second-semester Yale class; I remember hiding my hands under the seminar room table so the students in my Gothic Literature class wouldn't see them shaking. And new demons were lurking.

As he grew older he became convinced that his many enemies were intensifying their efforts to bring him down . . . This paranoid fantasy reminds me of Strindberg, who imag-

ined that his enemies were trying to get at him with electric
charges through the ceiling of his room.

—Richard Gilman on Wilhelm Reich's *American Odyssey:*
Letters and Journals, 1940–1947, New York Times Book Review,
September 5, 1999

In the months after his terminal cancer diagnosis, my father's prick-
liness, his neurotic vigilance, his defensive attitude toward life came
back in full force. Like Reich, like Strindberg, he developed paranoid fears: that his friend Sherwin Nuland had deliberately taken
away his hope by sending him a copy of his acclaimed book *How We
Die*; that various friends had turned on him; that he was being ousted
unceremoniously from various positions of power and authority. In
March of 1998, when he received a letter from Yale referring to him
as a terminated employee, he immediately jumped to the conclusion
that Yale Drama School was taking the opportunity presented by his
cancer diagnosis to let him go. His position there had always been
more precarious than it might seem; an untenured adjunct, he was at
once a pillar of the institution and subject to the whims of its admin-
istration. He was enraged by the phrase "terminated employee." He
hadn't been asked if he wanted to retire. He hadn't told them he was
done. Yasuko emailed to relate his fury and indignation and then
called me so I could hear his reaction for myself. "This is outrageous!"
he yelled. "Get me a lawyer, Sidda! Those bastards terminated me!
They think I'm too gaga to know! They think I won't catch on! Well,
I've still got a brain in my head and I can use it!" A fit of coughing
obscured the words, but the vitriol came through loud and clear. We
explained that the phrase "terminated employee" was a technical-
ity required to process his disability payments. Once he understood
that money would flow as a result of the designation, he calmed down
fairly quickly. But the way he'd gone full throttle into paranoia was
a scary caricature of the insecurity that had always shadowed him.

And yet despite all his perceived adversaries, his heartache, the thousand natural shocks his flesh was heir to, bit by bit my father regained a precarious hold on equanimity. The chemo was a resounding success, eliminating all visible tumors. He took great pride in being a good patient and in the Japanese doctors' devotion to him. That spring, he and Yasuko went to see the cherry blossoms and took an overnight trip to Nagasaki, his favorite place in Japan. And he was told he could travel to New York that summer for a six-week stay. All of this good news emboldened me to realize my most cherished dream and get pregnant in June of 1998, a month after my twenty-eighth birthday. That summer, Richard and I drove in and out of New York to see my father and Yasuko as I battled nausea and fatigue, and the day before they returned to Japan, just as my pregnancy reached the three-month mark, we told them that my father was going to be a grandfather and sent them off with something to look forward to the following summer.

The first half of 1999 brought a raft of good news and promising developments for all of us. At the urging of my dissertation advisors, I applied for an assistant professorship at Yale, and despite the fact that I'd completed only one and a half chapters of my dissertation and was bursting out of my maternity suit during the interview, I was offered the job. A month later, I gave birth to my first child, a boy we named Benjamin. Claire got engaged to her longtime boyfriend, Sasha. New tests showed that my father was still cancer free. He and Yasuko enjoyed their summertime stay in New York City more than ever, especially delighting in dandling Baby Benj, snug in his yellow Carter's sleeper, on their laps.

Around this same time, a rush of productivity propelled my father forward along multiple lines: an essay about the beginning of his relationship with Yasuko, an introduction to the Penguin Chekhov, a new introduction to *The Making of Modern Drama*. In that introduction, the grand imperturbability of claims like "The human voice, language, is a survivor . . . the chief executive instrument of consciousness" belied the agonizing effort it took to get his own voice on the page. His fingers moved more slowly, he could only work in brief spurts before his energy flagged, and it took him much longer to find just the right word. What gave him ammunition, sustenance, and the will to carry on were his fierce love for Yasuko and his equally fierce commitment to thinking, writing, being a critic.

> Consciousness will always be in need of, and always demand, enactment; and language, as someone (I think Coleridge) once said, is the armament of the mind, which I take to mean our chief protection against mortality.
>
> —Richard Gilman, new introduction to *The Making of Modern Drama*, written in the spring of 1999

My father's consciousness was desperately in need of enactment, and one of his chief protections against mortality was a book he was determined to write about Japan and his love affair with Yasuko. As Yasuko put it, "When Richard conceived the plan to write a book on Japan, he said he was thinking of setting things right for my sake, seeing my terrible and to him unanticipated suffering over my estranged children." She confided in me that my father had been deeply disheartened by his literary agent's lack of enthusiasm for the idea, and asked if I could introduce him to my graduate school friend Tina Bennett, who was now a top agent at my mother's literary agency. I had him send all the writing he had to me and to Tina. I read the pages with a sinking sense of how much would need to be done in order to stitch together disparate bits and pieces into a coherent book project. How strange it felt to be my father's editor—his critic—and even harder was seeing his typically finely wrought and sinewy prose in rough and shapeless form. I desperately tried to help, sending him twenty pages of editorial suggestions; Tina was generous with her time and her edits. My father took our criticisms in good stride, but Yasuko and I both knew that the effort required to transform the rich material into a compelling book might exceed his increasingly feeble grasp.

So feeble was he that when Claire announced that she and Sasha would get married in May 2000, my father sent her a long, heart-rending letter explaining that he wouldn't be able to come because Yasuko couldn't accompany him due to her teaching responsibilities. In it, he was compelled to enumerate the many indignities of his illness, his utter helplessness without Yasuko, and the myriad ways his body and mind had broken down. He ended the letter:

> There are so many other things I want to tell you, but I'll close by saying that I deeply want to be a strong, close father to you, and that I love you very very much. I'm sorry to be weak and geographically if not emotionally distant. I have been fighting for my very life these past few years and have very little energy left. Please understand that. Give my love to Sasha.
>   Much love,
>   Daddy

He was deeply concerned that Claire would be heartbroken as a result of his absence. In fact, she was relieved. She wouldn't have to worry about the tension involved in having him and my mother together, the stress of shepherding him physically and emotionally through a weekend of celebrations. Nicky walked her down the aisle, and a few months after the wedding she had a little afternoon party for my father at Sasha's family's apartment on Riverside Drive. At this point unable to walk without a cane and Yasuko's arm, our father was ensconced in a comfortable armchair, holding court as family and friends came to pay obeisance. He especially loved it that Sasha's family dogs, two Australian wolfhounds, wouldn't leave his feet. Carrie was the guest he was happiest to see; she brought him one of her famous pound cakes to take home and sat by his side, stroking his hand reassuringly and making him laugh by sharing memories of sweet little Priscilla and spunky little Claire.

Back in Japan, my father began work on a review of the collected Lionel Trilling for the *New York Times Book Review*, and as Yasuko reported, the fighting for his very life he'd mentioned in his letter to Claire took on an even deeper resonance:

> This is special good news: he is back to writing again. Once in the morning and once in the afternoon, he goes to his study and writes, little by little, but constantly. He's excited to realize that he *can* still write. He long has had a gnawing fear that he's lost the ability for concentration and lucid thinking. And I know he has a deep sense of the limited time given him. Of course he may be able to live many many years to come. Still we never know what's waiting in ambush. Now that he is writing, his morale is good, and this seems to be activating all his other functions, mental and physical. It's a heroic battle, without exaggeration.

The martial metaphors Yasuko used are reminiscent of the gladiatorial stance of my father and his 1960s and '70s compadres in art and criticism. Only now my father was without a cohort, without students, ill in a foreign country, tenuously holding on to his identity by putting words on the page. His battle to analyze and write became analogous to and inextricably bound up with his battle to live.

His Trilling piece, "The Foremost Authority," published in September of 2000, was the last review my father ever wrote, the last time he publicly inhabited the role of critic and exerted his own authority in print. He began to have more difficulty swallowing. He was weaker, less able to move on his own, unable to sit up at the computer for extended periods. There was no sign that the cancer had returned, but the debilitating effects of the treatments and the enfeebling effects of old age were taking a relentless toll.

The fall of 2001 was a grim time for my father. He was devastated by 9/11 and felt helpless and adrift so far away from New York City. And after a series of choking incidents, the doctors insisted that he needed a tracheotomy—which involved cutting a permanent hole in his throat into which a tube would be inserted to suction out his phlegm—and a feeding tube. He was also becoming increasingly confused and suspicious of people's intentions. He'd refuse to allow the nurses and doctors to care for him, would flail around trying to rip out his tubes, and would sometimes scream and yell and curse at Yasuko, asking what she had done to his wife. He was raging against the dying of the light, to be sure, but his rage was misguided, hurtful, and irrational. He received a diagnosis of dementia, caused either by the radiation or by new brain tumors.

With these alarming medical developments came another blow. "I'm sure now that your father will never be able to travel to New York again," Yasuko told me, Nicky, and Claire in an email, "so I've made arrangements to sell the apartment to our neighbors." She presented the sale as a fait accompli. When we heard how little she'd gotten for the apartment, which had nearly tripled in value since my father had bought it, we nearly shrieked in frustration. But how could we begrudge her anything she felt she needed to do? She hadn't told my father—"It might kill him if he knew," she said—and swore us to secrecy.

At virtually the same time Yasuko told us that Daddy would never be able to come to the States again, I discovered I was pregnant with my second child. Given that my health insurance was limited to a fifty-mile radius of New Haven, this happy news meant I wouldn't be able to take a trip to Japan. It seemed likely that I might never see my father again, never be able to say goodbye to him in person. I had lost him to an ocean, a country, a continent.

In January 2002, a call from a preschool to which we'd taken Benj for an interview alerted us to concerns about his speech and social behavior. A developmental evaluation at the Yale Child Study Center resulted in diagnoses of severe fine motor delays, moderate gross motor delays, a speech disorder, sensory integration disorder, and challenges with socializing and imaginative play. We were told that the precocious reading, spelling, and counting we'd thought were signs of our unusual little boy's brilliance were in fact symptoms of a disorder called hyperlexia, considered by many experts to be a subset of high-functioning autism. He would need occupational therapy, speech therapy, sensory therapy, and might never go to a regular school or attend college. Benj's present life was consumed by checklists and assessments, appointments and therapies. His future seemed terrifyingly at risk.

I kept all of this from my father and Yasuko. I thought that it might kill Daddy to learn that Benj faced so many challenges. And so I shared news of Benj's voracious reading without telling him about hyperlexia. I protected my father and Yasuko from any bad news, anything that might ruffle their fragile equanimity. Now more than ever, I felt that they needed me to be strong, successful, serene. They were thrilled that I'd gotten a tenure-track job offer at Vassar and that Vassar had given Richard a half-time position.

I don't know precisely when I last heard my father's voice, but over time it dwindled from a throaty whisper to a breathy murmur or exclamation to nothing at all. A man whom Anatole Broyard had called "a brilliant talker" in his memoir, *Kafka Was the Rage*, was now reduced to an immobile, unresponsive body. He was utterly silent, confined to a hospital bed that had been set up in the apartment's living room, unable to eat or drink, move, speak, or smile.

With my father in a waking coma and his condition essentially unchanging, I was able to throw myself into getting all the therapeutic supports available for Benj, adapting to a new job at Vassar and a new house in Poughkeepsie, and parenting sweet but high-needs Baby James. James was up three times a night, and I was exhausted, often sick, and increasingly sure that despite my joy in teaching, I wasn't happy as a professional academic. My marriage was also under severe strain as Richard and I coped with Benj's challenges in precisely opposite ways and his own issues with procrastination and perfectionism grew worse. But I continued to share only good news and positive developments—the publication of one of my dissertation chapters in the prestigious journal *ELH* (*English Literary History*), a bonus I received for teaching excellence, appearances at top academic conferences—with Yasuko, who insisted that my father understood it all and indicated his approval or delight with movements of his eyes. About my piece being published in *ELH*, she wrote:

> Dearest Priscilla, you keep giving your Daddy such pleasure and satisfaction. The deep emotion he felt when I was reading your wonderful news was expressed by the many tender

wrinkles around his eyes. And I know not only this news but
that you wanted to tell him about your achievement pleased
him a lot. I held the piece in front of him, and just by reading
the first page he had tears welling up. It will take time,
Priscilla. But the mere fact that he showed such desire to read
it means a lot.

Were his tears actually in response to my name, my words, my
achievement? Or were they involuntary, merely physical, and given
a beneficent interpretation by a loving wife and stepmother? There
was no way to know. How I longed to give my father pleasure and satisfaction. How I feared that pleasure and satisfaction were no longer
within his reach. And at the same time, I often hoped his reactions
were not the emotional responses Yasuko saw them as. I had written
several papers on Yeats's "Sailing to Byzantium" under my father's
tutelage, and he'd always especially loved these lines:

Consume my heart away; sick with desire
And fastened to a dying animal
It knows not what it is; and gather me
Into the artifice of eternity.

The idea of my father's heart being sick with desire yet fastened
to the dying animal of his body, the idea of him craving release from
the prison of his physical being, was almost unbearable. I was often
asked: Would it be better or worse if he had consciousness, emotions,
ideas locked inside his head? Far worse, in my mind. The thought of
him yearning to be gathered into the artifice of eternity and those
tubes and devices prolonging his life unnaturally haunted me. But
this was what Yasuko wanted. She was comforted by what she called
his "angelic presence" in the bed, the calm and quiet of their life
together, his slow, gentle journey into that good night.

In the last years of my father's physical decline, as he slipped slowly out of life, I didn't give myself time for sadness. I was finishing a dissertation, working as a tenure-track English professor, parenting two young boys, one on the autism spectrum, and dealing with a failing marriage. I couldn't allow myself to feel the full weight of my sorrow. "You mustn't be sad," I'd lovingly chided Harry Carson in the letter my father immortalized in print, and I'd lived by that mantra, for good and ill. This insistence on soldiering on through disappointment, trauma, and loss, this buoyant optimism, had served me well as I weathered my parents' split, Sarah's illness and death, Benj's special needs, and my father's diagnosis and diminishment, but they came at a cost. I didn't allow myself to truly feel or acknowledge the terror, disorientation, and profound sadness that must have accompanied these situations and experiences. And I certainly didn't share those feelings with others. I feared being a burden. I feared undermining the listener's own well-being. I feared appearing weak and vulnerable rather than strong and capable. I feared not being able to parent effectively if I leaned in to or came face-to-face with my own wounded child. I feared playing anything other than the role I'd been assigned at a very young age: the happy, resilient, reliable one who counseled and supported, cheered up and calmed others. Even though the role and the self were closely related, even though I'd been chosen for the role because it wasn't a stretch, playing it to the hilt took a toll.

Another role that had taken a toll was my identity as a professional academic. At the same time that our parents fostered our independence from cultural norms, they wanted for me and Claire the safety and security, the buffer and benefits, of academic credentials and institutional prestige. I had always greatly admired my father's idiosyncratic career path, forged on his own terms. Because he was on the fringe of academia, he didn't have to toe the line, pay his dues, use footnotes, and he'd appreciated these liberties that tenure-track faculty lacked. But for him, a sense of satisfaction in his distinctive career was always mixed with insecurity. When he gave a talk and his placard or name tag said "Dr. Gilman," he felt both proud and fraudulent, but he kept those placards, even displaying some of them on the shelves around his writing desk. And my mother had always lamented concentrating in theater and never getting to study philosophy or literature in depth. Whenever I'd been dissatisfied or unhappy in college or graduate school, I'd felt guilty because my parents would have killed to have the opportunities I did.

But my unease in academia was getting stronger. I adored teaching, but the idea of turning my dissertation into a book filled me with dread. My children were my priority, and for a parent, these years were the most important and demanding. And I yearned to write with greater immediacy and emotion, to use my words and ideas to connect, rather than to assert or argue or theorize. I was terrified of letting my mentors down if I chose to leave; when I'd dangled the possibility a few years earlier, several of them had been furious, others baffled. "Why, why would you disinvest yourself of all the prestige you've worked so hard to accrue?" one professor asked. But that prestige mattered not a whit to me anymore. Losing Sarah, Benj's special needs, my father's illness and decline, had put things into perspective.

When I sang "Tonight" and "Somewhere" from *West Side Story* to Benj and James at night, in the dark, the tears I stuffed down during the day couldn't help but slip out. These were songs I'd performed for my parents in the shows Claire and I had put on, songs that crystallized for me just what it was I had had with my father and was longing for with my husband and my son. Intense feeling and connection, two selves opening to and appreciating and elevating each other, dreaminess and exuberance, miracles and stars, the transformation of the ordinary into the extraordinary. My childhood, the early days of my romance with Richard, my dreams for my marriage, my life devoted to literature, my hopes for motherhood, had been full of light, with suns and moons all over the place.

But academia felt sterile and confining. My marriage had lost its romantic charge. My father was gravely ill, greatly diminished, without his energetic spark or imaginative fire. Benj was aloof and distant, uninterested in hugs or imaginative play. I wanted miracles to happen: A cure for my father's terminal cancer. A way to find myself back to the deep sense of kinship Richard and I had once had. Benj's emergence from the insulated world he lived in and the blooming of his capacity for love.

"Tonight" is the song of intensity, the onrush and euphoria of love; "Somewhere" the song of yearning for serenity and peace. I had neither joy nor tranquillity with my work, my father, my husband, or my child. I had to maintain a constant vigilance over Richard, whose procrastination and perfectionism meant bills didn't get paid, papers didn't get graded, groceries didn't get bought, and over my little boy, whose every move and utterance had to be documented for therapists and evaluations and whose days were filled with therapy sessions and hours upon hours of work with me and his father. I wanted a time and place where I could relax my vigilance. Where I didn't have to worry so much, or feel imminent threats to my loved ones, or the imminent loss of those I loved most.

My career and marriage offered me little nourishment. Benjamin's future was in peril. My father was on a grim march toward death. Would Benj ever be able to give and receive love? Would my caring for him ever matter? Could my father feel my love and care so many thousands of miles away? Could I find a new way of living, without the drum of anxiety, the thrum of fear, the listlessness and lack of hope? There was no one to take my hand. Richard and I never held hands anymore. Benj wouldn't hold my hand. My father's hand, withered and wasted, was across an ocean.

By the spring of 2004, Benj had made astonishing progress. The wonderful lab nursery school at Vassar, a cadre of ingenious, empathetic therapists, my and Richard's unswerving devotion, and my mother's tireless support had all helped him to bloom emotionally and socially. He was saying "I love you" and "Mommy," he was using his favorite *Frog and Toad* and *George and Martha* stories to help make sense of his experiences, he was developing a fascination with nature and a passion for music.

There was good news, too, about my father. Yasuko wrote to say that his miscellaneous writings had been collected by a former student and the book would be published by Yale University Press! But it had been a while since she'd heard anything about the publication and asked if I would check up on things. When I googled the title, I saw a biography that read, "The late Richard Gilman was a professor . . ." and I plunged into action; I felt an urgency to stop this before it went to print and do everything in my power to keep it from Yasuko. I immediately emailed both the former student and Yale University Press to tell them that my father was still alive and it would greatly distress my stepmother to have him presented this way.

It turned out not only that the former student who'd edited the collection had been fired from his university for plagiarism but also that his introduction was plagiarized—some of it from my father's work! Gordon Rogoff, stalwart as ever, had uncovered the misdeed and taken the book in hand. Perhaps, we agreed, the plagiarist had relegated my father to the grave so the book wouldn't need to be checked or approved. But the misrepresentation, so potentially hurtful to Yasuko, was uncannily accurate in that my father, for all Nicky could tell on his recent visit, had no consciousness at all.

And now I would see for myself. With five-year-old Benj thriving and James no longer a baby, I at last felt confident enough to leave them and embark on a trip to Japan. I tried to resist the quixotic hope that my father would respond or react to me. But I knew I needed to be in his presence nonetheless.

> Chekhov wishes to reveal how time, as we experience it, is always and only the present, how the future is always illusion, the past always absence or loss.
>
> —Richard Gilman, *The Making of Modern Drama*

> For love, all love of other sights controls,
> And makes one little room an everywhere.
>
> —John Donne

My first morning in Japan, I walked the few blocks from my hotel to the building where my father lay dying. As I rode the elevator to the apartment on the twenty-third floor, I steeled myself against being overwhelmed by the sight of Daddy; Nicky had warned me that it was horrifying. But nothing could have prepared for me for the first glimpse of my father lying in a hospital bed in the living room. His head was starkly bald (a lasting effect of the radiation), his blazing blue-green eyes staring blankly, his face—the most animated, expressive, alive face I have ever seen—frozen into a mask of impassivity. He lay absolutely still, with tubes suctioning mucus from his throat, giving him nourishment, and disposing of his waste.

The apartment smelled both stagnant and sterile and medical supplies sat on counters and shelves, but Yasuko had nonetheless created a cheerful and serene environment. He was swaddled in the blue-and-white sheets and blankets that had once covered Claire's and my twin beds in our country bedroom. Bookcases lined with my father's favorite books surrounded the bed, green plants hung from the ceiling and spilled out of pots in each corner, flowers filled the living room's balcony. Photos of me and Claire and my children bedecked the shelves, Nicky's paintings hung on the walls. Super Grover, faithful as always, dangled from one of the metal bed's posts. I had been expecting a depressing scene, but love had made my father's little room an everywhere.

I stood near my father's head and spoke to him in a jaunty voice, mustering the cheer I'd always summoned for him. I told him about James's love of Grover and Benj's passion for the Giants and Mets. I conveyed well wishes from friends and former students. Nothing I said changed his expression at all.

Later, I sat at the dining table with Yasuko, who served me green tea and delicious food she'd prepared. Acutely aware of my father lying several feet away, I was determined to keep the conversation light and pleasant, but Yasuko was so naturally empathetic that she soon elicited confessions from me. Her kind eyes and gentle, mellifluous voice unlocked something inside me and the words came tumbling out. I told her at last about the severity of Benj's challenges—the grim warnings that he might never interact socially or say "I love you," the incredible therapists and wonderful preschool that had helped him so much, how he was now blooming in ways that exceeded all predictions. I told her that after years of agonizing—so great were my reluctance to break our family and do to my children what my parents had done to me and Claire and my fear of plunging Richard into a despair akin to my father's—I'd decided to end my marriage. We would do it thoughtfully, with a mediator, and mutual respect and love, always. I told her that I was on the brink of leaving academia, dispirited by its lack of emphasis on truth and beauty, tired of its petty politics and rigid definitions of worth, cramped by the smallness of its universe and exhausted by the relentlessness of the tenure clock. I longed for a more family-friendly career and to write for a wider audience. I told her that being a tenure-track professor in an English department was a far cry from working in a drama department as an independent scholar, that literature in the academy was to be interrogated, not cherished, and that I'd felt my passion for art thwarted at every turn. My decisions to leave my marriage and academia were intertwined. I'd stayed in academia as long as I had in part because Richard had gotten jobs as a "trailing spouse." I confessed that ending my career as an academic represented my shedding the identity others had wanted for me. I'd come to realize that I'd taken on the role of an academic in large part in order to please my parents, then my professors, who'd become parental figures, and ultimately my husband, but that being an academic had never felt entirely comfortable or rewarding.

"What you say is exactly how I feel, being a professor!" she exclaimed. "My creativity seems to have dwindled a lot, especially since Richard stopped talking to me. He was a great bulwark against the tsunami of demands of that very limited academic world. I know your daddy would want you to break free from the oppressions of academia," she told me firmly, "and that he would be so proud of how you're handling the split from Richard." Yasuko not only understood, she gave me the support, the validation, the blessing my father couldn't. My eyes filled with tears.

Unable to converse with my father, I attempted to connect with him via poetry and music (it occurs to me now that these were also the two things that connected me to distant, aloof little Benj). I'd sing "Somewhere" and "Tonight," "Oh, What a Beautiful Mornin'" and "Edelweiss." Reading poems by Gerard Manley Hopkins, like my father a tortured Catholic who fought his sexual proclivities, celebrated "all things counter, original, spare, strange," and saw the spiritual and the aesthetic as intertwined, I found comfort in the words and lines and phrases I'd first explored in conversation with Daddy. One day I chose Dylan Thomas's "Fern Hill," a poem about the bliss of childhood on a farm in Wales, one that my father and I had exclaimed over together. I could barely get the words out, and as I came to the end, my voice faltered:

> Oh as I was young and easy in the mercy of his means,
> Time held me green and dying
> Though I sang in my chains like the sea.
> My father's eyes looked a little shinier.

And then I read "The Lake Isle of Innisfree" by his favorite poet, W. B. Yeats, the poem he had cited as the inspiration for his favorite trip ever, to Ireland with Yasuko, a few years after their marriage:

> I will arise and go now, and go to Innisfree,
> And a small cabin build there, of clay and wattles made:
> Nine bean-rows will I have there, a hive for the honey-bee;
> And live alone in the bee-loud glade.

> And I shall have some peace there, for peace comes dropping
>   slow,
> Dropping from the veils of the morning to where the cricket
>   sings;
> There midnight's all a glimmer, and noon a purple glow,
> And evening full of the linnet's wings.

I will arise and go now, for always night and day
I hear lake water lapping with low sounds by the shore;
While I stand on the roadway, or on the pavements grey,
I hear it in the deep heart's core.

I saw tears welling from my father's eyes. I wiped them away with tiny cotton squares that Yasuko handed me. I kissed him on his bald pate. And as I rose to go on the last night of my stay, I feared I was leaving him forever. But I knew that wherever I was, my father would be in my deep heart's core.

———

The drama is coming now, sir, something new, complex, most interesting.

—Pirandello, *Six Characters in Search of an Author*

In the fall of 2005, *The Drama Is Coming Now: The Theater Criticism of Richard Gilman, 1961–1991* was published, and Yale Drama School sponsored a book launch event on Yale's campus. Gordon and I chose a panel of readers including the two of us, David Epstein, and Stanley Kauffmann. Claire thought she would be too emotional to read, so she bowed out. On a beautiful Friday afternoon in late September, I drove up to New Haven with Sasha and Claire. I'd moved to New York City a month earlier in search of better special education schools for Benj, a richer social life in the wake of my split from Richard, the embracing presence of my extended family. I was on sabbatical from Vassar that semester and planned to commute upstate to teach my classes in the spring, but I'd already decided to resign from my position and join my mother's literary agency the following summer. I was glad my father would never have to know that I'd chosen to work alongside my mother as an agent, rather than as the critic and teacher he'd always wanted me to be. It felt odd to be traveling to Yale just as I was on the cusp of leaving academia forever.

Though ostensibly celebratory, the book launch felt like a proleptic memorial service. All of us at one point or another slipped into speaking of my father in the past tense and then hastily corrected ourselves, aware that Yasuko would watch the recording of the event. Some of the introductions hovered perilously on the verge of eulogy.

There was humor too. We laughed as Gordon read this from a piece celebrating fifty years of the *Village Voice*:

> Lest anyone think I have nothing but praise for Off-Broadway and Off-Off-Broadway, I offer some strictures and indictments. There was a near infinitude of boring occasions over these thirty years, theatrical epiphanies of appalling dullness, and there was widespread lack of skill, sometimes compensated for by ardor and ideality but more often not. And also: self-indulgence; juvenile acting-out; theory run amok; false gurus, fake avant-gardism, dreary imitations of Beckett, Ionesco, Pinter; a dispiriting hunt for modern "myths"; an equally dispiriting idea that you could devise "rituals" as though they were party games; an obnoxious belief that if you shouted "Love!" and "Freedom!" loudly enough you would bring them about; and other instances of nonsense, witlessness, and *dreck*.
>
> —"Jest, Satire, Irony, and Deeper Meaning:
> Thirty Years of Off-Broadway"

"Nonsense, witlessness, and dreck": my father's eviscerating critical voice filled the room with its wit and power. But at other moments, Gordon, David, and Stanley choked back tears and fought for composure as they expressed how very much they missed him.

And one passage from Stanley's speech struck me with its wisdom, its empathy, its penetrating appreciation of my father's essential vulnerability:

> There's some congruence between true, serious criticism and belief in something large or dear or dangerous. For Dick, to enter the universe of art, to enter its service as best one can as a critic, is to manifest some belief, or at least—maybe more important—some hunger for belief. That for me is the key to all Dick's work. I can't separate it—this book or that book or the other book—from faith, sex, and mystery. He put it on record that his spiritual life is part of the tissue of his artistic life . . . When I took down my copy of *Faith, Sex, Mystery*, I found that I'd stuck in it a copy of the review of the book from the *New York Times* by the novelist Mary Gordon. She said about the book: "It has nothing of the museum piece about it: rather, it is the cry of the living, wounded soul, hungering for the promise of a larger life."

In that pre-memorial moment, it seemed that this indeed had been my father's struggle: to reconcile his intellectual rigor and insistence on lucidity and precision with his hunger for belief, his spiritual yearnings, his sense of something beyond the capacity of words to describe or the mind to grasp and master. He erected organic but increasingly hardened carapaces of eloquence and authority to protect the sensitive, vulnerable parts of himself. By the time of *Faith, Sex, Mystery* and even more in his Chekhov book, he was coming out of that shell, allowing himself to lay bare his "living, wounded soul" and his hunger for a larger life, for what he called "an opening into eternity."

At the reception, when I caught sight of my father's former student Sandra Boynton and her daughter Caitlin, who had been one of my most cherished students at Yale, I finally burst into tears. It touched me that they had come to support both Daddy and me. It spoke to the continuity of his and my teaching lives. Their warmth and kindness penetrated the composed, performative façade I'd adopted during the event and elicited the sadness I'd been suppressing.

Over the next year, Richard and I settled our divorce in the most amicable way possible. We wrote a parenting plan that covered everything from financial arrangements to our parenting philosophy, devised a flexible joint custody arrangement, and agreed to a nesting setup until James was six (the kids stayed in my apartment, Richard rented a studio close by, and I stayed at my mom's on nights he was with them). I did everything I could to avoid the scenario and the situation that had so weighed on me and Claire. My boys would never have to compare their mother's luxurious abode to their father's temporary, provisional, depressing ones, never have to see their father cry with shame or sadness at not being able to provide them with comfortable rooms or delicious meals, never have to sleep over in unfamiliar, unsettling surroundings. Most important, they would never have to feel pulled between two warring parents. Richard and I attended every conference together, sat side by side at school events, spoke daily about Benj's and James's experiences, needs, challenges, and triumphs. We would spend holidays together (and one day even live in the same apartment building).

Our solidarity had been crucial in helping the boys weather the many transitions—to a new city, a new home, and new schools. After a rough first year, Benj was now thriving in his special education school. James was a sweet and hilarious four-year-old with a pack of buddies at the wonderful Upper West Side preschool Claire and I had attended. I was now the proud aunt of Sanja and Sebastian, Claire and Sasha's beautiful baby twins.

Although I missed teaching, I'd felt an enormous sense of liberation once I stepped off that tenure track. Work at the literary agency allowed me to become an advocate for voices and visions I believed in. My agent friend Tina, who was now my colleague, had suggested I combine talks I'd given at literary romanticism conferences with those I'd delivered to parents and educators at early childhood conferences, so after a year or two of intermittent work, I finally had a piece called "The Anti-Romantic Child" that Tina was sending to magazines.

One afternoon in late October, Yasuko wrote to say that my father seemed to be declining and might only live another few months. We'd received warnings like this several times before, but I began thinking about traveling to Japan to see him. The next night was the wedding of one of my closest high school friends. I danced exuberantly with my friends and arrived home a bit giddy. Sitting in my desk chair in my slinky black dress, scrolling through my email, I saw one with no subject from Yasuko and opened it:

> Dear Nick, Priscilla, and Claire,
>   Your daddy passed away last night (12:12 a.m., Oct. 29). No struggle, no pain. Suddenly he stopped breathing, without any sign of doing so. In peace. He had reached the limit and decided to leave.

Nearly ten years after being diagnosed with terminal lung cancer and given seven months to live, my father's body had at last given out. Even though I had long prepared myself for this inevitability, even though he hadn't spoken or moved in over four years, this stark announcement of his death felt unreal and impossible.

Claire was staying at a hotel in DC that weekend with Sasha and their four-month-old twins; I called the front desk and had them wake her up. Hearing her voice broke through the numbness and opened the floodgates for me; we both sobbed uncontrollably into the receiver. After hanging up the phone, I lay in bed unable to sleep, soaking the pillow and sheets with tears. The intensity of my emotion surprised me. My father had had no quality of life for years. We'd had no real relationship for years. There had never been a possibility he would improve. But a line from a letter by John Keats kept running through my head: "Land and Sea, weakness and decline are great separators, but death is the great divorcer for ever." My father and I had been separated by land and sea for years. His weakness and decline had rendered him unable to communicate with me. But this was the great divorcer, for ever.

The next day I spoke to Nicky and emailed back and forth with Yasuko. She had already had my father cremated and had planned a Catholic wake for the next day. There was no way any of the children could get to Japan in time. I was deputized to call or email all of my father's friends and family in the US, and was strong, clear, comforting to his stricken friends. I emailed relevant information to the *New York Times*' obituary department, including the confirmation that my father's year of birth was 1923, not 1925. But in between the doing, I was overtaken by grief. I'd find myself doubled over in my chair, moaning, gasping for air between sobs.

I pulled myself together for the boys, who arrived home from a weekend at my mother's country house around 6 p.m. They'd heard about my father's death from my mother, and both tentatively offered their own means of consolation. James asked if I wanted to sleep in his bed that night; Benj offered to sing for me or play me some guitar pieces. I tried to protect the boys from my grief—reassuring them I'd be OK, then crying in the bathroom with the water running. But their sweet solicitousness and innocent certainty that my father was now in heaven were disarming in ways I couldn't protect myself against. James would wipe his little hands across my tear-stained cheeks or throw his arms around my waist, burying his head in my stomach and telling me over and over: "Mommy, you still have us! You'll always have us!" Benj was only just getting comfortable with showing physical affection, and his hugs were brittle and awkward. Coincidentally, we were on the last few chapters of *Charlotte's Web* that week, and when I read the last bit to him, I couldn't hold back the tears anymore:

> Wilbur never forgot Charlotte. Although he loved her children and grandchildren dearly, none of the new spiders ever quite took her place in his heart. She was in a class by herself. It is not often that someone comes along who is a true friend and a good writer. Charlotte was both.

As Benj tentatively stroked my arm, he said in his sweet gravelly voice: "Your father was a true friend and a good writer, too, Mommy." His genuine empathy showed me how far he'd come and touched me at my core. Terrific, radiant, humble little Benj—how my father would have loved him.

In the days following my father's death, calls from old friends came in at the agency, and my mother accepted the condolences graciously, reminisced about old times affectionately, then passed the phone to me. I could hear her telling Wilfred Sheed, Lionel Tiger, Christopher Lehmann-Haupt how hard my father's prolonged and horrific decline had been on me, how much I'd loved him. I was amazed that she was speaking of my father without the contempt that had laced her voice ever since they had separated. Her ability to move, at last, beyond criticism to kindness pierced me almost as much as my grief at losing him. Why couldn't she have shown this empathy—for him and for me and Claire, who loved him—while he was alive??

> Grief, when it comes, is nothing like we expect it to be . . . Grief has no distance. Grief comes in waves, paroxysms, sudden apprehensions that weaken the knees and blind the eyes and obliterate the dailiness of life.
>
> —Joan Didion, *The Year of Magical Thinking*

My mother had been the first to go to Joan's apartment on the night John dropped dead of a sudden heart attack, and ever since had been Joan's steadfast companion, encouraging her to channel her grief into writing, gently coaxing her back into the dailiness of life by taking her out to dinner and lunch. I had read *The Year of Magical Thinking* in galley proof a few months before it was published in October of 2005. Staying at my mom's Connecticut weekend house, I had answered the phone call breaking the news that Joan's daughter, Quintana, had died at thirty-nine. I had gone to John's heartbreaking memorial and then to Quintana's. And now those waves, paroxysms, apprehensions Joan had described were mine. One of the first condolence notes I got was from Joan. "My Dearest Priscilla," it began, "I know how much you loved your very brilliant father. Life must feel unreal right now. I love you very much." The waves swept over me.

I lost my father over and over until he died, but almost as soon as he left the physical world, he came back—suddenly, shockingly, painfully. The grief leveled me, ravaged me, sent me reeling. I could hear his voice in my head for the first time in years, I could remember again how he'd been when he was well. Notes from friends and former students poured in; beautiful obituaries distilled what made him distinctive, their anecdotes and adjectives—"elegant and contentious voice," "eloquent and exacting," "critical sharpness and personal warmth," "an enthusiastic raconteur who eschewed theory and jargon for a more humanistic and personal view of drama"— conjuring up all his impressive and endearing uniqueness. My eyes were blinded by tears again and again.

Yale Drama School offered to sponsor a memorial service for my father at Symphony Space on the Upper West Side the following March. It would be held in the theater next to the movie auditorium where he'd so often taken us as little girls. A committee was convened to plan the event, and meetings were held every third Friday afternoon at Gordon Rogoff's apartment. With some of our father's colleagues and former students, Claire and I sat around Gordon's dining table, where we'd eaten pizza and butter almond-ginger ale ice cream sodas with our father those Saturday nights so long ago, and laughed, reminisced.

One day a few weeks before the service, a mailer arrived for me from Japan. I tore it open to find a note from Yasuko paper-clipped to a large manila envelope. "Here are the contents of a box labeled GIRLS that your daddy brought with him to Japan. I can imagine how deeply the evidence of your father's love for you two will move you." I opened the envelope with trembling hands. Photos of me and Claire tumbled out, all the ones he'd stuck on the dingy walls of his sublets. Tape marks were still visible around their edges. There were Yale Drama School envelopes marked "Girls' Hair" with long blond strands visible through the thin paper, report cards, letters and postcards we'd sent him from sleepaway camp, drawings, all the consoling notes on Hello Kitty or Snoopy stationary that I wrote him after the separation, and then there was this poem, written out in my childish handwriting on a piece of my father's typing paper:

Loneliness

Loneliness is when no one listens,
When no one seems to know who you are.
Loneliness is a grey sky no one looks at,
A balloon when no one's holding the string.
Loneliness is strange to me,
A distant thought.
  —*Priscilla Gilman, age 9*

Loneliness was no longer strange to me. Without my father in the world, would anyone know who I truly was?

ACT 5

GLIMPSES AND GLIMMERINGS, RECKONING AND RECOMPENSE

What we miss—what we lose and what we mourn—isn't it this that makes us who, deep down, we truly are.

—Sigrid Nunez, *The Friend*

You must go on, I can't go on, I'll go on.

—Samuel Beckett, *The Unnamable*

Voices, ghostly faces, in the light still. The theater in Beckett's hands has abandoned events, direct clashes, inquiries, representations. What remains is the theatrical impulse itself, this thrust toward the truth about our condition: that it consists in enactment, presence, the painful necessity to remain visible. "Tell him you saw us," Didi says to Godot's messenger. To be seen, heard, by a Godot, by each other, and, in the darkness, ourselves: this is an obligation, a fate, and, finally, a story.

—Richard Gilman, *The Making of Modern Drama*

The day of my father's memorial was bright and temperate for March. Having the event in a theater rather than a private home or a religious space helped me stay calm, steady, and composed. Even as it was filled with strong emotion, painfully vivid memories, and people who brought the past back to me, it was nonetheless a production, and as one of the producers, directors, and actors, I could not cry. I wanted to preside over the event with grace, warmth, and a welcoming energy that would invite others to feel at ease.

During the memorial, sitting hand in hand with Claire, I listened to my father described by André Gregory as "brilliant, irascible, charming, cantankerous, warm, difficult, and fascinating." I heard him celebrated for his "generous, overflowing imagination," his "mystical stew of erudition, piercing insight, and sudden wit," his "moral passion." I nodded in recognition as friends described the way he "wore eccentricities like so many badges of honor" and combined "a divine innocence" with "an equally divine sophistication."

And then it was the three children's turn. Nicky spoke of how my father taught him about humor by taking him to Marx Brothers, Buster Keaton, Chaplin, W. C. Fields, and Laurel and Hardy movies, imparted to him an existentialist sense of the absurdity of life, instilled in him a love of travel and adventure, bequeathed to him an "ironic, inquisitive, humorous, and slightly pugnacious attitude toward life." Then Claire got up to speak. She spoke movingly of Daddy's religion of childhood and reminisced about the magical childhood he'd given us; many of the anecdotes were things we'd discussed as I helped her shape the piece. The end of her eulogy, however, caught me off guard with the accuracy and courage of its insight:

> He never expressed disappointment in us . . . Indeed, I don't believe he ever felt any. Strangely enough, this attitude could sometimes make it difficult to be his daughter. It was a tall responsibility to be the best. And since that's what he believed us to be, we felt we had to deliver. Not in our achievements, mind you—he never pressured us in that way—but in our spirits, in our energy, in our joy of life. But I realize, too, that this was really our own issue, brought on by our fear of adding to his sadness following our parents' divorce. I know he would have embraced and absorbed any failing—and certainly did whenever we allowed him to—precisely because he could see no failing in us. With his abiding faith, he challenged us to pursue a moral life. More importantly, he taught us to be unafraid of showing love, risking failure, and seeking the truth. I love you, Daddy.

I was the final child to speak. Standing on the stage, I drew on all my experience as a performer and all my experience performing composure for my father. I began my eulogy with the opening lines of Wordsworth's "Ode: Intimations of Immortality":

> There was a time when meadow, grove, and stream,
> The earth, and every common sight,
> To me did seem
> Apparelled in celestial light,
> The glory and the freshness of a dream.

And then, in true Richard Gilman fashion, I went from high literature to sports:

> "Being a fan," he wrote, "means practicing a form of sympathetic magic, by which you suffer with, draw strength from, and generally share in the vicissitudes and personas of modern-day champions and heroes." He had always been our biggest fan and we his, and as we had drawn strength from him, so we suffered with him, as we basked in his sympathetic magic, so we had shared, wholeheartedly and without qualification, in his vicissitudes.

I ended with the closing lines of my father's *New York Times* article on me and the Giants followed by my own address to him: "So, Daddy, I say to you today: 'Didn't I tell you? I still love you. More than ever.'"

I made it down the stairs, to my seat and into Claire's waiting arms; then, as a friend played Bach's Cello Suite No. 1, we watched the slideshow of our father's life that we'd put together. Photos of him as a sweet-faced young boy, a young man excitedly banging away on a typewriter, delighting in dogs, sitting on a porch swing engrossed in a book, flashed past. There he was grinning ecstatically at Nicky and me and Claire as babies, reading to us as little girls curled up on his lap, throwing a football to me on the lawn in Weston, with a flower in his buttonhole at his wedding to Yasuko, beaming proudly at Claire's college graduation, cuddling Koko, and then, finally, in a wheelchair, bald and gaunt, gazing out a hospital window at a cherry tree in bloom.

The photo that opened and closed the slideshow had been taken in the living room of our apartment at 333 Central Park West. The seventies vibes are strong: my father is sitting on a wicker lounge chair, in head-to-toe denim and Wallabees. His hair is long and curly and a bit wild, he holds his heavy black-rimmed glasses in one hand as he gazes off over his shoulder, deep in thought, a subtle smile playing at the corners of his mouth. The photo had run with his obituary in the *New York Times*—we'd chosen it because it captured him in his prime, because it exemplified the core of who he was. It restored to us his celestial light.

Video footage from his 1979 appearance on *The Dick Cavett Show* provided welcome relief from the poignancy of the Bach-accompanied photo montage. Slim, tall, and more conventionally handsome than I'd remembered, my father was so funny, so clever, severe and seductive by turns. He deftly ducked and dodged Cavett's attempts to pin him down, he passionately defended ambiguity and mystery.

And if the Cavett appearance captured my father in all his critical authority, Gordon Rogoff's eulogy celebrated his capacity for romanticism. Gordon showed how Yasuko brought out the boyish passion in my father, allowed him to believe, despite all obstacles and threats, in a happy ending.

> I see him now as I'm not quite certain he saw himself: a delirious romantic, constantly falling in love with literature, plays, performers, paintings, football players, poker, and finally,

with Yasuko, the wonderful interpreter given to him when he was visiting Japan for the first time. On the Metro-North, he told me about what happened to him; between Stamford and Bridgeport, I saw him transformed into a giddy adolescent—the boy I never knew . . . And what was wondrous about the tale is that it already seemed so plausible, fraught with what the critic might have called "dramatic possibility." He had to know, as always, that drama comes with conflict, and in his later letters to us he even used phrases such as "the plot of my romance," even asking us to "bear with me: this is the sketch of a forthcoming romance-suspense series!" And finally: "Oh, what a tangled web we weave!" Best of all was the conclusion to one letter: "This is all crazy, of course, but then who wants to live rationally all the time!" (And, uncharacteristically, this was the third sentence ending with an exclamation point.)

Yasuko gave the final eulogy. She told us that while she had known "many Richards," his last face was that of a "boy-sage, a combination of innocence and serene dignity." She ended in her typically gracious, generous way: "Thank you for missing him. He loves to be missed." Oh that line! How he loved to be missed indeed.

In our words of loving tribute, in the photographs and video footage, the wounded giant had regained his dignity.

A few weeks after the memorial, my boys, now eight and almost five, announced that they wanted to watch *The Wizard of Oz* for the first time. I told them that although I dearly loved the film, I couldn't watch it with them. I set them up in front of the TV and fled to my bedroom. Once there, I put earplugs in and barricaded myself against the strains of its songs, the timbre of Judy Garland's singing, the voice of Ray Bolger as the Scarecrow.

When people asked me what my favorite movies were, I always included *The Wizard of Oz*. But I hadn't actually watched it in full since my parents' split. I couldn't. Because no movie so flooded me with a sense of longing and loss.

It was a movie our family watched every year, religiously. When I was nineteen, I wrote:

> I can never hear Judy Garland singing "Over the Rainbow" without tears coming to my eyes, I guess because I associate it with the illusion of happiness and security I had as a young child, when we lay in my parents' huge bed, I leaning my head on my father's shoulder, my sister curled up inside my mother's arm, and watched *The Wizard of Oz* on our Sony TV.

Why this movie, this song more than anything else? Well, it's about dreamy romanticism, and I am a romanticist after all. It's about longing for something better, purer, truer. It's about a land that I heard of once in a lullaby—the lullaby of my enchanted childhood, the land of play and make-believe and magic I'd created with Claire and that my father presided over and reveled in. And yet despite the beyond-the-rainbow dream of that childhood space, it was also true that I'd wished and wished on stars when it came to my father. As a little girl and for many years after, I'd think to myself: My father had a brain, he had a heart, he had courage in spades. If he only had an X. What was it he lacked? What was it he needed? What void in him could I fill? What need in him could I meet? What hurt in him could I assuage? How could I be the wizard who fixed the problem and restored him to his glorious, essential self?

The summer between seventh and eighth grades, I was cast as Dorothy in a summer camp production. I immediately wrote letters to my parents announcing the great news; my mom sent me a congratulatory card with ruby slippers embossed on the front, and my father's note on Yale Drama School stationary ended with this: "I'm so proud of you, Sidda. But you know, you've always been my Dorothy." Parents weren't allowed to visit for shows, and my father wouldn't have spent the money on planes and hotels in any case. But when I came home from camp late that August and arrived at his apartment, tanner and taller and more grown up than I'd been just a month earlier, the first thing he asked me to do after hugging me was to sing him "Over the Rainbow."

In my childhood, my father was always the Scarecrow to me: lithe and nimble, with "magic brains of a very superior sort," resourceful and plucky, and the one Dorothy will miss most of all. I had a Wizard of Oz play set—my favorite seventh-birthday gift—complete with an Emerald City backdrop and action figures. Before I went to sleep at night, I always arranged Dorothy and the Scarecrow holding hands or linking arms. Soon after my father moved out, I allowed my mother to give the play set away to a friend with young kids; I did so with no complaints or conscious sadness.

Now, in the wake of my father's memorial and with my children newly passionate about *The Wizard of Oz*, I found myself missing that Scarecrow doll more than I had in many years. And so, just a few days after I had tried to block out the film that most evoked my father, I invited it back into my life, searching furiously online for a Scarecrow like the one I had played with as a child. When I found it at last, I burst out crying, and when it arrived in the mail I gently and reverently lifted it out of the box and set it on a shelf over my desk, next to a photo of my father. Looking at its smiling, kind face, its disheveled exuberance, I could almost hear my father's excited, affectionate voice in my head, sense his game, always-up-for-an-expedition spirit, feel his arm in mine. My father and I often walked with arms linked just the way Dorothy and the Scarecrow did. And when we set out together, down College Street in New Haven or Broadway in New York, I always felt uplifted, as if at any given moment we could jump up and click our feet together and land back on the ground lightly. We were off to see the Wizard. We had infinite possibility before us. We were on an adventure, following a yellow brick road. And now that road was gone. We would never walk together again. My father was the one I would miss most of all.

In the acknowledgments to my first book, I thanked "my father, who taught me how to see, how to read, and how to love." I meant that as the highest tribute. My father taught me to empathize with outsiders, to see the essence, the vulnerable core of people, to be a fierce advocate for those who feel or fall outside the mainstream. He taught me to love ardently and unabashedly, loyally and with every aspect of my being. But there was a darker aspect to his tutelage. He taught me to love the insecure, the damaged, the needy. And after his death, my yearning for him drew me away from men who were whole, healthy, and secure toward those who suffered, struggled, teetered on the verge of insolvency or insanity, and desperately wanted me to nurture, bolster, save them.

Before my father died, I had mostly chosen men based on how they buffered me against the risks attendant on being with someone like him. I shied away from anyone who lived an unhealthy life, anyone who might cheat, anyone who struggled with compulsions and addictions. Richard had many of my father's best qualities while correcting for his most dangerous and unattractive flaws.

But in the months and for several years after my father's death, in my grief and disorientation, I connected with damaged, charismatic, complicated men who reminded me of him. I had a series of passionate roller-coaster flirtations, charged friendships, and romantic relationships with mercurial, artistic men plagued by insecurity, addictive tendencies, anger issues, or all three. I basked in the adoration they shone my way when they were in a buoyant mood. I've always been a sucker for songs about healing, calming, or lighting up men: Tom Petty's "Here Comes My Girl," Billy Joel's "She's Got a Way," Neil Young's "Mellow My Mind." My boyfriends would text or email me these songs with a note that said a version of "You do this for me" or "You are this for me." I had a smile that healed them, I mellowed their minds. Men would "get healthy" for me—one stopped drinking after we started dating, another daily pot smoker never smoked again after our first date. When they told me they no longer needed mood- or mind-altering substances because they had me, I felt both powerful and concerned. I'd urge them to meditate, get into therapy, exercise, or find other stress-reduction methods that wouldn't put all the burden for their wellness on me.

I stayed longer than I should have in these entanglements because there was something both gloriously and sickeningly familiar about the way I felt with these men. I loved their romantic ardor, their commitment to the arts, their devil-may-care sense of adventure and fun. I empathized, excused, made allowances for their outbursts of anger, their alternation between lighthearted playfulness and melancholic quietude, their irritability or impatience. As my father's daughter, I'd become an expert manager, skilled at discerning the warning signs—the hints that a mood was headed south, that the potential for upset or disappointment or offense was hovering—and either distracting or consoling. This ability served me well in navigating the shoals of academia, as an agent handling sensitive or testy writers, as the mother of boys in their terrible twos and their teens. But it also became too comfortably second nature for me as I brought those "skills" to my interactions with moody, temperamental men who needed managing. Walking on eggshells, tiptoeing around topics, coaxing someone into a good mood felt familiar to me. Because my father had told me he'd commit suicide were it not for me and Claire, when a man

I was dating tried to kill himself in front of me after I expressed some hesitation about the relationship, it felt both utterly terrifying and weirdly normal.

After my father's death, I gave my attention, my care, and my love away impetuously and recklessly; I drained my reserves, spent myself, laid waste my powers. The Charlotte to a host of Wilburs, I poured myself into cheering men up and reminding them how terrific they were, allowing my radiance to dim in the process. But eventually, I pulled back and away from each of these men. I saved myself. My psychiatrist told me I had "good survival skills."

In one therapy session, as I was agonizing over whether to end things with a brilliant, endearing, yet troubled guy, my psychiatrist broke in abruptly. "You don't need to be in a relationship with F to hold on to your father."

What? Where had *that* come from? F was nothing like my father. Or was he?

My therapist's questions in subsequent sessions became a rigorous inquisition for me:

Do you have guilt that you couldn't care for your father when he was dying?

Could taking care of these men emotionally be a way of making up for what you perceive to be your failure to save your father's life?

When you were a little girl, did you think that if your mother had made more of an effort, been more understanding, given him the second chance he asked for, he wouldn't have fallen apart?

Is it possible that your stepmother and your father's love against all odds and obstacles made you seek relationships steeped in difficulty and faced with extreme challenges?

Do you see that your experience with Benj and James, how you've nurtured their miraculous growth and helped them overcome so many challenges, may have reinforced your belief that if you work hard enough, you can save or rescue people?

Don't you deserve to be cared for, nurtured, and supported the way you care for, nurture, and support these men?

Would you ever have wanted to be married to your father?

Once the connection between losing my father and getting entangled with troubled men became clear, I read everything I could in the literature of Al-Anon and codependence. I attended Co-Dependents Anonymous meetings and worked with a therapist who specialized in codependency. I did an intensive teacher training to become a certified mindfulness and loving-kindness meditation teacher. My father would likely have scoffed at it all. But it was what I needed to break his spell and dispel his ghost, even as it helped increase my empathy and tenderness for the struggling soul he had been and for my mother's suffering in her marriage to him.

> [Nina] lives now in the recognition that nothing rescues and nothing ransoms, that she can expect no external force or human connection to embolden or give a warranty to her art, which will exist as the outcome of her acts of making it, of her free and responsible choice. What is true of her art is also true of her life ... [She] will live open-eyed and disenchanted, working, making herself, being what she is.
>
> —Richard Gilman on Chekhov's *The Seagull*,
> from *The Making of Modern Drama*

In a therapy session a few years after my father's death, my psychiatrist announced that she'd taken my "case" to her monthly psychiatrist meeting at which members presented their patients for the others' input. Their response? "Tell Priscilla she needs to stop being the supporting player in other people's dramas. She needs to write and direct and star in her own life." "Whoa! Did they know who my father was?" I asked. "No," she replied. "But this is the metaphor they chose."

In 2011, *The Anti-Romantic Child: A Story of Unexpected Joy* was published and launched me on a new career as a writer, public speaker, and advocate for children and autistic people. I would never have been able to effectively parent two children with special needs—Benj autistic, James dyslexic and dysgraphic—or devote myself to advocacy for those who aren't typical or "normal," had I not had my father's example in both thought and life. He celebrated individuality, originality, strangeness; he opposed reductive categories and labels; he took writers on their own terms. That's exactly what I try to do with my children, and exactly the message I convey in my talks to parents and teachers. The way that my father approached Brecht and Büchner is the way that I approach Benj and James, the children on whose behalf I give talks and write pieces, my students.

For I am still a teacher of literature. I lead book groups, helping others to love many of the books my father taught me to love, and I've taught poetry in public schools, to medical students at Mount Sinai, and in prisons. I teach classes on everything from Virginia Woolf to Milton, Jane Austen to Toni Morrison, for Yale Alumni College, where some of my students were my father's students many years ago. One of my most moving teaching experiences was at Still Waters in a Storm, an after-school program for at-risk immigrant children in Bushwick, Brooklyn, founded by one of my father's favorite students and inspired, that student says, by my father's legendary Criticism Workshop.

All three of my father's children are now, in one way or another, critics. After writing a few book reviews for the *Chicago Tribune, O, The*

Oprah Magazine, and the *New York Times Book Review*, I'm now a book critic for the *Boston Globe*, where I do my best to avoid the adjectives—haunting, stunning, gripping, striking—my father wanted banned from reviews. After getting a PhD in art history, Claire also left academia and is now chief curator of the Drawing Center in SoHo, where, like our father, she champions innovative, unconventional, or outsider art. Nicky has made a career swerve from painting to food criticism, publishing an acclaimed book about street food in Mexico City, writing food pieces for publications ranging from the *Guardian* to *Food & Wine*, regularly reviewing restaurants on his blog, and always taking care to deflate hype, convey enthusiasm, and approach his subjects with rigor and wit. As he puts it, all three of us are carrying on "the Gilmanian Critical Tradition."

Yasuko, too, has become a published critic. With a shrine to my father in her apartment and the memory of his faith in her as a living force, she spent the years after his death lovingly translating *The Making of Modern Drama* into Japanese and writing her first book, a study of *King Lear*, the play she and my father loved most.

I think of him tearing up as he recited *King Lear* to me:

No, no, no, no! Come, let's away to prison.
We two alone will sing like birds i' th' cage:
When thou dost ask me blessing, I'll kneel down,
And ask of thee forgiveness: so we'll live,
And pray, and sing, and tell old tales, and laugh
At gilded butterflies.

He told me and Claire of the play when we were very young, and called us "my two Cordelias." My father often said that the scene of Lear howling in anguish as he carries Cordelia's dead body onstage wrenched him more than any other in literature. And if I was a

Cordelia to him, he was King Lear to me, both "the great image of Authority" and "a very foolish fond old man," prone to "ungovern'd rage" and capable of immense sweetness, intellectually sophisticated yet innocent and utterly without pretense. He was easily provoked, he demanded loyalty, he could be cruel and arbitrary. But he was also loving and longing, flawed and worthy. Can I make him stay a little? If I can make him live again, "it is a chance which does redeem all sorrows / That ever I have felt."

> [Brecht's] work will never fail to exhibit a love, crafty, sober, theoretic, or impassioned as the case may be, for the human struggle to find a way through errors into a fullness of life.
> —Richard Gilman, from *The Making of Modern Drama*

In an obituary for my father, the *Los Angeles Times* hailed his "uncompromising critical voice"; this would have pleased him no end. But while he believed in the virtues of mercilessness, he would want our mercy. He would want mine, and his ex-wives', and all of ours. He knew he had done wrong. He hated his temper, his susceptibility to envy, his stinginess. He loved this line from Chekhov's notebook: "He alone is all right and can repent who feels himself to be wrong." My father felt himself to be wrong. He never defended himself for yelling or raging. My mother and numerous friends of his have told me that he never felt justified in his infidelities or relationships with students, that he saw them as injuries to those he loved, sins. He lived with a strong sense of shame about his sexuality, his emotional vulnerabilities, what he saw as his failure to make good on his religious beliefs. In *Faith, Sex, Mystery*, he described himself ruefully as "a lapsed Jewish-atheist-Catholic. Fallen from all three, a triple deserter!" He was guilty of error. He struggled to find his way through errors into a fullness of life.

Recently, I confronted my mother about calling my father's love for me narcissistic projection and telling me that it wasn't real. She instantly admitted she'd been wrong.

"He certainly loved you for who you were, Sid," she told me. "I just wanted to protect you from feeling you had to caretake him and from making the same mistakes I had. You know, I had a lot of apprehension about marrying him. A few weeks before our wedding, I was standing with Jacob and Lore Segal on the corner of Barrow Street near where we lived in SoHo and Jacob asked, in a tone of great concern, 'Lynn, are you sure you should marry him? You're so much *stronger* than he is.' In fact, I wasn't sure. When I first dated him, he had several meltdowns, crying and distraught about his life and work. I had to help him get over his writer's block, make sure his mood was OK. Always, I felt responsible for his stability. That he might break apart if I didn't manage everything well."

I understood, because that's how I'd felt, too.

A few weeks later, I asked my mother to put her reasons for marrying my father down in writing for me, and she sent me this:

> Why did I marry him? Well, he had a brilliant and refined mind which I respected and admired. I knew he would be an excellent father to you girls. Basically he was a kind and ethical man.

That simple phrase "excellent father" and that brief sentence "Basically he was a kind and ethical man" broke me. I put my head down on my desk and sobbed. I had been waiting almost forty years for her to say these things. And now she had affirmed them, clearly and directly. This was a balm like no other.

All the world's a stage,
And all the men and women merely players;
They have their exits and their entrances;
And one man in his time plays many parts.

—Shakespeare, *As You Like It*

My assumptions in this book are that drama ought to matter
to us as a source of consciousness, that great plays can be as
revelatory of human existence as novels or poems, that such
plays aren't discrete objects to which we "go" but analogues of
our lives which we encounter.

—Richard Gilman, *The Making of Modern Drama*

t's the spring of 2018, and I'm standing in the wings of a professional theater in downtown New York City. I'm in the second of my three costumes—this one a paisley flowy blouse and white jean shorts, with my hair in a long French braid, large silver earrings dangling from my ears, and a jaunty red scarf pulled through one of the jean shorts' belt loops. James, in similarly bohemian garb, stands behind me. This is his first high school musical and we are doing it together.

A few months earlier, I'd received an email from the theater director at his school announcing that the musical auditions would be open to the entire school community: students, alums, parents, teachers, and staff. We would be the first school to mount a production of a new musical based on Shakespeare's *As You Like It*, with a book by Laurie Woolery and music and lyrics by Shaina Taub, that had premiered at the Public Theater and Shakespeare in the Park. After asking James if he'd be OK with my trying out—"I wouldn't be OK if you *didn't*, Mom!" he'd lovingly exclaimed—I'd auditioned with a Cole Porter classic, "Take Me back to Manhattan," that my father had especially loved to hear me sing. Benj, on a gap year before starting college at Vassar, had traveled to the audition with me and accompanied me on the guitar.

James and I were both cast in small feature parts and tapped as understudies for the lead roles of Touchstone and Duke Senior. For the past three months, I'd immersed myself in mastering dance steps, holding harmonies, learning lines. I'd forged close friendships with the other moms in the show and with the wonderful teenage cast members.

As I began work in earnest on a book about my father, *As You Like It*'s themes of intergenerational conflict and forgiveness, inclusion and acceptance, a daughter's finding her father after a transformative journey, could not have felt more appropriate. The idea of a child and parent being restored to each other also resonated for me with Yasuko, who had at last found her children and reunited with them, becoming a grandmother in the process.

My Yale application essay on an extracurricular activity I was most passionate about had ended: "Shakespeare said 'All the world's a stage'; for me, the stage has also been a world." The stage had indeed been for me a kind of Arden, an alternative realm to the competitive world of academics. But after coming to Yale, other than singing in the Freshman Chorus and its Chamber Singers during my first year,

I'd never again set foot on a stage as a performer. Now, the stage was once again a virtual Arden for me to create, cavort, and grow in. In the production notes for *As You Like It*, Taub describes her Arden as "the mythical sanctuary where we all need to travel in order to heal." Being in this show had helped me to heal.

Performing in *As You Like It* felt like the culmination of my rediscovering my love for singing and acting since having children. Reading to them, I'd given each Oz character a distinctive voice, each lyrical passage in *Charlotte's Web* or *The Cricket in Times Square* a poetic resonance. Every night, I'd sing them songs from *Oklahoma!*, *West Side Story*, and *The Sound of Music* and standards by Cole Porter, Irving Berlin, and Gershwin. As Benj developed into an accomplished guitarist and singer, he and I sang together often, and two years earlier we'd professionally recorded an album of Christmas music. How my father would have loved it all.

In the show's opening number, "All the World's a Stage," I played a young mother. I stood with a baby doll cradled in my arms as Jaques the clown sang of the trajectory of human life. And in each performance, as I stood frozen in tableaux, then turned to face the audience and look out into the vast sea of faces, including my beaming mother's, the lyrics struck me with a sense of recognition and rightness.

> And then we're kids
> not yet capable of hate
> freely dancing with each other
> unaware inside our youth
> of a difference between make-believe and truth
> . . . .
> Then we get bigger
> and think before we play
> give each other stage fright
> and worry what the critics have to say

We hide in costume
pretend we blend in with the scenery
and act the way we're taught we oughta be
. . . .
Then we're almost grown-ups
trying to fill our parents' shoes with broken soles
we question our roles
can't seem to find our light
sick of waiting in the wings of the same life
night after night
longing for a duet
with someone who truly sees you
. . . .
All the world's a stage
and everybody's in the show
nobody's a pro
all the world's a stage
and every day, we play our part
acting out our heart
year by year, we grow
learning as we go
trying to tell a story we can feel
How do you make the magic real?

In all of my endeavors—from parenting to writing, advocating to performing—I'd drawn on the best of my father's teaching and his being. But I had finally learned to let go of my worry about what the critics would say. I had at last chosen my own life path, not the one marked out for me by my parents and my professors. Happily single, I nonetheless hoped that, like my father, I would one day get to sing a duet with someone who truly sees me. And I hoped that the story of my father would make his magic real.

Something mysterious spills over.

> —Richard Gilman, *Faith, Sex, Mystery*

think back now on the dedication to *Faith, Sex, Mystery*: "For my daughters, Claire and Priscilla, who will understand some of this book now and the rest of it in time." Do I understand it all? Would my father even want me to? He often cited this line from Chekhov approvingly: "It's only fools and charlatans who know everything and understand everything." My father repeatedly gestured toward the ineffable, the mysterious, something larger and greater than what can be analyzed, judged, or mastered. A realm, a force, a state beyond the power of criticism.

My father never valorized complete understanding; his description of Hamlet is apropos here:

> We'll never get to the bottom of *Hamlet*, which is just the play's glory. We'll never completely sound out Hamlet either. As he lies dying he tells Horatio: "Things standing thus unknown,

shall live behind me." Ah, sweet, fertile, forever partly hidden prince.

—Richard Gilman, "Tales of Hamlets Then and Now," *New York Times*, May 6, 1990

I could say the same of my father. Sweet, fertile, forever partly hidden he will remain. He would want it that way.

Toward the end of his memoir, he wrote:

> I only know that I don't want to die as an act purely of nature, of this world; I want my poor value to exist past me, somewhere else. I want my tears to be wiped away and those of the people I love. I want to make sense of everything, but more than that, to make peace with it.

It strikes me now that he is alluding here to the ending of *Uncle Vanya*, when Sonia tenderly wipes away her own and her uncle's tears. I believe—I yearn to believe—that writing about Chekhov helped prepare him for his own illness and dying, for his own grappling with mortality, just as reading him on Chekhov teaches me how to grieve him and gives me solace:

> But the full music establishes itself, the rhythm moves between sorrow as sorrow and as an unexpected, unwished for but liberating opening to the inmost self. Lyricism doesn't transform or redeem the weight of sorrow, it doesn't even physically lighten it. What it does is place it, environ it, bring it into intimacy with the soul which, tested by grief, learns about itself. At the same time lyricism makes visible the hidden and speaks of how grief makes us human; the beauty that inheres in sorrow is our recognition of mortality, which happiness obscures . . . "We'll rest. I know we will." But rest,

peace, is already there, besieged, infinitely fragile, in Chekhov's art.

—Richard Gilman on the ending of *Uncle Vanya*, from *Chekhov's Plays: An Opening into Eternity*

Didn't I tell you, Daddy? I still love you. More than ever.

ACKNOWLEDGMENTS

To Tina Bennett, a character in these pages, my friend since our first year in Yale University's English & American literature PhD program, my colleague at Janklow & Nesbit, and then my literary agent, I owe profound thanks. She is the one who always believed I could write for more than just other academics, who saw that I was falling in love with Richard before I did, who came up with the idea of combining my papers for literary conferences with my talks to schools and parents into an article and eventually a book proposal called *The Anti-Romantic Child*, who urged me relentlessly and lovingly to write a book about my father. She pushed me to go to dark and scary places, to bring not only my father but also little Priscilla back to life, to tell the truth in the way my father would have wanted.

Eric Simonoff, my friend since our days working together at Janklow & Nesbit, came on as my agent midway through the process with this book and bolstered me with his immensely reassuring presence, his enormously appreciative and sensitive reaction to the book, and our hours-long conversations about everything from novels we'd been reading to our children. Every chat was a boon and a gift. Eric has been a pillar of strength and good humor. He is the very definition of a mensch and I love the heck out of him!

Also at William Morris Endeavor: Criss Moon, Eric's assistant, has been a witty, clever, and effervescent presence. Caitlin Mahoney and Fiona Baird knocked my proverbial socks off with how well they understood the book and how warmly they embraced it.

My team at W. W. Norton has been simply spectacular. Jill Bialosky has my deepest gratitude for her unwavering support of this book from the moment she began reading the proposal, for her extremely rigorous and careful edits, for her uncanny ability to ask the hardest questions that elicit my deepest and most authentic feelings. Jill is demanding yet kind, tough yet tender, cerebral yet ardent. She gave me the courage to look backward and revive the ghosts of my days.

John Glusman could not have been more supportive and gracious to me and my book; Matt Weiland and Bob Weil were also early champions. Drew Weitman was astonishingly efficient, cheerful, and smart, a great pleasure to work with in every way. Erin Lovett is a dream publicist: warm, passionate, shrewd, and indefatigable in her efforts. Michelle Waters impressed me immediately as a congenial spirit; her ingenuity and amiability make her a delight to converse and strategize with. Ingsu Liu and Kelly Winton designed a cover that made me teary; it perfectly encapsulates what I tried to accomplish with this book. Amy Robbins was an exacting and meticulous copyeditor. Thanks also to Lauren Abbate and Rebecca Munro for their fine work on the book's production.

Many friends made contributions large and small. Stephen Klein, dream librarian, answered all of my research requests with unruffled alacrity, hunting down obscure reviews and articles with aplomb. Rick Hilles's extravagant enthusiasm heartened me. Josh Skaller was a sympathetic and sagacious reader and interlocutor as I wrote. David DiRienz brought his creative genius and stringent editorial eye to many a page and idea. Francesca Stanfill read a late-stage draft with sensitivity and keen intelligence and reassured me about my portrait of my mother, her dear friend and agent. Ann Beattie was a bountiful source of encouragement and laughter. Mina Hamedi, my mother's fabulous assistant, gave thoughtful and extremely helpful feedback on the manuscript. Delia Ephron was the first person other than my agent to whom I disclosed the title and book idea; her affirmation gave me confidence that *The Critic's Daughter* could work as a book. The late Gil Shiva, one of my mother's closest friends and a great admirer of my father's writing, assured me that I could write about their divorce in a way that was honest yet loving.

Lore Segal was a fount of anecdotes and insights about my parents both as individuals and as a couple and a brilliantly incisive reader of my book as it evolved.

Nalaini Sriskandarajah and Clarice Kestenbaum provided perspective and direction, wisdom and empathy as I navigated my way through this most painful story.

Many of my father's former students and colleagues generously shared stories and memories about his teaching and mentorship, quotations and passages from his work with me. Thank you to David Akroyd, Shelley Berc, Mark Bly, Art Borreca, Sandy Boynton, David Bruin, Becke Buffalo, James Bundy, Michael Cadden, Lonnie Carter, Meiling Cheng, Dare Clubb, Gabrielle Cody, Martha Cooley, Royston Coppenger, Julia Devlin, the late Morris Dickstein, Chris Durang, Garrett Eisler, Sasha Emerson, the late Guy Gallo, Liz Giamatti, Oscar Giner, Eve Gordon, Margaret Gray, Joe Grifasi, Jessica Mann Gutteridge, Lars Hanson, William Hauptman, Liza Henderson, Steve Hendrickson, Mead Hunter, the late Albert Innaurato, Bret Israel, David Kaplan, Richard Kramer, Jon Krupp, Rocco Landesman, Marc Linn-Baker, Mark Lord, Allen Lowe, Jeff Magnin, James Magruder, Framji Minwalla, Bob Montgomery, Daniel Mufson, Steve Oxman, Kim Powers, the late Michael Roloff, Laura Ross, Edwin Sanchez, Bob Schneider, Christina Sibul, Douglas Soderberg, Michael Stevens, Edith Tarbescu,

Laurie Treuhaft, Russell Vandenbrouke, Adam Versenyi, Jeff Wanshel, Andrew Wood, and most of all to Elizabeth Bennett, Rustom Bharucha, David Epstein, Shawn Marie Garrett, David Alan Grier, Stephen Haff, Allan Havis, Susan Jonas, Jonathan Kalb, Charlie McNulty, Jill Morris, Marc Robinson, Gordon Rogoff, and Catherine Sheehy for seeing and appreciating, supporting and loving my father so well.

Thank you to Mary Gordon and Andre Gregory for being such wonderful friends to my father and for their beautiful eulogies at his service.

I'm so grateful to Shaina Taub and Laurie Woolery for the gift of *As You Like It*, their warm and wise presence in our rehearsals and at our performances, their inspired work as artists in the theater. My father would have given their show a rave review and them his most genial hugs.

The mellifluous and marvelous Jamie Leonhart helped me find, hone, and polish my voice. Our creative kinship is just one aspect of an incredible friendship that began in high school when we sang in the NYC Vocal Jazz Ensemble together!

My boys are blessed beyond measure in their father and I in an ex-husband. Richard Prud'homme's steadfast love, playfulness, patience, brilliance, and purity of heart have been instrumental in our children's growth, and his top-notch editorial skills helped me through many a thorny revision.

Thank you to my mother for putting the agent in her over the ex-wife and mother and encouraging me to write the story of my father and our relationship, for her willingness to revisit some very painful things as I queried her, for being a fierce advocate for Benj and James and loving them with every ounce of her being.

Yasuko will always have my boundless gratitude, admiration, and love. She made my father truly happy, gave him a reason to fight, brought him a peace and serenity he'd never before experienced. No man has ever had a more faithful, attentive, or loving wife.

Claire Gilman is the best sister anyone could ever ask for and has patiently tolerated my endless questions about everything from the names of stores to details about experiences we shared with our father. She is Tacy to my Betsy, Bert to my Ernie, Toad to my Frog, Amos to my Boris, Cinderella to my Prince, Martha to my George. She is my best chum, pal, buddy, as our father would laughingly say, my most trusted confidante and dearest friend. Streaks of love fly to her from me every single day.

Nicholas Alexander Gilman is the funniest person I have ever met, and the most multi-talented. He answered my countless email queries about our father with vividly evocative descriptions, humor, and that inimitable Nicky charm; he had me rolling in the aisles, as the Marx Brothers did for him!

Benj and James, you have become two young men who my father would have adored and been so very proud of. I wish he were here to watch Giants games and tennis matches with you, debate the relative merits of *Oklahoma!*, *West Side Story*, and *Sunday in the Park with George* with you, listen to you both sing so beautifully, marvel at Benj's mastery of the classical guitar and James's performances in plays and musicals. I wish he were here to have lunch with you every week at Yale, Jamesie, and discuss your Directed Studies papers with you as he did with me. He lives on in you both in so many ways.